THE CHURCH

TRIUMPHANT

AT THE END

OF THE AGE

THE CHURCH TRIUMPHANT AT THE END OF THE AGE

Characterized by Revival, Restoration, Unity, World Evangelization, and Persecution

by Nate Krupp

"... Hallelujah! For the Lord our God, the Almighty, reigns. Let us rejoice and be glad and give glory to Him, for the marriage of the Lamb has come and His bride has made herself ready."

— Revelation 19:6b-7

The Church Triumphant

Destiny Image Publishers
P.O. Box 351
Shippensburg, PA 17257

"Speaking to the Purpose of God for this Generation"

I.S.B.N. 0-914903-38-1

For Worldwide Distribution
Printed in the U.S.A.

DEDICATION

This book is gratefully dedicated to the many who have so greatly influenced my life and ministry: especially, my parents, Dad and Mom Krupp; The Navigators; my wife, Joanne; her parents, Dad and Mother Sheets; our children, Gerry and Beth; The Wesleyan Church; Youth With A Mission; The Foursquare Church; the hundreds of churches that we have had the privilege of working with over the past twenty-five years, which placed within me the hunger to search out and deal with the issues addressed in this book; and most of all, Jesus Christ, my Lord.

iii

TABLE OF CONTENTS

PART III — UNITY 133

PART IV — WORLD EVANGELIZATION 151

PART V — PERSECUTION 211

APPENDIX

CHARTS

TABLES

FOREWORD

Few men have had the variety of experiences Nate Krupp has known. In 1961, God brought him into a full-time ministry of challenging and training churches to more effectively evangelize their communities which resulted in his founding of Lay Evangelism, Inc. That work led to successful city-wide Lay Evangelism Training Crusades. In the late 1960's he concentrated his evangelistic activity on the inner city of Chicago, becoming a one-man mission to the ghettos.

Nate has ministered to the Body of Christ for more than twenty-five years. He has been a faithful voice calling the Church to be all that God would have her to be — in order to see the world evangelized and to present to Jesus a Beautiful Bride.

Nate's rich experiences with the Navigators, The Wesleyan Church, Lay Evangelism, and Youth With A Mission have contributed to his writing nine books that have blessed thousands of people on every continent. I have had a close-up look at this man and his ministry and can heartily endorse it. Nate's strength of character and commitment to the Lord have personally enriched my life.

The Church Triumphant has been twenty-five years in the making. In these pages, Nate shares the things God has poured into his life in the areas of revival, restoration of the Church, and world evangelism. May God use this book to encourage His Church to do great exploits and triumphantly bring back the King!

Loren Cunningham
President
Youth With A Mission International

PREFACE

When we talk about "end-times," some Christians think of storing up food. For others, it means revival, or fulfilling the Great Commission. Over a period of two decades the Lord has been gradually speaking to this writer that the Church at the end of the Age will be a triumphant Church and will be characterized by revival, restoration, unity, world evangelization, and persecution. Allow me to tell the story.

The author began his full-time Christian ministry in 1961 by traveling from church to church throughout North America, challenging and training people for personal evangelism. As time went on, he began to see that personal evangelism (or any kind of evangelism) would not take place until the Church experienced awakening. For the awakening to be sustained, some fundamental changes need to be made in the life of the Church; thus the need for reformation, or the restoration of New Testament Christianity.

Then there is the whole question of unity. Why did we have so many denominations? Why all the seeming competition? How is one to evaluate the ecumenical movement? What was Jesus praying for in John 17:20-23?

I was greatly affected by The Navigators as a young Christian (1957-60). Through them, God began to give me a world vision. Then, in 1976, God brought my wife and me into contact with Youth With A Mission, and the vision for evangelization of the entire world increased. God broadened the burden from personal evangelism and made it a burden for world evangelization.

In the 1970's the Lord began to speak to me about coming persecution of the Church world-wide and that God's people needed to be awakened to this possibility — and needed to be prepared. At that time I wrote *The Omega Generation,* which was published in 1977.

In 1979 I began to see how these five characteristics fit together to form a single, balanced picture of the Church triumphant at the end of the Age. So, the message of this book — revival, restoration, unity, world evangelization, and persecution — has been in the making in my heart for over twenty years. I began to teach on these five characteristics as a total teaching in 1979, put them into booklet form in 1980, and then began to gather material and look for time to expand the booklet. From October, 1983, through June, 1984, the Lord graciously opened up a nine month slot of time to write. Copies of the manuscript were then sent to over twenty Christian scholars and leaders for their input, which has been very helpful in preparing the final draft. Final revisions were made in the summer and fall of 1986 while residing at YWAM's Pacific and Asia Christian University, where it was accepted as a thesis for a Masters degree in Christian Ministries.

There have been three passages of Scripture that the Lord especially spoke to me: "So I prophesied as He commanded me, and the breath came into them, and they came to life, and stood on their feet, an exceedingly great army."[1] (Ezekiel 37:10); "Then the Lord answered me and said, 'Record the vision and inscribe it on tablets that the one who reads it may run. For the vision is yet for the appointed time; it hastens toward the goal, and it will not fail. Though it tarries, wait for it; for it will certainly come, it will not delay,'" (Habakkuk 2:2-3); and "Write therefore the things which you have seen, and the things which are, and the things which shall take place after these things." (Revelation 1:19). I have endeavored to be obedient. But this book is in no way to be considered "the final word." There is much that God will yet show to His people, and do, as we move toward the final days of the end of this Age. If this book provokes thought, prayer, discussion, and Spirit-led action, it will have accomplished its mission.

Many have helped in this project. I especially want to mention Ann Chapman, Marge Gaffney, Tracey Hoyt, Sandra Leonard, Kathleen McConnell, and Sue Nelson, who typed the several drafts of the manuscript; Wilma Eads, who checked for English style and correctness; Maureen Greene and Rogie Harter, for proof-reading; the Tacoma YWAM family, who released me to do the writing; the Pat McCullough family, in whose summer home we lived during the months of study and writing; Bill and Patricia Parker, whose financial support kept food on the table; Wilson Turner, for editorial assistance; and Andy Beach, Gene Hackett, and Eric Vogal whose typing and computer skills produced the finished draft.

I also want to thank the many Christian leaders who reviewed the manuscript and shared vital suggestions, especially Rev. Ron Boeheme, Mr. Dale Buehring, Dr. Raymond L. Cox, Dr. Robert Crandall, Dr. Loren Cunningham, Mr. James Dawson, Rev. Gale Erwin, Mr. Jay Ferris, Rev. Paul Filidis, Rev Armin Gesswein, Rev. Robert C. Girard, Rev. Denny Gunderson, Rev. Tom Isenhart, Rev. Dick Iverson, Mr. Graham Kerr, Rev. David King, Mr. Paul H. Krupp (my father), Rev. Ronald Lowrie, Dr. J. Edwin Orr, Rev. John Pentecost, Rev. David Rees-Thomas, Mr. Richard Owen Roberts, Rev. Randy Roth, Rev. Dale Rumble, Rev. Hans Schnabel, Dr. Howard A. Snyder, Dr. C. Peter Wagner, Rev. Arthur Wallis, and personnel at the U.S. Center for World Mission, and a number of YWAM leaders. Of course, I assume full responsibility for the finished project. And I especially want to thank my dear wife, Joanne, for her helpful encouragement in many ways during the months of writing.

So, here it is — what I hope is an accurate, balanced, and concise, but fairly complete, overview of the Church triumphant at the end of the Age. As you prayerfully read it, it is my prayer that it will be used by the Holy Spirit to contribute to the evangelization of the world and to present to Jesus a glorious Church. And I pray that all of us will be challenged to believe God for great and mighty things (Jeremiah 33:3).

Nate Krupp
Tacoma, Washington
July 1987

INTRODUCTION

We are living in momentous times. Wars are occurring in many parts of the world. We face the growing threat of global, nuclear war; or the possibility of unilateral, nuclear disarmament. There is the growing hunger-famine problem, and the potential of solving it. There is the uncertain world economic situation. There are unparalleled, unusual, and almost unpredictable weather phenomena: earthquakes, volcanoes, storms, changing weather patterns. Israel is a nation again after almost two thousand years of being scattered. There is the world population explosion. There is the birth and coming to age of nations in the Third World. There is the electronics-computer revolution that provides for unprecedented information storage and transfer, and also the vehicle for potential world control. One can scarcely keep up with all that is happening. What does it all mean? Could we be at that time in history that the Bible calls "the end of the Age"?

Where does the Church fit in to all of this? Is it to be just a sterile, isolated institution that is scarcely noticed? Something that is known by its pretty steeples and is consulted at the time of the children's christening or the old folks' funerals? Or is it to be the greatest force in history? The Bible says, "... These are in accordance with the working of the strength of His might which He brought about in Christ, when He raised Him from the dead, and seated Him at His right hand in the heavenly places, far above all rule and authority and power and dominion, and every name that is named, not only in this age, but also in the one to come. And He put all things in subjection under His feet, and gave Him as head over all things to the Church, which is **His body, the fullness of Him** who fills all in all." (Ephesians 1:19-23).

This writer believes the the Church of the Living God will increasingly become the greatest force on earth. It will do great spiritual exploits; be reckoned with, and listened to, by world leaders; and change the course of history. The greatest chapters of the Church's history are yet to be written. They will be days of revival, restoration, unity, world evangelization, and persecution. That is what this book is all about.

PART 1 — REVIVAL

"So rejoice, O sons of Zion, and be glad in the Lord your God; for He has given you the early rain for your vindication. And He has poured down for you the rain, the early and latter rain as before . . . And it will come about after this that I will pour out My Spirit on all mankind; and your sons and daughters will prophesy, your old men will dream dreams, your young men will see visions. And even on the male and female servants I will pour out My Spirit in those days."

— Joel 2:23, 28-29

"And when they had prayed, the place where they had gathered together was shaken, and they were all filled with the Holy Spirit, and began to speak the word of God with boldness."

— Acts 4:31

"There is a sense in my spirit that we are on the verge of a new visitation of God right here in North America that is going to not only affect our continent, but others as well." [1]

— Ralph Mahoney

"History is silent about any great revival that did not begin in prayer." [2]

— J. Edwin Orr

1

1

DEFINITION AND BIBLICAL BASIS

Introduction

What do you think about when you hear the word, "revival"? For some it brings back negative feelings of some scary hell-and-brimstone message at a camp meeting where sinners were exhorted to come forward and repent. For others it stirs up the excitement of days gone by when God came by His Spirit and changed the course of a nation.

So, what is revival? What does it have to do with us today in the Twentieth Century? Let us see.

Definition of Revival

The words, "revive, revived, reviving," occur 30 times in the New American Standard translation of the English Bible. The King James translation additionally lists Romans 7:9 and 14:9. (See Appendix 1 for a listing of them.) In all of these cases, the basic meaning of the Hebrew words, "chayah" and "michyah," and the Greek words, "anathallo" and "anazao," is "to live," "to live again," and "to come to life." The English word, "revival," is derived from two Latin words, "re," which means "again," and "vivo" which means "to live;" thus the literal meaning "to live again." [1]

The American College Dictionary defines "revival" as the "restoration of life." More specifically, "revival of religion" is defined as "an awakening, in a church or a community, of interest in and care for matters relating to personal religion." [2]

Various Christian writers have defined revival in these ways:

"God came." [3]

"A visitation of God." [4]

"Revival then is such a display of God's holiness and power that often human personalities are overshadowed and human programs abandoned. It is God breaking into the consciousness of men in majesty and glory." [5]

"We shall consider 'revival' as that special season of refreshing when many believers simultaneously experience deep Holy Spirit conviction, causing them to make private and public confession of sin, along with a renunciation of it . . . and the whole experience bearing fruit in the salvation of the lost." [6]

"God at work, restoring His Church to health." [7]

"It is God visiting a segment of His people with cleansing from sin and the filling of the Spirit." [8]

"The divine intervention of God in human affairs which changes the course of history." [9]

"Revival is an 'awareness of God' that grips the whole community, and the roadside, the tavern, as well as the church, becomes the place where men find Christ." [10]

"It is the sovereign outpouring of the Holy Spirit in which Christians are turned to their 'first love' for Christ." [11]

"Is nothing else than a new beginning of obedience to God." [12]

" . . . times of refreshing . . . from the presence of the Lord."

— Acts 3:19, New American Standard Bible.

Let's combine these into a single definition: revival occurs when God, the Holy Spirit, moves upon a person, local church, community, nation, or the whole world in an extraordinary way which results in Christians being greatly awakened and drawn closer to God; in multitudes of new people being brought to Christ; in the social climate of that area being greatly changed for the good; and in many new workers being thrust forth into the harvest.

Characteristics of Revival

As further definition and explanation of revival, the following characteristics of a true revival are given. These are two lists

3

composed by respected men of God of recent history: one, an English Methodist leader, Dr. A. S. Wood, and the other, an English Baptist leader, Charles Spurgeon.

Characteristics of Holy Spirit Revival,
by Dr. A. Skevington Wood —

1. An intensified awareness of God.
2. An acute sensitivity to sin.
3. A jealous concern for the truth.
4. An absorbing concentration on prayer.
5. An enhanced standard of conduct.
6. A strengthened loyalty to the Church.
7. An exciting realization of unity.
8. An augmented zeal in evangelism.
9. And a passion for social justice. [13]

Genuine Revival, by Charles Spurgeon —
1. An uncommon eagerness to hear the Word of God, and an unusual readiness to speak and be spoken to about the interests of the soul.
2. An unusual sense of sin and personal unworthiness, together with a readiness to unite in prayer for pardon and holiness.
3. A singularly cordial appreciation of the atoning sacrifice of Christ, and a joyful acceptance of the personal Savior.
4. Personal consecration and covenanting with God in the Spirit of grace, accompanied by reformation of life and manner.
5. Great delight in secret and social prayer, and in all the ordinances of God.
6. An uncommon sense of the nearness of God, with joy in the Holy Ghost, and abounding with thanksgiving and praise.
7. Increased fervor of love and deepened sense of unity among Christians.
8. An extraordinary concern for the salvation of others, and boldness in testifying the grace of God in His Son. [14]

Revivals in the Old Testament

There were times recorded throughout the Bible when God met with and renewed His people in extraordinary ways. In the Old

Testament we find times when God worked on behalf of His people bringing renewal. Since this was not yet the Age of the Holy Spirit, which began on the Day of Pentecost, they were not times of revival, in the strictest sense of the word. But, in another sense, they were, for they were times when God undertook for His people in an unusual way. The following are some striking examples.

1 Samuel 7:4-10. Israel had been in constant threat of foreign aggression by the Philistines for many years. A major Philistine invasion loomed ominously. The prophet Samuel responded to the crisis and urged the people to return to God with heartfelt repentance and commitment. The entire nation was called to assemble at Mizpah. On that day they fasted and confessed, "We have sinned against the Lord." Samuel sacrificed a burnt offering and fervently interceded, crying out to God on Israel's behalf. The Philistines drew near to engage Israel in battle, but God supernaturally threw them into a panic and they were routed before the Israelites. So the foreign aggressor was subdued and cities that had been captured from Israel were restored.

2 Chronicles 5-7. The historic dedication of the temple took place under Solomon's leadership. All the men of Israel were summoned and came together for the festival. The entire assembly gathered before the ark and so many sheep and cattle were sacrificed that they could not be recorded. A vast group of musicians and singers joined in unison as with one voice to give praise and thanks to God. Then the glory of the Lord fell upon the temple. Sometime later God appeared to King Solomon at night and gave him the famous covenant promise of 2 Chronicles 7:14, "If My people who are called by My Name humble themselves and pray, and seek My face and turn from their wicked ways, then I will hear from heaven, will forgive their sin, and will heal their land."

2 Chronicles 15:8-15. In the midst of zealous national reform, King Asa assembled the nation in the capital city, Jerusalem. Thousands of animal sacrifices were offered up and the people made a covenant to seek God wholeheartedly. They ministered to God with much joyful worship. As a result God gave them rest on every side from their enemies.

2 Chronicles 20:1-19. A vast army from Edom was coming against Judah. Disaster and debacle were imminent. King Jehoshaphat resolved to inquire of the Lord and proclaimed a fast for all Judah.

People came from every town to seek God. The King fervently led in prayer and the men of Judah with their wives and children stood before the Lord. The prophetic word came forth. Then the people fell down and worshipped. Many then stood up and praised the Lord with a very loud voice. Because of the time of prayer and fasting, God gave them a miraculous, overwhelming victory in battle and rest on every side.

2 Chronicles 30:1-27. King Hezekiah sent word to all Israel and Judah to come to Jerusalem to celebrate the Passover which had been neglected for many years. Some people mocked and ridiculed but others humbled themselves and came. A very large crowd assembled in the capital. Sacrifices were offered and leaders prayed. There was much worship and joyful celebration. Sweeping national reforms followed.

2 Chronicles 34. Idolatry had been prevalent for many years. Finally the Book of the Law was found. King Josiah called all the people of Jerusalem and Judah to gather together. God's word was read from a large platform. The people made a covenant to seek God. As a result, the nation followed God for a generation.

Ezra 10:1-17. The nation was deep in sin through disobedience and unfaithfulness. All the men were commanded to come to the capital, Jerusalem. The people gathered and the leaders prayed, wept, confessed, and prostrated themselves before God. This gathering took place in the rain. The people committed themselves to change their ways. Because of the repentance and consecration, God allowed them to remain in the land.

Nehemiah 8. The entire nation assembled in Jerusalem. Ezra read God's word aloud from sunrise to noon. The people worshipped God and prostrated themselves. Leaders explained the word and the people wept. Then the people went away with great rejoicing to celebrate because of their new understanding of God's requirements for their lives. This national gathering led to national reforms and the reinstitution of godly traditions.

Nehemiah 9. The whole nation gathered, fasting in sackcloth and ashes. The people confessed their sins and the wickedness of their fathers. God's word was read aloud for three hours, and worship and confession of sin took place for another three hours. As a result, the people made a covenant in writing to follow God.

Jonah 3. The prophet Jonah had publicly declared in the foreign city-state of Nineveh its imminent destruction by God. The people of Nineveh believed Jonah and a national fast was called. The entire population, from the greatest to the least, put on sackcloth and ashes. For three days not a single person or beast ate or drank. They called upon God earnestly and turned from their evil ways. God had compassion on the city and national judgment was averted. [15]

Revival and the Church Age

A very important passage of Scripture on the subject of revival is Joel 2:23-32, written by the prophet Joel, about 800 years before Christ. He says,

So rejoice, O sons of Zion, and be glad in the Lord your God; for he has given you the early rain for your vindication. And He has poured down for you the rain, the early and latter rain as before. And the threshing floors will be full of grain, and the vats will overflow with the new wine and oil. Then will I make up to you the years that the swarming locust has eaten, the creeping locust, the stripping locust, and the gnawing locust, my great army which I sent among you. And you shall have plenty to eat and be satisfied, and praise the name of the Lord your God, who has dealt wondrously with you; then my people will never be put to shame. Thus you will know that I am in the midst of Israel, and that I am the Lord your God and there is no other; and my people will never be put to shame. And it will come about after this that I will pour out My Spirit on all mankind; and your sons and daughters will prophesy, your old men will dream dreams, your young men will see visions. And even on the male and female servants I will pour out My Spirit in those days. And I will display wonders in the sky and on the earth, blood, fire, and columns of smoke. The sun will be turned into darkness, and the moon into blood, before the great and awesome day of the Lord comes. And it will come about that whoever calls on the name of the Lord will be delivered; for on Mount Zion and in Jerusalem there will be those who escape, as the Lord has said, even among the survivors whom the Lord calls.

The Apostle Peter quotes Joel 2:28-32, recorded in Acts 2:17-21, on the Day of Pentecost, stating that Joel's words were then being fulfilled. The Church was "birthed" by a mighty outpouring of the Holy Spirit on the Day of Pentecost. And the Church would continue to be given new life and power by further outpourings of the Spirit throughout its history. The Church Age could also be called "the Age of the Holy Spirit" or "the Age of Revival."

Many, including this writer, believe that the greatest outpouring of the Holy Spirit will be at the very end of the Church Age, just before Jesus returns. (More on that in Chapter 4.)

Revivals in the New Testament

After the initial outpouring of the Holy Spirit on the Day of Pentecost, there were further times when God, by His Spirit, came upon His people to bring new life. Peter and John had been put in prison for preaching the Gospel and healing the lame man (Acts, Chapters 3 and 4). When released, they returned to their fellow believers and told what had happened. They all went to prayer, in desperate need of God's help, and the Holy Spirit came in a mighty way, shaking the building they were in and freshly filling all of them. Acts 4:31 says, "And when they had prayed, the place where they had gathered together was shaken, and they were all filled with the Holy Spirit, and began to speak the word of God with boldness." This resulted in unity (4:32), liberality (4:32), powerful witnessing (4:33), and abundant grace (4:33).

There are other times in *Acts* when the Holy Spirit was poured out: Acts 8:14-17, 9:17, 10:44-48, and 19:1-7. This writer sees each of these as an occasion when believers were experiencing "the baptism with the Holy Spirit" or being initially "filled with the Holy Spirit" rather than a time of revival of an already Spirit-baptized group of believers.

Within 60 years, by A.D. 90, much of the Church was in need of revival, as seen in the letters to the seven churches (Revelation, Chapters 2 and 3). Five of seven of these churches, the churches of Smyrna and Philadelphia being the exceptions, were called to repent. They were in need of a fresh humbling, repenting, and infilling of the Holy Spirit. They needed to experience revival.

2

REVIVALS THROUGHOUT CHURCH HISTORY
(A.D. 100-1900)

Not only do we see mighty revivals —outpourings of the Holy Spirit — in the Bible, when God came in an extraordinary way, but we also see them throughout Church history.

Early Church History

A.D. 300 — Asia Minor[1]

Some historians estimate that God so moved in Asia Minor (today's Turkey), that by A.D. 300 nearly half of the population were Christian.

400's — Ireland[2]

For thirty years St. Patrick preached the Gospel throughout Ireland, and established churches, monasteries, and schools from which missionaries were sent forth for four centuries. So many turned to God that Ireland was called "the Isle of Saints."

1100's — Waldenses[3]

In the late 1100's there was a movement, led by Peter Waldo, that experienced a revival which resulted in great evangelistic activity. They preached in houses, streets, market places and spread with extraordinary rapidity throughout much of central Europe. (More on the Waldenses and other groups mentioned in this chapter can be found in Chapter 8.)

1300's — Bohemia[4]

In the 1300's and 1400's in Bohemia there was a spiritual awakening associated with the preaching of John Hus which developed into a religious fellowship known as Unitas Fratrum, or Bohemian Brethren, comprising 80,000 people.

1400's — Italy[5]

In the late 1400's in Italy, Savonarola, an Augustinian monk, began to preach against the sins of the city, Florence. God honored his preaching with a mighty revival that transformed the city.

1300-1500's — The Reformers

There was much that God did through John Wyclife, Martin Luther, John Calvin, John Knox, and others during this period of time. It involved both revival and restoration. This writer has chosen to put this in the section on Restoration (see Chapters 8 and 9).

1620's — Ulster, Northern Ireland[6]

In 1625 a great awakening came to Ulster as a result of a band of faithful ministers who spent many days and nights in prayer.

The First Great Awakening — 1727-1780
The Thirteen American Colonies and Europe

1727 — Herrnhut, Germany[7]

In 1722 Count Nicholas Ludwig von Zinzendorf offered his estate as a home for religious refugees. About 300, many of whom were descendants of the Bohemian Brethren, came from Moravia under the leadership of Christian David and established a community called Herrnhut, or "The Lord's Watch." They had some difficulty getting along and in May, 1727, began several months of meeting together in small groups to seek God and to exhort, reprove, and pray for each other. On August 13 there was a great outpouring of the Spirit upon them that brought great unity to their midst. It also resulted in beginning a ministry of intercession that lasted for over a hundred years. It also resulted in the sending, over the next two hundred years, of thousands of their number as missionaries to every continent.

10

Probably no other Christian group in history has sent so large a percentage of its membership to overseas missions as have the Moravians. All the result of revival! A chart giving an overview of the great awakenings in modern times is found on page 12.

1734-1760 — The Thirteen American Colonies[8]

Many of the first European settlers to America in the 1600's were genuine Christians. (Further details of this are available in *The Light and the Glory*. See Bibliography for this and other pertinent books.) Now a new generation had arisen who were less concerned about Christ and His kingdom. But a faithful remnant was praying.

Under Solomon Stoddard's (1643-1729) ministry, pastor of the church at Northhampton, Massachusetts, and grandfather of Jonathan Edwards, there had been local awakenings in parts of Massachusetts and Connecticut between 1679 and 1718. And for twenty years there were small, regional breezes of revival: in the Dutch Reformed and Presbyterian churches in New Jersey, among Baptists in Pennsylvania, Virginia, and the Carolinas; and elsewhere.

In 1734 in Northhampton, Massachusetts, Jonathan Edwards began a series of stern messages where he named the town's sins and preached on justification by faith in Christ alone. A great concern about eternal issues came to the community. People gathered in their homes to pray. Shops closed and people began to individually find their way to Christ and His salvation. Before long, scores of communities in New England were being affected. His famous message, "Sinners in the Hands of an Angry God," stated, "You hang by a slender thread, with the flames of divine wrath flashing about it, and ready every moment to singe and burn it asunder; and you have nothing to lay hold of to save yourself, nothing to keep off the flames of wrath, nothing of your own, nothing that you have ever done, nothing that you can do, to induce God to spare you one moment."

In 1738 George Whitefield arrived from England and added fuel to the revival flames. He preached up and down the colonies from Georgia to Maine during seven trips to America from 1738 to 1770. Much of his preaching was out-of-doors. There was no "invitation." He simply spoke and waited for the Holy Spirit to move. People were converted and jumped up to tell about it.

This revival, which has come to be known as The First Great

CHART 1
GREAT AWAKENINGS IN MODERN TIMES

	Date	Place	Person Remembered	Characteristics	Results
1st	1727-1780 1727	Hermhut, Germany	Count Zinzendorf and Moravians	Unity, prayer	100 year prayer, missions
	1734-1760	U.S. 13 Colonies	Jonathan Edwards, George Whitefield	Prayer, preaching	Prepared colonies to become nation
	1740-1780	Great Britain	Wesleys, Whitefield	Outdoor preaching	Saved England, Methodist Church
2nd	1792-1842	Europe			Great Century of Protestant missions New denominations
	1857-1859	U.S. West U.S. East	Charles Finney	Campmeetings	Social effects
3rd	1857-1859	New York City & U.S. Europe	Jeremiah Lanphier	Laymen, prayer	1 million converts, social, missions
4th	1904-1930	Wales United States	Evan Roberts	"Bend me" Evangelical stream	Nation transformed
		World-wide	Parham & Seymour	Pentecostal stream	Pentecostal movement 5 million converts
5th	1947-Present	Many	Many	First Sprinklings of	end-time deluge
	Near Future	World-wide	The Body	Last!	Jesus returns!

12

Awakening, continued until about 1760. During that time there were added to the churches twenty-five to fifty thousand new converts (ten to twenty percent of the population); 150 new Congregational churches were started; and other groups were multiplying also. The awakening had an immediate effect upon education. Of the nine colleges established in the Colonies 1740-1770, six were birthed by the awakening: Brown, Columbia, Dartmouth, Pennsylvania, Princeton, and Rutgers.[9] The Awakening prepared the way for the colonies to become a new nation in 1776, and anti-slavery advocates began to arise in the major church groups in the South.[10]

1740-1780 — Great Britain[11]

In the early 1700's the teachings of deism and naturalism were sweeping Great Britain. Morals were at a low ebb. At Oxford University there was a small group, including John and Charles Wesley, meeting each evening from 6-9 p.m. for Bible study and prayer. Two days a week were set aside for fasting and prayer. On May 24, 1738, John Wesley had his "heart-warming" experience of full assurance of salvation through Jesus alone.

Great Britain was in desperate need: immorality, inhuman treatment of children (three out of four died before their fifth birthday!), drunkenness, poverty, filth, illiteracy, and unbelief in God were all rampant. In 1739 George Whitefield and John Wesley began to preach to open-air crowds as large as twenty thousand. Over the next forty years, a mighty revival came to Great Britain through the labors of the Wesleys, Whitefield, and others. These early "Methodists" literally gave themselves to prayer: most spent two hours a day in prayer and a few spent four to eight hours daily in intercession. They preached the Gospel out-of-doors, where the people were. The singing of the large crowds could sometimes be heard two miles away and Whitefield's voice for one mile. They gathered weekly in small groups to exhort one another. George Whitefield preached 18,000 times to over 100 million people. John Wesley rode over 250,000 miles on horseback (a distance equal to ten times around the globe) and preached over forty thousand times. Charles wrote over six thousand hymns. At John Wesley's death in 1791, there were 72,000 followers in Great Britain and over fifty thousand in the United States. Some scholars believe that because of revival, England was spared the political revolution that France was soon to experience.

The Second Great Awakening — 1792-1842
Europe and the United States[12]

Toward the close of the century, there was again in Europe and the United States a decline in morals and interest in spiritual matters. Some of this was due to the humanistic teachings of Voltaire and others.

In England, starting in about 1784, seven years before revival came, there were a growing number of people in all denominations devoting the first Monday evening of each month to praying for revival. By late 1791, England was in the midst of a spiritual awakening. About the same time there were major stirrings in Scotland and Wales, and in Ireland in the late 1790's.

In the early 1800's the Holy Spirit was moving in Norway, Sweden, and Finland. After Napoleon's defeat at Waterloo in 1815, the revival also spread to Switzerland, France, Holland, and Germany. There were also moves of God's Spirit as far away as South Africa and India.

In the United States the need for revival was increasingly apparent, and in 1794 a group of New England ministers issued a circular letter enjoining all Christians to spend the first Tuesday of each quarter in prayer for revival. Prayer groups were springing up everywhere. In Ohio, Kentucky, and Tennessee many were spending a day a month in prayer plus a half-hour each Saturday evening and Sunday morning.

Moves of God's Spirit began to take place: from New England to Georgia, and in the West (Ohio, Kentucky, and Tennessee). In the western territories of Kentucky and Tennessee and in the southern states, Virginia, the Carolinas, and Georgia, the crowds that gathered to hear itinerant evangelists were so large that outdoor meetings were held in what was the beginning of "camp meetings." One of these, in Cane Ridge, Kentucky, in 1801, had crowds of up to twenty-five thousand people from many denominations. The power of God was manifested in physical ways: people jerking, or being struck down, lying on the ground, sometimes for hours.

There were awakenings that also were occurring on college campuses. Especially at Yale, under the leadership of President Timothy Dwight, the grandson of Jonathan Edwards, there were five major awakenings between 1802-1815.

Toward the end of the Second Great Awakening there was a resurgence of Holy Spirit outpouring. It began in Boston and New

York, immediately added one hundred thousand to church membership, and soon touched many parts of the world.

The ministry of Charles G. Finney was part of this resurgence. He was converted in 1821 at the age of 29, while a lawyer. He was shortly thereafter mightily baptized with the Holy Spirit and immediately began to preach. Over the next fifty years, close to five hundred thousand were converted through his logical, powerful preaching. One of the greatest revivals ever to occur in a single city occurred in Rochester, New York, in 1830. Most of the churches came together; there was much prayer; Finney preached; and about a thousand, or 10% of the city, were soundly converted, including many leading professional and business people. Behind the scenes were those who gave themselves to prayer day and night.

There were outpourings in England, Scotland, Ireland, and Wales. In 1834 there was a major awakening in Tonga. In 1837 the Spirit was poured out in Hilo, Hawaii, resulting in about 27,000 being added to the Church throughout the Hawaiian Islands between 1837 and 1842. The resurgence of the 1830's also touched Fiji, Samoa, Indonesia, India, Ceylon, and parts of Africa.

One of the results of the Second Great Awakening was the emergence of whole new denominations: in the United States the Cumberland Presbyterian Church, Disciples of Christ, Churches of Christ, Christian Church, and United Brethren in Christ; and in England, the Plymouth Brethren and the Catholic Apostolic Church (sometimes called the Irvingites).

Another result of the Second Great Awakening in Europe and in the United States was the effect on missions. In England, through the efforts of William Carey, the Baptist Missionary Society was formed in 1792. Over the next twenty years numerous missionary agencies came into being in Great Britain and the United States, with pioneer Protestant missionaries going to India, Burma, China, the South Pacific, and elsewhere. There was also the beginning of the Sunday school movement and the starting of Bible societies.

A third effect of the Second Awakening was the general effect upon the improvement of society: the drive for the emancipation of the slaves, the protection of prisoners, the improvement of working conditions, the safe-guarding of women and children; and the providing of hospitals, asylums, orphanages, schools and colleges.

The Third Great Awakening — 1857-1859
The United States and Great Britain[13]

From 1845 to 1855 religious life in the United States was in decline. Many people lost faith in spiritual matters at this time due to the extremes and unfulfilled predictions of the Millerite apocalyptists, who had predicted that the return of Christ would occur on one of several dates. Additionally, the slavery question and discovery of gold in the West were of more importance to many than seeking God.

The first signs of revival began to occur in various parts of Canada and the United States in the summer and fall of 1857. But it is a businessman in New York City that is most notably connected with the Third Great Awakening.

The Dutch Reformed Church was considering closing their eighty-year-old church at Fulton and William Streets in downtown New York City, since most of the original families had moved away, and the neighborhood was now mostly made up of transient immigrants and laborers. They decided to make one last effort. They hired Jeremiah C. Lanphier, a 49-year old merchant with no experience in church work, at $1,000 a year, to knock on doors in the neighborhood and see what he could do. He knocked on doors for three months. A few new families came, but it was slow, wearying, discouraging work. Then he got the idea of opening a room in the church building once a week, at noon time, for those businessmen who might like to spend a few minutes in prayer. The small sign he put outside read, "Prayer Meeting from 12 to 1 o'clock. Stop 5, 10, or 20 minutes, or the whole hour, as your time permits." On the first Wednesday noon, September 23, 1857, only Lanphier was there until 12:30. But before the hour was over, there were six. On the second Wednesday there were twenty. During the third week, a financial crisis and panic began at Wall Street —banks failed, businesses closed, the railroads went into bankruptcy. Man's extremity was God's opportunity! There were forty at the Wednesday noon prayer meeting that week, and they decided to start meeting daily in a larger room. In a short time there were 3,000 attending, and they were using the entire building. Within six months 10,000 businessmen (out of a population of 800,000) were gathering daily in many places throughout New York City for prayer.

In November, 1857, revival came to a local church in Hamilton, Ontario, Canada. In December a three-day Presbyterian Convention meeting in Pittsburgh was considering the need for revival. Soon prayer meetings were being held across the nation. From Maine to California, Christians gathered to pray for revival. In many towns church bells summoned the people to prayer morning, noon, and night. In Chicago (a city of 100,000) two thousand men met at noon for prayer. In Albany, New York, the state legislators started their own early morning prayer meeting.

The revival was front-page news. Front-page headlines of leading newspapers read as follows:

New Haven, CT — "City's Biggest Church Packed Twice Daily for Prayer"
Bethel, CT — "Business Shuts Down for Hour Each Day: Everybody Prays"
Albany, NY — "State Legislators Get Down on Knees"
Schenectady, NY — "Ice on the Mohawk Broken for Baptisms"
Newark, NJ — "Firemen's Meeting Attracts 2,000"
Washington, D.C. — "Five Prayer Meetings Go Round the Clock"
New Haven, CT — "Revival Sweeps Yale"

Christians prayed for revival, and revival came! A mighty outpouring of God's Spirit swept the nation. Every major denomination was awakened. Over one million people were converted to Christ out of a national population of thirty million. **There were several New England towns where not a single unconverted adult could be found.** Many denominations saw their membership jump — the Baptists by ten percent, the Methodists by twelve percent. The revival was born in prayer, was interdenominational, and was essentially a laymen's movement. The late Perry Miller, of Harvard University, called it "the event of the century."[14] The Awakening occurred mainly during the two years of 1858 and 1859, but the effects were still being felt in the 1860's. By the end of the Civil War (1861-1865), one-third of the Confederate Army were professing Christians.

The news of the revival in America spread to England, Scotland, Ireland, Wales, South Africa, New Zealand, Australia, and India, resulting in similar prayer meetings and awakenings. There were other far-reaching results of this major awakening. It quickened the American conscience on the slave issue. It gave a great spiritual boost to the young YMCA movement and to D. L. Moody's ministry. In

England it influenced William Booth, and his Salvation Army that was just getting started; affected Hudson Taylor, who received his vision for inland China in 1865; and helped give birth to laws protecting the factory workers, and to the Red Cross. It also gave impetus to the birth of the Christian Endeavor Movement and the Student Volunteer Movement, both of which had world-wide impact on the youth of the day. And there were many who were converted to Christ on both sides of the Atlantic during this Third Great Awakening who ended up on the mission field all over the world.

3

REVIVALS IN MODERN TIMES *(1900-PRESENT)*

The Fourth Great Awakening — 1900-1930

The Third Great Awakening had waned in the 1860's although the effects from it were still being reaped. Humanism was on the rise. The Western world was enjoying the fruit of the Industrial Revolution and was becoming preoccupied with materialism. The Church had begun to lose her cutting edge and voice of leadership in the world. It was time once again for God to act.

Prayer Preparation

As with all revivals, the Fourth Great Awakening was preceded by many of God's people praying. In the latter part of the nineteenth century there was a growing number of Christians in many parts of the world earnestly seeking God for a deeper relationship with Him; and that He would pour out His Spirit upon the earth. In 1875 the Keswick movement, with its teaching on the deeper-life, began in England.[1] The emphasis on holiness that was part of Methodism, and which spread in various forms to most other groups as part of the foundation for the Third Great Awakening (1858-59), was still part of the American scene.[2] The various groups that emerged and merged from 1886 to 1919 to become the Church of the Nazarene all had a deeper-life emphasis.[3] Thus, on both sides of the Atlantic, there

there was the theological foundation for a deeper experience with God, and there were a growing number who were hungering for God. Frank Bartleman, who was to later report the Pentecostal revival at Azusa Street, and others like him, were spending nights in prayer, praying for revival, in the latter part of the nineteen century and the early 1900's.[4]

Dr. R. A. Torrey, pastor of Moody Church in Chicago and superintendent of Moody Bible Institute, with song leader Charles Alexander, went to Australia in 1899 for an evangelistic campaign. When they arrived, they discovered 1,700 weekly home prayer meetings in progress. These evangelistic efforts in Australia and New Zealand were quite fruitful with thousands coming to Christ. After the close of the meetings in Melbourne, a lady who had helped to organize the Melbourne prayer groups visited England. While there, she was invited to speak at the Keswick Convention. She told of the 1,700 prayer groups. The hearts of those attending the Convention were deeply stirred, and a decision was made to form prayer groups throughout the British Isles, to pray for revival.[5]

John Hyde, known as "Praying Hyde," arrived in India from America in 1892. He and a few others were spending much time in prayer for an awakening throughout India.[6] In 1902 in Calcutta, India, two lady missionaries heard Dr. Torrey speak on prayer; and by the spring of 1905, many Khassians (a people of India) were also praying for revival.[7]

1904 — Wales[8]

The first place where the Fourth Great Awakening touched was Japan in 1901. But the first major outbreak occurred in the small country of Wales in the British Isles in 1904. It was preceded by several years of local awakenings and many prayer meetings. These prayer gatherings were rather informal, each participant obeying the promptings of the Spirit. One might read a portion of Scripture, while another would testify, another would pray, and someone else might suggest a hymn to sing. These informal prayer gatherings would usually go on for two or three hours.

At this time, Evan Roberts was in college preparing for the ministry. But he was soon too hungry for the baptism with the Holy Spirit and burdened for souls to continue his studies. God did baptize him with His Holy Spirit, and he was soon talking of going through Wales with a Revival Team, was talking about a great revival that was coming to Wales, and was praying for 100,000 converts.

The Lord led young Roberts to commence some ministry at his home church. Before long there were dozens of prayer meetings daily in every part of the district. People began to gather nightly at the church building. Sometimes Roberts would bring a simple message, sometimes he would only pray, and sometimes he would do nothing while others prayed or did whatever the Spirit prompted them to do. Often these meetings would go on until the early hours of the morning. Word of this spread, and soon all of Wales was ablaze with prayer meetings and spontaneous church meetings, sometimes with Evan Roberts, sometimes without. They were characterized by Robert's now-famous prayer, "Lord, bend me," meaning "Make me a broken vessel." Four things were stressed by Roberts: confession of all past sins, repentance and restitution, surrender to the Holy Spirit and consequent obedience, and public profession of Christ. There were seven characteristics of the revival:

1. Honor to the Holy Spirit as a presiding presence.
2. The plain preaching of Christ and of sound Gospel doctrine.
3. The prominence given to prayer, individual and united.
4. The dependence upon God, rather than upon men.
5. The absence of stereotyped program and set method.
6. The readiness for blessing by a willingness to remove obstacles.
7. The direct dealing with the unconverted.[9]

The main thrust of the awakening lasted for two years (1904-1906). Many entire congregations were quickened. One hundred thousand (what Roberts had prayed for!) were added to the churches. Five years later, 80,000 were still active. Many taverns went bankrupt as drunkenness plummeted. Crime decreased so that in some districts the police and judges had nothing to do. An awesome sense of God's presence brooded over towns, in one case for two years. Twenty-five years later the atmosphere of revival still lingered in parts of Wales. In 1906 Evan Roberts was led to retire from public ministry, and gave the rest of his life (he died in 1951) to private prayer for world-wide revival.

1905-1910 — The Awakening Becomes World-Wide

Word of the awakening in Wales spread around the world; and so did the awakening. In England, the Archbishop of Canterbury called for a nationwide day of prayer. Between 1903-06 most English denominations increased by ten percent. The revival swept Scotland and Ireland. Revival came to all of Scandinavia (Norway, Sweden, Finland, and Denmark) — where some said it was the greatest move of the Spirit since the evangelization of the Vikings. In Norway, the Parliament passed special legislation to permit laymen to conduct communion because the clergy could not keep up with the number of converts desiring to participate. It also touched France, Germany, and other European nations.[10]

Word of the awakening reached the United States. The religious press reported it. And Welsh-Americans, especially in Pennsylvania, received word from their relatives in Wales. In late 1904, revival broke out in Wilkes-Barre, and other communities in Pennsylvania. In 1905 the revival spread throughout the entire nation. On January 20, a day of prayer was called in Denver. At 10 a.m. the churches were filled, and by 11:30 a.m. most of the stores were closed. A vote of the Colorado Legislature postponed business in order to attend the prayer meetings. Every school was closed, twelve thousand crowded into the four theaters in the city to pray, and the whole city went to prayer. In Schenectady, New York, women from prayer meetings formed teams to witness in the taverns. In Philadelphia the Methodists had 10,000 converts by spring. In Atlantic City the pastors reported that there were **only fifty unconverted adults out of a population of 50,000**. In Portland, Oregon, over 200 stores closed from 11 a.m. to 2 p.m. each day so that the city could be involved in prayer meetings. Ship captains ceased bringing their ships to Portland because so many sailors were being converted and leaving their ships. In Paducah, Kentucky, the First Baptist Church had a thousand converts in two months, and the aged pastor died of overwork! At Princeton College over 1,000 of the 1,384 students regularly attended weekly religious meetings. At Drake University in Iowa, one-third of the student body was involved in Bible study and prayer meetings. In the Midwest the Methodists were reporting the greatest revivals in their history. Every store and factory closed in Burlington, Iowa, to permit employees to attend prayer meetings. In Los Angeles, united meetings reached 180,000.

The Grand Opera House was filled at midnight as drunks and prostitutes sought to be saved. In Atlanta, 1,000 businessmen united for prayer. On November 2, stores, factories, and offices closed in the middle of the day for prayer. The Supreme Court of Georgia adjourned.

As a result of the Fourth Great Awakening, Church membership in the United States increased by over two million in the seven major Protestant denominations. This did not include the gains by a number of new holiness and pentecostal denominations.[11]

The awakening swept Canada from coast to coast. In India every province was touched and the Christian population increased seventy percent. Korea experienced three new waves of revival in 1903, 1905, and 1907 which caused the membership in churches to quadruple in ten years. Every province in China was touched. The awakening came to Indonesia, Malaysia, the Philippines, Manchuria, Japan, the islands of the South Pacific, Australia, New Zealand, Canada, Brazil, Chile, and much of Africa.[12]

The Pentecostal Stream of the Fourth Great Awakening[13]

At the same time that God was pouring out His Spirit in much of the world, in a traditional evangelical manner, He was also uniquely pouring out His Spirit on some in a way that included certain gifts of the Spirit, including speaking in tongues (glossolalia).

There were several instances of speaking in tongues throughout the 1800's in Europe and North America.[14] In 1898 Charles Parham, a former Methodist minister, started a Bible school in Topeka, Kansas. In a study of *The Acts* by Parham and his forty students in December, 1900, they concluded that "the evidence" of receiving "the baptism with the Holy Spirit" was "speaking in tongues." During a watch night service, just past midnight on New Year's Day, 1901, an 18-year old student, Agnes Ozman, spoke in tongues after hands were laid on her and prayers offered for her to be baptized with the Holy Spirit. Soon Parham and other students experienced this, and Parham formulated his thesis that "speaking in tongues is the initial evidence of the baptism of the Holy Spirit." From 1901 to 1905, Parham and his "Apostolic Faith" workers preached their Pentecostal message in the Middle West. From 1901 to 1908, they grew to a following of 25,000 from Missouri to Texas. In 1905 Parham moved his school to Houston, Texas.

One of Parham's students in Texas was a Black man, William Seymour. In 1906 Seymour received an invitation to preach in a Black Nazarene Church in Los Angeles. Los Angeles was "ripe" for revival. Joseph Smale, pastor of First Baptist Church had visited the Welsh revival. Phineas Bresee had recently founded the Pentecostal Church of the Nazarene (which was actually holiness rather than pentecostal), later to be renamed Church of the Nazarene. Frank Bartleman, who would later report on the outpouring at Azusa Street, and others were spending nights in prayer for revival.

When Seymour preached on Acts 2:4 and claimed that "speaking in tongues was the evidence of the baptism of the Holy Spirit," he was locked out of the Nazarene Church. He was taken in by a sympathetic Black family; and, in a prayer meeting in their home, Seymour first spoke in tongues. Meetings were conducted in this home, but as the crowds grew, they found a small abandoned Methodist Church building at 312 Azusa Street. Services began in the building in April, 1906. They were held daily from 10 a.m. until after midnight for three and a half years, with three altar calls given daily for those who wanted to be saved, sanctified, baptized with the Holy Spirit, healed, or delivered from demonic bondage. In addition to speaking in tongues, other gifts of the Spirit were experienced. Messages in tongues were interpreted into English, words of wisdom and knowledge were manifested, as were gifts of healings and discerning of spirits. There was a strong emphasis on the blood of Christ, and seekers were not encouraged to seek the gifts of the Spirit until a definite experience of sanctification had been received. There were also manifestations of "holy laughing," "holy dancing," and "singing in the Spirit."

As word of these activities at Azusa Street spread, people came from around the world to experience their own "Pentecost." Within a few years, the movement had spread to Europe, Africa, Asia, and South America. These "Pentecostals" soon found themselves rejected by the traditional holiness and evangelical churches, and by 1920 a number of Pentecostal denominations had emerged. On into the 1920's there also arose The International Church of the Foursquare Gospel through the preaching and healing crusades of Aimee Semple McPherson.

Results of the Fourth Great Awakening

The Fourth Great Awakening touched more people in more countries than any previous one. As a result of this world-wide outpouring of the Spirit in the early 1900's, over five million people were converted to Christ. Also, a whole new wave of missionaries was sent out world-wide, whose fruit would be borne in future decades.

First Sprinklings of a Soon-Coming, World-Wide, End-Time Revival

Since 1947 God has been pouring out His Spirit in various parts of the earth. This writer believes that these are just "sprinklings" that are preparing the way for a mighty end-time "deluge." (More on this deluge in the next chapter.) Let's look at some of these "sprinklings."

1947-1953 — Western Canada and the United States[15]

In February, 1947, there was an outpouring in North Battleford, Saskatchewan, that spread to many parts of North America. It was dubbed "the latter rain movement," and later also centered in Bethesda Temple in Detroit. It was characterized by much worship, prophecy, singing in the Spirit accompanied by a heavenly choir, and the operation of all the gifts of the Spirit. God was beginning to drop a few sprinkles of the rain that was to come.

1949 — Los Angeles[16]

Youth For Christ grew from Saturday night youth evangelism rallies in Chicago after World War II into a nationwide movement. In Southern California, pastors were gathering together to pray for revival. A three-week evangelistic tent campaign in 1949, with YFC evangelist Billy Graham preaching, extended to nine weeks. Many were converted, including some well-known Southern California personalities. Billy Graham was soon invited to conduct crusades in major cities across the United States and overseas. There were signs of a growing awakening.

November, 1949 — Hebrides Islands, Scotland[17]

In November, 1949, on the Island of Lewis in the Hebrides Islands, in the northwest part of Scotland, two sisters in their eighties were burdened for their local church, particularly because the young people were no longer part of the church. They began to spend Tuesday and

Friday evenings in prayer from 10 p.m. until three or four in the morning. The pastors of the island, with about 37,000 inhabitants, likewise were concerned for the spiritual state of the island. They met to consider the situation and passed a resolution calling on the people to pray.

The two sisters, one of them blind, challenged their minister to gather with his elders on Tuesday and Friday evenings also to pray. So they began to meet in a barn while the ladies were likewise praying in their humble cottage. These men met for prayer for a month and a half. Two passages of Scripture that were strongly impressed on them were:

"For I will pour water upon him that is thirsty, and floods upon the dry ground . . . " (Isaiah 44:3a KJV),

and

"Who shall ascend into the hill of the Lord? Or who shall stand in his holy place? He that hath clean hands, and a pure heart; who hath not lifted up his soul unto vanity, nor sworn deceitfully. He shall receive the blessing from the Lord..." (Psalms 24:3-5a KJV).

They interpreted the phrase, "the blessing," to be the blessing of revival, and prayed with that understanding. As these men and the two sisters continued to pray, the presence of God began to be felt throughout the community.

Duncan Campbell, a Scottish evangelist, was invited to come to the island. On the first night of his arrival he went to address a group of about 300 who had gathered in the church building. The meeting began at 9 p.m. and was finished about 11 p.m. When he went to leave the building, he discovered another 600 gathered outside. The Holy Spirit had visited the local dance hall, compelling all one hundred there to go to the church building. The other 500 had been strangely awakened, got out of bed, and also went to the meeting. The meeting lasted until four in the morning. Many found God that night. As the meeting was concluding, a request came for Mr. Campbell to come to the police station where four hundred people had gathered, without even knowing why they were there. As Mr. Campbell and a few others made their way to the police station, they passed people along the road who were crying out to God for mercy. When they arrived at the police station, they found many likewise crying out to God.

This sovereign awakening spread to all parts of the island. Work stopped for two hours each day as people gathered to pray. Evening meetings at the church buildings and home meetings often continued all night. This continued for three years. Revival swept the entire island. Seventy-five percent of the converts were converted outside the church buildings. In one village the Holy Spirit moved and people were saved in every home. An alcoholic schoolmaster on another island was strangely drawn to take a boat and to go to a house meeting in that village. He was converted around midnight. In another home, a father, mother, two daughters, and a son were all converted. Another daughter, in the medical profession in London, was converted at the very same time as she was walking down the street in London. Thus the entire family was converted at the same time!

1949-1951 — United States Christian Colleges[18]

During 1949-1951 a number of U.S. Christian colleges and seminaries experienced awakenings including Asbury College, Baylor University, Bethel College, Houghton College, Northern Baptist Theological Seminary, North Park College, Northwest College, Northwestern College and Seminary, Seattle Pacific College, Simpson Bible College, St. Paul Bible College, and Wheaton College.

1952 — Nagaland, India[19]

Christianity came to Nagaland, in eastern India, in 1872 through American Baptist missionaries. Over the years the Church had lost its spiritual life. In 1952 a great revival broke out. It started through some illiterate, native preachers and spread like wildfire from village to village until the entire area was engulfed. People left their jobs by the thousands to attend prayer meetings. The economy was threatened as offices, fields, and trades were vacated. Services were held from sundown until late into the night. There was great conviction of sin. People walking down the street were smitten and dropped on their faces to cry to God for mercy. There were many healings. The gifts of the Spirit began to operate — prophecy, healings, tongues, interpretation, and discernment. Many were converted, there was much singing, and the whole moral climate of the area was changed. Theaters were all but closed. Cigarette dealers were on the verge of bankruptcy. Theft and juvenile delinquency practically ceased. Nagaland was once one of the most troubled states in India. It became one of the most peaceful. Since 1970 the Spirit has been moving afresh in bringing the people of Nagaland to Christ and in miraculous manifestations. It is now estimated that 98% of the population of 800,000 are born-again and the revival is spreading to Burma and Nepal.

1951-1970's — The Charismatic Renewal[20]

Starting slowly, here and there, and continuing to build, the charismatic renewal soon became the talk of Christendom world-wide in the 1960's and 1970's. In June, 1951, the Holy Spirit led David du Plessis to the Headquarters of the World Council of Churches in New York City. Out of that, as his prejudices against "the liberals" melted, he became God's prophet to prepare the way for the leaders of the mainline Protestant denominations, Greek Orthodox, and Roman Catholics, to be open to the Holy Spirit and His gifts.

In October, 1952, Demos Shakarian, a dairyman in southern California, invited 21 Pentecostal laymen to breakfast at Clifton's Cafeteria in Los Angeles. Out of that was born the Full Gospel Businessmen's Fellowship International which has been a catalyst for evangelism, lay participation, unity, and the charismatic renewal throughout the world.

In March of 1959 the Lord spoke to Harald Bredesen, pastor of a Reformed Church in Mt. Vernon, New York, and his associate, Pat Robertson (now President of The Christian Broadcasting Network), and a small group of others, that they could no longer keep their experience with the Holy Spirit secret. Contact with Dr. and Mrs. Norman Vincent Peale resulted in John Sherrill writing the book, *They Speak With Other Tongues.*

In April of 1960, in Van Nuys, California, Father Dennis Bennett shared with his Episcopal Church his recent experience with the Holy Spirit. Articles were carried in "Newsweek" and "Time" magazines, and the charismatic movement gained national attention. Soon people of all denominations were experiencing a renewal and a deeper experience with God which they called "the baptism in the Holy Spirit."

In February of 1967 the Holy Spirit fell on a group of Duquesne University faculty and students, and the renewal had begun among Roman Catholics. Over six million Catholics in the United States consider themselves charismatic with millions more around the world.

That same year, 1967, a women's movement called Women Aglow began in Seattle, Washington. Also a part of the charismatic renewal was the Jesus People movement that touched thousands of drug-culture young people all over the world in the 1960's. In addition to the charismatic renewal, there has also been a growing evangelical renewal movement in the mainline denominations.

A recent Gallup poll indicated that 29 million Americans claim to be either pentecostal or charismatic. In 1981 there were an estimated 75-100 million pentecostal-charismatics around the world, and by 1985 the estimate had reached 150 million. This portion of the Christian Church is by far the fastest growing on every continent. But this charismatic renewal is only part of God's "sprinklings" that are leading us toward a mighty "rain" of the Spirit that will soon take place.

1965 — Indonesia[21]

On September 26, 1965, about 200 people were gathered in a Presbyterian Church on the island of Timor in Indonesia. As they were praying, suddenly the Holy Spirit came just as He had on the Day of Pentecost, almost 2,000 years ago: they heard the sound of a mighty, rushing wind; they saw the flames; they experienced "the baptism in the Holy Spirit;" and people were speaking languages they had never learned. Sin was dealt with very deeply. Miracles began to take place: water turned into wine, people walked on water, people were raised from the dead, food multiplied. Teams began to go out to tell others what was happening. As the awakening spread to other Indonesian islands, tens of thousands turned to Christ.

1967 — Zululand, South Africa[22]

Concerned about his lack of lasting fruit from evangelistic tent meetings, a German Lutheran evangelist and some of his Black Christian friends began to search *The Acts* and seek God for answers. The Lord led them into a prolonged time of prayer. They hardly took time even to eat or sleep as hours and days were spent in repentance from impure lives. As they continued to seek the Lord, there was a mighty outpouring of the Holy Spirit. Thousands turned to Christ as the Word was proclaimed, many were healed, and set free from demons. At one high school, 610 of 640 students had deep experiences of repentance and conversion.

1970 — United States Christian Colleges

In the Spring of 1969, J. Edwin Orr spoke on "Evangelical Awakenings" at an American Association of Evangelical Students convention held at Asbury College in Wilmore, Kentucky. In January, 1970, a number of students began to arise early in the morning to pray for revival. On Tuesday, February 3, 1970, close to 1,000 students at Asbury had gathered for their daily chapel time. The dean of the college, who was scheduled to preach, felt impressed not to. Instead, he opened the floor for anyone who wanted to, to stand and share what God was doing in their lives. A growing number of students had been praying individually and in small groups for a spiritual awakening. A few students had even been stating that a great outpouring of the Holy Spirit was imminent. Students began to share — some telling what God was doing in their lives, others making public confession of sin. At the close of the chapel hour, it was announced that those who wanted to stay and pray should gather around the front of the auditorium. Hundreds stayed. Most prayed. But a line began to form as others lined up to share at the microphone of their new-found experience with God. The chapel service continued into the afternoon, and classes were suspended for the rest of the day. In the early evening the crowd in the auditorium grew to about 1,500, while classrooms in the basement became meeting places for smaller prayer groups. Word of the revival soon spread across the street to Asbury Seminary where an all-night prayer meeting was called, and a similar move of the Spirit occurred at the seminary chapel service the next day (Wednesday). Classes were soon canceled at both college and seminary for the rest of the week. The spontaneous time of prayer and testimony continued day and night at both chapel auditoriums. Over the weekend they merged at the college.

News of the revival spread throughout North America. Soon prayer requests were being received by telegram, letter, and phone calls from all over the United States and Canada. Hundreds of visitors came from across the continent. Several local churches joined in on Sunday. Classes were resumed after chapel on the following Tuesday, one week after it all began, but months later there were still those who visited the chapel to pray throughout the day and those who gathered in the evenings to share and pray together.[23]

Soon teams were going out to share at other colleges and churches.

By the summer of 1970, at least 130 colleges, seminaries, and Bible schools had been touched by the fires of revival. Some of the colleges where outpourings were repeated include Anderson College, Azusa Pacific College, Fort Wayne Bible College, Houghton College, Nazarene Theological Seminary, Northern Baptist Theological Seminary, Olivet Nazarene College, Oral Roberts University, Seattle Pacific College, Southwestern Baptist Seminary, Spring Arbor College, Taylor University, Trevecca Nazarene College, and Wheaton College.[24] Teams from many of these schools were in turn going out to share in local churches in their area. In the summer of 1970, teams went out to share the story of revival on the five other continents.

1971-1972 — Western Canada[25]

In the fall of 1971 there was an awakening that began in Saskatoon, Saskatchewan, Canada, in connection with an evangelistic crusade conducted by twin brothers, Ralph and Lou Sutera, that soon spread to most of Canada and some parts of the United States. The exciting details of this are available in the book, *Flames of Freedom.*

1972 — Papua New Guinea[26]

About 400 students from all over Papua New Guinea, from twenty-two different missions and churches, were enrolled at the Papua New Guinea Bible Institute. A week of special spiritual emphasis was scheduled for the first week of October. On the first night (Monday) about half of the student body came forward to pray. On Tuesday night conviction deepened, and a large number were at the altar groaning over their sins. Students began to make confession and restitution of the sins of stealing, cheating, and breaking school rules. Toward the end of the week the students pled with the principal that the meetings be continued. On Sunday evening, October 12, God poured out His Spirit. Wave after wave of God's glory descended. It was electrifying. Holy pandemonium broke out. Students were shouting, jumping, and running throughout the congregation. On Wednesday evening over 1,000 people gathered from all over the area. On Friday, classes were dismissed to allow the students to go back to their villages to make restitution and to share what God was doing. In village after village, God poured out His Spirit.

The story could go on, telling of outpourings of God's Spirit that have taken place in various parts of the world in recent decades. It is important to note that sometimes these outpourings of the Spirit have been accompanied by various manifestations, or gifts, of the Spirit, and at other times they have not. God is sovereign. He chooses when, where, and how to pour out His Spirit. We need to be open to His sovereign choosings. All of these are just "sprinklings" of a mighty, world-wide deluge that is soon to come.

4

A SOON-COMING, MIGHTY, WORLD-WIDE, END-TIME REVIVAL

What a glorious expectation for God's people — a soon-coming, mighty, world-wide, end-time revival! We need it! There are growing evidences that it is on the way! But there is that which we can, and must do, to prepare the way.

The Need for an End-Time Revival

World Need

Who can deny the need for a mighty spiritual awakening? We are surrounded by evil and need of every kind: war, military and political tyranny, terrorism, violence, famine, oppression of the poor, situation ethics, immorality, homosexuality, an AIDS epidemic, pornography, abortion, idolatry, materialism, gambling, drug abuse, alcoholism, injustice, selfcenteredness, financial debt and insecurity, humanism, and the possibility of global nuclear war and total annihilation of the human race. The world is approaching the point of total financial, moral, and spiritual bankruptcy.

An Unfulfilled Commission[1]

There are five billion people (as of mid-1986) on planet earth and increasing by about eighty-one million per year (222,000 per day). Approximately **ninety-four percent are unsaved.**

Two-thirds of the five billion have never heard the Gospel of our Lord Jesus Christ. Over 16,000 distinct groups of people are still waiting to be evangelized. Three thousand languages, of more than five thousand, do not yet have one verse of Scripture.

An Impotent Church

The Church of Jesus Christ is God's agency on earth. We are Christ's Body — His heart, mouth, hands, and feet. We should be fulfilling the Great Commission. We should be fighting evil and meeting human need. But the Church is all too often so involved in its own life, problems, and self-survival to even be aware of world need, let alone be ready or able to do much about it. People are looking for moral and spiritual answers. Some are turning to the Church and finding answers, but some are turning to the Church and not finding answers. Some are turning elsewhere — the cults, the occult, eastern religions, witchcraft, humanism — and finding false answers.

How will we, the Church of Jesus Christ, ever get the Gospel to every person, in every nation, in this generation (Mark 16:15)? What can cause the Church to become that effective, life-changing, nation-shaking, hell-defeating agency that we read about in *The Acts?*

There is hope — for the Church — and for the world. There is a hope —one hope: a mighty spiritual awakening. As a speaker in the British House of Commons recently said, "I hope and pray for revival. It's still the only hope of the world."[2] *Nothing can turn the tide of the world's evil and need, and the Church's impotency and disobedience, but a heaven-sent, God-ordained, Christ-exalting, Holy Spirit-breathed, mighty, world-wide revival. We are at a point in history where it is either world revival or world destruction!*

Biblical Basis for an End-Time Revival

Is there a Biblical basis to believe for a mighty, world-wide, end-time revival? As we have seen in Chapter One, Joel 2:23-32 is a very important passage on the subject of revival. In verse 28, God says that He will pour out His Spirit on all mankind. This was initially fulfilled in Jerusalem on the Day of Pentecost, as explained by the Apostle Peter in Acts 2:14-21. But that is not the complete fulfillment. In Joel 2:23 the Scripture talks about "the early and latter rain." This is comparing the Church Age to the weather pattern in the Middle East, where there are two periods of rain. In the fall there is the early rain to prepare the soil for the planting of the crops. Then in the spring there is a later, or "latter," rain to prepare the crops for harvesting. This is also mentioned in Deuteronomy 11:14, Proverbs 16:15, Jeremiah 5:24, Hosea 6:3, Zechariah 10:1, and James 5:7. So it is in The Church Age. There was the "early rain" of the Spirit in Jerusalem on the Day of Pentecost, recorded in Acts 2:1-47, to begin The Church Age. There will also be a "latter rain" of the Spirit upon the Church and the world

34

("all mankind" in Joel 2:28) to end The Church Age. This last outpouring will be a mighty, world-wide outpouring upon all mankind just before Jesus returns.

Other Christian writers, speaking of a great, latter-rain revival, state:

"The latter rain, in prophetic sense, is a mighty revival of the Church in the last days of the present age.... The dispensation of mercy is about to close, and the evil days of the great tribulation loom, dark and forbidding before the world. Before those days can come the world must receive the last call of the Spirit of God. This it will receive through the channels of the fully restored Church.... It will be a glorious Church without spot or wrinkle.... A mighty revival will sweep the world."[3]

"By comparing Scripture with Scripture, we shall see that this glorious restoration is speaking of the great world-wide move of the Spirit of God at the end of the Gospel Age, just before the Second Coming of the Lord Jesus Christ. ... the revival for which we pray - the revival we so desperately need - will be nothing short of a world-wide outpouring of the Holy Spirit." [4]

"Zechariah spoke of the 'latter rain' (10:1), which, some think, refers to the end times when the final fulfillment of Joel's prophecy (2:28) will take place. The Spirit was poured out on all flesh at Pentecost according to Acts 2:17. Multitudes were converted and the Christian faith dealt the death blow to the anti-Christian Greek and Roman culture. The same Spirit is to be poured out on all flesh before the second advent of Jesus Christ. Therefore, we can expect great things to happen." [5]

This last, great, world-wide outpouring of the Holy Spirit will result in an awakened, purified, spiritually-powerful Church. It will result in a Church completely restored to the Christianity of the New Testament. It will result in unity coming to the Body of Christ. It will result in the fulfillment of the Great Commission. And it will result in the world-wide persecution of true believers. These are the themes of the rest of this book.

Other Passages
There are many passages that are examples of people praying for

revival: Psalms 80:18; 85:6; 119:25, 37, 40, 88, 107, 149, 154, 156, 159; 143:11; and Habakkuk 3:2; to name a few. Isaiah 59:19-20 gives us an end-time sequence: increased satanic activity, God pouring out His Spirit, and Christ returning to earth. (This is especially clear in the Amplified translation.) In Hosea 6:1-3, revival is promised to those who diligently seek God.

What About the Laodicean Church in Revelation 3:14-22?

There are those who teach that the seven churches described in Revelation, Chapters 2 and 3, are seven chronological periods in Church history, with the final Church period before Jesus returns being one where the Church is lukewarm. This teaching leaves little room for revival, and in fact, gives us a picture of the Church barely making it to the end of the Age. But there is no place where the Bible says that these are seven periods in Church history. They were seven messages written by the apostle John to the messengers of seven churches in Asia in the A.D. 90's.

Five Simultaneous Trends in the Last Days

This writer believes that there will actually be five trends taking place simultaneously in the last days. First, world conditions will continue to get worse, with seemingly no solutions (Matthew 24:6-7, 12; Luke 21:25-26; 1 Timothy 4:1-3; 2 Timothy 3:1-7, 13; 2 Peter 3:3-4; Jude 18, etc.). Second, in order to try to solve these problems, a world government will develop, which will become political-economic-religious in nature, and will be anti-Christ (Revelation, Chapter 13). Many nominal Christians will become part of this system (Matthew 24:10-12; Luke 21:16; 2 Thessalonians 2:3). Third, because men and nations will continue in their sin and rebellion against God, God's judgment will continue to fall, accelerating into a Great Shaking of all of society (Hebrews 12:25-29). **Every system of man will crumble. Only the Kingdom of God will remain.** Fourth, Israel will continue to be restored to her land (Isaiah 43:5-7, 56:8; Jeremiah 31:8-11, 33:10-13) and come to know her Messiah (Zechariah 12:10-13; Romans, Chapter 11). Fifth, the true Church will experience revival, restoration, unity, and world harvest, along with persecution.

Growing Evidence of a Coming, End-Time Revival

There are a number of growing evidences that we are building up to a mighty, end-time revival.

Growing Emphasis on Prayer [6]

There is a growing emphasis on prayer today, and much of it is prayer for revival. Campus Crusade for Christ has had a 24-hour prayer ministry since 1951. On January 31, 1983, a number of Christian leaders in the United States met in Chicago under the sponsorship of Inter-Varsity Missions to discuss a cooperative effort to mobilize Christians in united prayer for spiritual awakening and world evangelization. On February 3, 1983, Dr. J. Edwin Orr spoke at the evening session of the annual National Prayer Breakfast on the need to pray for a national revival. On June 5-11, 1984, there was an International Prayer Assembly for World Evangelization in Seoul, Korea, where 3,200 prayer leaders from 69 nations gathered to consider how to mobilize a world-wide prayer movement to pray for revival and world evangelization. They also learned more about the daily early-morning prayer meetings attended by over a million South Korean Christians.

Growing Interest in Spiritual Things

There is a growing, world-wide interest in spiritual matters. Note the recent developments.

President Reagan declared 1983 the Year of the Bible during his February 3 address at the National Prayer Breakfast in Washington, D.C. Three days earlier he addressed a session of the National Religious Broadcasters Convention on the theme of the Bible. His 21-minute speech was interrupted by applause fifteen times. Here are excerpts:

"In a time when recession has gripped our land, your industry, religious broadcasting, has enjoyed phenomenal growth. Now, there may be some who are frightened by your success, but I'm not one of them. As far as I'm concerned, the growth of religious broadcasting is one of the most heartening signs in America today. When we realize that every penny of that growth is being funded voluntarily by citizens of every stripe, we see an important truth. It's something that I have been speaking of for quite some time — that the American people are hungry for your message because they are hungry for a spiritual revival in this country. When Americans reach out for values of faith, family, and caring for the needs, they're saying, 'We want the Word of God. We want to face the future with the Bible.' " [7]

Other recent quotes from national periodicals include:

"Talk of prayer, meditation, worship and Bible study have replaced social crusades in many a church. Pastors, once caught up in the administrative tangle of managing congregations, are ceding some of those duties to others and spending more time honing their skills as shepherds of souls."

"What these trends indicate, observers say, is a new-found determination by those of religious faith to 'search out the sacred' in a society that has increasingly moved away from its religious underpinnings."

"The word spirituality is what you hear on the lips of pastors and lay people, and it cuts across many denominations," says the Rev. Don Browning, professor of religion at the University of Chicago Divinity School.

"There's an authentic hunger in people, a feeling that something is missing in their spiritual depths," explains the Rev. Tilden Edwards. The Episcopal priest directs Shalem Institute, a Washington, D.C., program founded to train lay people interested in serving as spiritual directors.

"Other believers simply want more from their faith than what they get at a weekend service. A movement spreading fast through churches and synagogues fosters meetings by small groups to discuss faith and what religious beliefs mean for each individual. 'Congregations and parishes tend to be too big to relate in a meaningful way to people,' notes Msgr. Thomas Kleissler of the Catholic Archdiocese of Newark, New Jersey. There, some 40,000 Catholics meet regularly in groups of 10 to 12 to pray, study Scripture and tell of their efforts at spiritual growth and the problems of living their faith at work and in the community." [8]

" 'There's much more emphasis on spirituality now,' says the Rev. Colin W. Williams, professor of religion at Yale Divinity School. 'The confident secularism of the '50's and '60's has passed, and people are asking questions about what is transcendent, what is life's meaning.' "

"This trend is taking on particular importance in liberal mainline churches — the United Methodists, United

38

Presbyterians, Episcopalians, and Christian Church (Disciples of Christ) — which have suffered major declines in membership since the mid-1960's."

"Faith Alive, a mostly Episcopalian organization based in York, Pennsylvania, sends 300 lay volunteers to hold 100 "renewal weekends" annually in churches all over the United States. Leaders tell participants of their own spiritual awakenings, sometimes touching cautiously on their controversial beliefs in charismatic 'gifts of the Holy Spirit' such as faith healing and the inspired language known from the Bible as 'speaking in tongues.' "

"Vitality also is seen in bulging enrollments at Protestant seminaries of all kinds."

"W. Fred Graham, a Presbyterian professor of religious studies at Michigan State University, reports 'more students wanting courses on the Bible than we can handle.' "[9]

"Similarly, some 20,000 Catholics have joined the Focolare movement, which again emphasizes small groups who either live together or meet often for prayer and social ministry to the elderly, poor, and other needy people."

"Lay people also have been the force behind the expanding Marriage Encounter movement, in which teams of couples meet in weekend retreats to improve essentially good marriages through better communications. Since 1972, some 800,000 couples have taken part." [10]

There is a network of Christian leaders and workers that is forming throughout the United States, called Coalition on Revival, that hopes to be a "movement to encourage spiritual awakening in America" through "nationally uniting awakened believers and churches around the country, bringing the United States and the world under a greater power of individual and corporate prayer, bringing reformation to the nation through education and activity, training and mobilizing believers in evangelism and missions." [11]

Growing Talk About Revival

Everywhere this writer has been since 1982 there has been growing talk among Christian leaders of a soon-coming, mighty, world-wide, end-time revival. Dr. Ben Jennings, coordinator for the 1984

International Prayer Assembly for World Evangelization, recently said, "Many of us believe a great worldwide revival is imminent."[12] Evangelist James Robison recently stated, "I believe the greatest revival in the history of the church is on its way. As I have traveled across this country, I have begun to feel it in my bones. Everywhere I go, I see new, dramatic, unmistakable evidence of the awesome work of preparation now being carried out by the Holy Spirit." [13]

There have also been several significant books written in recent years stating this very thing. (A list of these books can be found in the Bibliography.)

Preparing the Way

This is the most important section of this entire book. It deals with preparing the way for a soon-coming, mighty, world-wide, end-time revival. Please read it prayerfully.

Recognize the Need for Revival

The first step of preparation is to recognize the need for revival: in your own life, in your family, in your church, in your community, in your nation, throughout the world. The greatest need on every level is **revival**. Go back and prayerfully read page 33 and 34, and ask God to show you how desperately you need reviving; and how greatly revival is truly the greatest need of the hour in every level of society world-wide!

Realize the Possibility of Revival

Many Christians really don't see a genuine, world-wide spiritual awakening as a possibility. If you are one of them, we suggest that you go back and re-read previous pages of this book, especially pages 34-36. Revival is not only a possibility — **God longs to send revival.** He is **waiting** for His Church to get prepared. Will you begin to believe God for revival? Will you begin to cry out to Him for it? Will you get prepared?

2 Chronicles 7:14

How do we work with God in preparing the way for revival? It's all so clear in 2 Chronicles 7:14 (KJV), "If my people who are called by My name, shall humble themselves, and pray, and seek My face, and turn from their wicked ways; then will I hear from heaven, and will forgive their sin, and will heal their land."

Being A Christian

"If my people who are called by My name . . . . " Revival is something that happens to God's people. The effects include the conversion of the multitudes and the transformation of society, but revival begins as an awakening of God's people. So, it begins with us — "My people who are called by My name." God longs to send a mighty, spiritual awakening to this earth. But he is waiting; waiting for His people to do three things: "humble themselves," "pray and seek His face," and "turn from their wicked ways." Revival results from three very simple, but profound, conditions: 1) humility, 2) prayer, and 3) repentance and holiness.

Humility

First God says, "If My people who are called by My name will humble themselves." The Bible says much about humility, and its opposite, pride. Some of the key passages are:

Psalm 12:3 — May the Lord cut off all flattering lips, the tongue that speaks great things.

Psalm 25:9 — He leads the humble in justice, and He teaches the humble His way.

Psalm 35:13 — . . . I humbled my soul with fasting . . .

Psalm 37:11 — But the humble will inherit the land, and will delight themselves in abundant prosperity.

Psalm 75:5-7 — Do not lift up your horn on high, do not speak with insolent pride. For not from the east, nor from the west, nor from the desert comes exaltation; but God is the Judge; He puts down one, and exalts another.

Proverbs 16:5 — Everyone who is proud in heart is an abomination to the Lord; assuredly, he will not be unpunished.

Proverbs 16:18-19 — Pride goes before destruction, and a haughty spirit before stumbling. It is better to be of a humble spirit with the lowly, than to divide the spoil with the proud.

Proverbs 27:2 — Let another praise you, and not your own mouth; a stranger, and not your own lips.

Isaiah 2:11 — The proud look of man will be abased, and the loftiness of man will be humbled, and the Lord alone will be exalted in that day.

Isaiah 57:15 (KJV) — For thus saith the high and lofty One that inhabiteth eternity, whose name is Holy; I dwell in the high and holy place, with him also that is of a contrite and humble spirit, to revive the spirit of the humble, and to revive the heart of the contrite ones.

Micah 6:8 — He has told you, O man, what is good; and what does the Lord require of you but to do justice, to love kindness, and to walk humbly with your God?

Matthew 5:3 — Blessed are the poor in spirit, for theirs is the kingdom of heaven.

Matthew 18:4 — Whoever then humbles himself as this child, he is the greatest in the kingdom of heaven.

Matthew 23:12 — And whoever exalts himself shall be humbled; and whoever humbles himself shall be exalted.

John 13:14 — If I then, the Lord and the Teacher, washed your feet, you also ought to wash one another's feet.

Romans 12:3 — For through the grace given to me I say to every man among you not to think more highly of himself than he ought to think; but to think so as to have sound judgment, as God has allotted to each a measure of faith.

1 Corinthians 1:28-29 — And the base things of the world and the despised, God has chosen, the things that are not, that He might nullify the things that are, that no man should boast before God.

1 Corinthians 13:4 — ...Love does not brag and is not arrogant.

Galatians 6:14 — But may it never be that I should boast, except in the cross of our Lord Jesus Christ, through which the world has been crucified to me, and I to the world.

Ephesians 4:1-2 — I, therefore, the prisoner of the Lord, entreat you to walk in a manner worth of the calling with which you have been called, with all humility and gentleness, with patience, showing forbearance to one another in love.

Philippians 2:3 — Do nothing from selfishness or empty conceit, but with humility of mind let each of you regard one another as more important than himself.

James 4:6 — ...God is opposed to the proud, but gives grace to the humble.

1 Peter 5:5-6 — You younger men, likewise, be subject to your elders; and all of you, clothe yourselves with humility toward one another, for God is opposed to the proud, but gives grace to the humble. Humble yourselves, therefore, under the mighty hand of God, that He may exalt you at the proper time.

So away with all forms of pride: pride of appearance, pride of nationality, pride of knowledge, pride of accomplishments, and pride of spirituality. We must humble ourselves under the mighty hand of God (1 Peter 5:6). We need to die to our own rights, to wanting our own way. We must recognize that all we are and have is because of God's mercy and love, and not because of anything that we have done. We must ask God to make us open, flexible, patient, meek, gentle, teachable — all the fruit of true humility. Churches must repent of all that they do out of pride, which leads to competition, rather than from humility, which results in cooperation. We need to turn from our self-centered, self-promoting, self-exalting lifestyle to a lifestyle of humility and of **exalting Jesus only.**

Prayer

God's second requirement of preparation for revival is prayer. " . . . and pray, and seek my face." The Bible says:

Psalm 27:8 — When Thou didst say, "Seek My face," my heart said to Thee, "Thy face, O, Lord, I shall seek."

Psalm 145:18 — The Lord is near to all who call upon Him, to all who call upon Him in truth.

Isaiah 55:6 — Seek the Lord while He may be found; call upon Him while He is near.

Jeremiah 33:3 (NKJV) — Call to Me, and I will answer you, and show you great and mighty things, which you do not know.

Matthew 6:6 — But you, when you pray, go into your inner room, and when you have shut your door, pray to your Father who is in secret, and your Father who sees in secret will repay you.

Matthew 7:7-8 — Ask, and it shall be given to you; seek, and you shall find; knock, and it shall be opened to you. For every one who asks receives, and he who seeks finds, and to him who knocks it shall be opened.

Matthew 21:22 — And everything you ask in prayer, believing, you shall receive.

Mark 11:24 — Therefore I say to you, all things for which you pray and ask, believe that you have received them, and they shall be granted you.

Luke 18:1 — Now He was telling them a parable to show that at all times they ought to pray and not to lose heart.

John 14:12-14 — Truly, truly, I say to you, he who believes in Me, the works that I do shall he do also; and greater works than these shall he do; because I go to the Father. And whatever you ask in My name, that will I do, that the Father may be glorified in the Son. If you ask Me anything in My name, I will do it.

John 15:7 — If you abide in Me, and My words abide in you, ask whatever you wish, and it shall be done for you.

Philippians 4:6-7 — Be anxious for nothing, but in everything by prayer and supplication with thanksgiving let your requests be made known to God, and the peace of God, which surpasses all comprehension, shall guard your hearts and minds in Christ Jesus.

1 Thessalonians 5:17 — Pray without ceasing.

Hebrews 4:16 — Let us therefore draw near with confidence to the throne of grace, that we may receive mercy and may find grace to help in time of need.

Hebrews 11:6 — And without faith it is impossible to please Him, for he who comes to God must believe that He is, and that He is a rewarder of those who seek Him.

James 4:8 — Draw near to God and He will draw near to you. Cleanse your hands, you sinners; and purify your hearts, you double-minded.

James 5:16 — Therefore, confess your sins to one another, and pray for one another, so that you may be healed. The effective prayer of a righteous man can accomplish much.

1 John 5:14-15 — And this is the confidence which we have before Him, that, if we ask anything according to His will, He hears us. And if we know that He hears us in whatever we ask, we know that we have the requests which we have asked from Him.

Revelation 5:8 — And when He had taken the book, the four living creatures and the twenty-four elders fell down before the Lamb, having each one a harp, and golden bowls full of incense, which are the prayers of the saints.

What a tremendous privilege and opportunity — prayer! We have access to the heart of the God of the universe. What a privilege we have to spend time in the presence of a holy, loving, all-powerful heavenly Father—gazing upon and worshipping Him. Yet most of us are content with five minutes a day. He is waiting, longing, for His people to come before Him, to seek His face, to wait upon Him in prayer.

This writer is convinced that **prayerlessness is the greatest sin in the Church of Jesus Christ today.** Such was not the case with the great men and women of God in the past. John Wesley spent two hours each morning in prayer beginning at 4 a.m. John Fletcher often spent all night in prayer. Martin Luther spent two to three hours each morning in prayer. John Welch, the Scottish preacher, thought the day ill-spent if he did not spend eight to ten hours in prayer.[14] Dr. A. T. Pierson once said, "From the Day of Pentecost, there has been not one great spiritual awakening in any land which has not begun in a union of prayer, though only among two or three: no such outward, upward movement has continued after such prayer meetings have declined; and it is in exact proportion to the maintenance of such joint and believing supplication and intercession that the word of God in any land or locality has had free course and been glorified." [15] A. W. Tozer said it well, "Revivals are born after midnight." [16] **God is looking for those who will give themselves to prayer day and night until revival breaks forth.**

Ask God what you are to do about this matter of prayer. Are you to set aside a certain time for prayer each day? Are you to start a daily, family prayer time? Are you to talk with your pastor about starting a daily, morning prayer time, or a weekly or monthly church-wide or city-wide night of prayer for revival? A list of some possible prayer topics and Scripture references for times of prayer is given in Appendix 2. Sources for further information on prayer are listed in Appendix 3. A list of organizations specializing in helping God's people prepare for revival is given in Appendix 4.

Repentance and Holiness

God made it so clear — "... humble themselves, and pray, and seek my face, and turn from their wicked ways." You may say, "I'm a Christian. What do you mean, 'my wicked ways'?" Let's see what the Bible says about turning from our wicked ways:

Genesis 17:1 — Now when Abram was ninety-nine years old, the Lord appeared to Abram and said to him, "I am God Almighty; walk before Me and be blameless."

Exodus 19:6 — And you shall be to Me a kingdom of priests and a holy nation.

Psalm 15:1-5 — O Lord, who may abide in Thy tent? Who may dwell on Thy holy hill? He who walks with integrity, and works righteousness, and speaks truth in his heart. He does not slander with his tongue, nor does evil to his neighbor, nor takes up a reproach against his friend; in whose eyes a reprobate is despised, but who honors those who fear the Lord; he swears to his own hurt, and does not change; he does not put out his money at interest, nor does he take a bribe against the innocent. He who does these things will never be shaken.

Psalm 24:3-5 — Who may ascend into the hill of the Lord? And who may stand in His holy place? He who has clean hands and a pure heart, who has not lifted up his soul to falsehood, and has not sworn deceitfully. He shall receive a blessing from the Lord and righteousness from the God of his salvation.

Psalm 32:5 — I acknowledge my sin to Thee, and my iniquity I did not hide; I said, "I will confess my transgressions to the Lord."

Psalm 34:14 — Depart from evil, and do good; seek peace, and pursue it.

Psalm 51:17 — The sacrifices of God are a broken spirit; a broken and contrite heart, O God, Thou wilt not despise.

Proverbs 28:13 — He who conceals his transgressions will not prosper, but he who confesses and forsakes them will find compassion.

Matthew 5:6, 8, 29-30 — Blessed are those who hunger and thirst for righteousness, for they shall be satisfied .... Blessed are the pure in heart, for they shall see God .... And if your right eye makes you stumble, tear it out, and throw it from you; for it is better for you that one of the parts of your body perish, than for your whole body to be thrown into hell. And if your right hand makes you stumble, cut it off, and throw it from you; for it is better for you that one of the parts of your body perish, than for your whole body to go into hell.

Matthew 7:13-14, 21-23 — Enter by the narrow gate; for the gate is wide, and the way is broad that leads to destruction, and many are those who enter by it. For the gate is small, and the way is narrow that leads to life, and few are those who find it . . . . Not every one who says to Me, 'Lord, Lord,' will enter the kingdom of heaven; but he who does the will of My Father who is in heaven. Many will say to Me on that day, 'Lord, Lord,' did we not prophesy in Your name, and in Your name cast out demons, and in Your name perform many miracles?' And then I will declare to them, 'I never knew you; depart from Me, you who practice lawlessness.'

Acts 24:16 — In view of this, I also do my best to maintain always a blameless conscience both before God and before men.

Romans 6:15-16 — What then? Shall we sin because we are not under law but under grace? May it never be! Do you not know that when you present yourselves to someone as slaves for obedience, you are slaves of the one whom you obey, either of sin resulting in death, or of obedience resulting in righteousness?

Romans 12:1-2 — I urge you therefore, brethren, by the mercies of God, to present your bodies a living and holy sacrifice, acceptable to God, which is your spiritual service of worship. And do not be conformed to this world, but be transformed by the renewing of your mind, that you may prove what the will of God is, that which is good and acceptable and perfect.

2 Corinthians 6:17 — "Therefore, come out from their midst and be separate," says the Lord. "And do not touch what is unclean; and I will welcome you."

2 Corinthians 7:1 — Therefore, having these promises, beloved, let us cleanse ourselves from all defilement of flesh and spirit, perfecting holiness in the fear of God.

2 Corinthians 10:5 — We are destroying speculations and every lofty thing raised up against the knowledge of God, and we are taking every thought captive to the obedience of Christ.

Ephesians 4:22-24 — . . . that, in reference to your former manner of life, you lay aside the old self, which is being corrupted in accordance with the lusts of deceit, and that you be renewed in the spirit of your mind, and put on the new self, which in the likeness of God has been created in righteousness and holiness of the truth.

Philippians 4:8 — Finally, brethren, whatever is true, whatever is honorable, whatever is right, whatever is pure, whatever is lovely, whatever is of good repute, if there is any excellence and if anything is worthy of praise, let your mind dwell on these things.

Colossians 3:8-10 — But now you also, put them all aside: anger, wrath, malice, slander, and abusive speech from your mouth. Do not lie to one another, since you laid aside the old self with its evil practices, and have put on the new self who is being renewed to a true knowledge according to the image of the One who created him.

1 Peter 1:16 — You shall be holy, for I am holy.

1 John 2:15-16 — Do not love the world, nor the things of the world. If any one loves the world, the love of the Father is not in him. For all that is in the world, the lust of the flesh and the lust of the eyes and the boastful pride of life, is not from the Father, but is from the world.

Charles G. Finney, the evangelist-revivalist in the mid-1800's, gives us a list of things of which, as Christians, we may need to repent:[17]

1. Ingratitude
2. Lack of love for God
3. Neglect of the Bible
4. Unbelief
5. Lack of prayer
6. Neglect of fellowship
7. The manner in which you have performed spiritual duties
8. Lack of love for souls
9. Lack of care for the poor and lost in foreign lands
10. Neglect of family duties
11. Lack of watchfulness over your witness
12. Neglect to watch over your brethren
13. Neglect of self-denial
14. Love of things and possessions
15. Vanity
16. Envy
17. Bitterness

18. Slander (gossip)
19. Levity (a spirit of excessive humor)
20. Lying
21. Cheating
22. Hypocrisy
23. Robbing God
24. Bad temper
25. Hindering others from being useful
26. False gods and other religions

Revelation, Chapters 2 and 3, gives us an interesting list of things of which we may need to repent:

Revelation 2:4 — leaving your first love
Revelation 2:14 — committing acts of immorality
Revelation 2:20 — tolerating false teachers
Revelation 3:2 — not doing all that God wants
Revelation 3:15-16 — being lukewarm

Will you determine this day to begin to wholeheartedly humble yourself, to pray and to seek God's face, and to turn from your wicked ways, that you might participate in preparing the way for a soon-coming, mighty, world-wide, end-time, outpouring of the Holy Spirit? Why not set aside a day or more soon to get alone with God. Spend the day humbling yourself before God, seeking His face, and turning from your wicked ways. And know that He will hear you, forgive your sins, and heal your land. Hallelujah!

PERSONAL ASSIGNMENT-REVIVAL

Questions to Answer

1. Define "revival."

2. How does Joel 2:23-32 speak to the subject of revival?

3. When were the four major awakenings since 1700?

4. What are the conditions for revival according to 2 Chronicles 7:14?

Questions for Meditation and Application

1. Is a major, spiritual awakening on its way?

2. What changes do you need to make in your life so that it is characterized by humility, prayer, and holiness?

3. Are you doing all that God would have you to do to prepare the way for revival in your life, family, church, community, and nation?

Assignment

1. Read some additional material on the subject of revival. (See the Bibliography of this book for a list of available books.)

2. Set aside a day soon to seek God for revival in accordance with 2 Chronicles 7:14.

3. Ask God what He would have you to do to see an outpouring of His Spirit come to your city, nation, and the entire world.

PART II — RESTORATION

"... I will restore to you the years that the locust hath eaten ... and ye shall eat in plenty, and be satisfied, and praise the name of the Lord your God ... and ye shall know that I am in the midst of Israel, and that I am the Lord your God, and none else: and my people shall never be ashamed."

— Joel 2:25-27 (KJV)

"... until the period of restoration of all things ..."

— Acts 3:21

"But steadily, relentlessly, the mighty Spirit of God has been moving on, restoring that which was lost and heading things up toward that great revelation of the Body of Christ in unity and fullness — even one Body, fully matured 'unto the measure of the stature of the fullness of Christ.' "[1]

— Frank Bartleman

"In the midst of all the decay and confusion around us, both in the world and the Church, may God help us to look heavenward and catch sight of His great purpose — even a Church in the purity, power, and principles of New Testament Christianity."[2]

—Arthur Wallis

5

THE PRINCIPLE OF RESTORATION

The second thing that will characterize the Church triumphant at the end of the Age is restoration. Restoration is closely related to revival. On the crest of each wave of revival is that which God is restoring at that time to His Church.

Definition

The American College Dictionary defines the word, "restoration," as "a bringing back to a former, original, normal, or unimpaired condition;" and further states that "restore" means to "bring back to a state of health, soundness, or vigor."[1]

The Hebrew word most often translated "restore" in the Old Testament is the word, "shub." It has the basic meaning "to turn back, return." It is most frequently translated: return (263 times), returned (151 times), restore (59 times), again (54 times), turn (53 times), bring back (45 times), and brought back (31 times).[2]

The Greek word most often translated "restore" in the New Testament is the word "apokathistemi," and means "to restore, give back."[3] The noun form is used only once, in Acts 3:21: " . . . until the period of restoration of all things . . ." The verb form is most often used in connection with Jesus healing people (Matthew 12:13, Mark 3:5, 8:25, Luke 6:10); meaning that their bodies were being restored.

Thus, we can define "restoration" as "a returning or bringing back

52

to a former, original, normal, unimpaired state of health, soundness, or vigor."

God, A God of Restoration

As we study the pages of the Bible, we see that **God is a God of restoration**. When Abimelech mistakingly took Abraham's wife Sarah to be his wife, God spoke to him in a dream and told him to **restore** her to Abraham (Genesis 20:7). The Israelites prayed to God for **restoration** from their calamities (Psalms 60:1, 80:3, 7, 19). David cried out for God to **restore** to him the joy of salvation (Psalm 51:12). God was committed to **restoring** the nation Israel to their land, inheritance, and blessings when they backslid, if they would but return to Him (Deuteronomy 30:2; Psalms 85:1, 4, 126:4; Isaiah 1:26, 49:8; Jeremiah 15:19, 16:15, 27:22, 29:14, 30:3, 30:18, 31:23, 33:7; Ezekiel 16:53; Joel 3:1, Amos 9:14, etc.). The 23rd Psalm mentions, "He **restores** my soul." God **restored** Job's fortunes (Job 42:10). Nebuchadnezzar is **restored** to sanity and his throne after he acknowledged God (Daniel 4:34-37). Several people are **restored** to health by God (Isaiah 38:16; Jeremiah 30:17; Matthew 12:13, 15:31; Mark 3:5, 8:25; James 5:15, etc.). Those who fall into sin, God desires to see **restored** (Galatians 6:1). The disciples were expecting Elijah (John the Baptist) to **restore** all things (Matthew 17:11). Just before Jesus' ascension, the disciples were asking Him if now was the time that He was going to **restore** the Kingdom to Israel (Acts 1:6). God's plan of **restoration** of His people, Israel, also included the calling of the Gentiles (Acts 15:12-21). And someday Jesus will return to earth to **restore** all things to their condition before Adam's fall (Acts 3:18-21, Romans 8:18-23). **What a God He is —committed to a full restoration of all things!**

Restoration, A Principle in Our Judeo-Christian Society

We find the principle of restoration all through the Bible. Reuben wanted to **restore** Joseph unharmed to his father (Genesis 37:22). Joseph predicted that the cupbearer would be **restored** to his place of responsibility (Genesis 40:9-13). Moses **restored** Pharoah's hand (Exodus 4:7). One who commits a robbery is to **restore** what he took (Leviticus 6:4). And so forth, through the rest of the Bible (Numbers 35:25; Deuteronomy 22:2; 1 Samuel 12:3; 2 Samuel 9:7, 16:3; 1 Kings

12:21, 20:34; 2 Kings 8:6; 2 Chronicles 24:4; Ezra 2:68, etc.). This principle of restoring things to their rightful place, based on the Biblical principle, is a part of the Judeo-Christian heritage. We find it in our conscience, our laws, and in our understanding of proper social behavior.

The Restoration Concept of Church History

In this section we want to look at the principle of restoration as it relates to Church history. This writer believes that all of Church history is a cycle, or circle.[4] The early Church that we read about in *The Acts* could be called the early, apostolic, New Testament Church. It was characterized by a certain level of purity, spiritual authority and power; by certain purposes; by certain principles and patterns; and by a certain degree of fruitfulness. We will look at this early Church in more depth in Chapter 6.

It was not long until this early Church began to fall away from this purity, spiritual authority and power, purposes, principles and patterns, and fruitfulness. In fact, it began to fall away even during New Testament times. Five of the seven churches mentioned in Revelation, Chapters 2 and 3, were called to repent. The Church continued to decline, reaching a low point during the Dark Ages. Frank Bartleman says it this way:

> "So it was with the early Church. When they ceased to go forward, they started wandering in a circle and became lost in the Dark Ages. The devil found he could not destroy them or stop their march by persecuting and killing them; so he removed the cross, offering them titles, positions, honor, salaries, profits of every kind — and they fell for it." [5]

(The decline of the Church is the subject of Chapter 7.) You can see this decline, and the concurrent and subsequent restoration, visually on Chart 2 on page 58 and Table 1 on pages 59-62.

But God is a God of restoration! His plan is to have "a glorious Church, without spot or wrinkle" (Ephesians 5:27) that is "a mature man, to (or with) the measure of the stature of the fullness of Christ" (Ephesians 4:13), "a bride" who "has made herself ready" for Her marriage to the Lamb, Jesus Christ (Revelation 19:7). He is committed to seeing the Church restored to that which it was in its early days.

Starting in the A.D. 150's and accelerating about A.D. 1200, the Holy Spirit has been restoring the Church to New Testament Christianity. (See Chapters 8 and 9.) This restoration process is still taking place. (See Chapters 10 and 11.) When Jesus returns to earth, He will return for a Church like He left, like the early Church; in purity, in spiritual authority and power, in purposes, in principles and patterns, and in fruitfulness. Hallelujah! Here is how others have said it:

"God is not just dealing with the Church in this manner because of a lack of something better to do. God has a glorious plan which He is in the process of working out in His dealings with man. Each new visitation brings us just that much closer to the end product. Each new step or portion of truth brings us ever closer to that fully restored Church that will be a fit, or suitable, Bride for His Son. The Church will indeed be a help meet for the Son of God. It will be a glorious Church without spot or wrinkle or any such thing (Ephesians 5:27)." [6]

— Dick Iverson

"Jesus is coming soon, coming for a perfect church, clad in power, in glory, for the perfect tree with every gift and fruit hanging in luscious, mellow, developed perfection upon her branches . . . . Let us get back to Pentecost and go on to the fullness of Pentecostal power and glory recorded in God's Word, for Jesus is coming soon, very soon, for His perfect, waiting Church, His bride, unspotted with the world, His tree with its unblemished and perfect fruit." [7]

— Aimee Semple McPherson

"Ever since the early Church fell from New Testament purity and life, she has been like a backslider, fallen from the summit of apostolic days — though destined to return and yet enter into the full blessing of the Father's house . . . . But steadily, relentlessly, the mighty Spirit of God has been moving on, restoring that which was lost and heading things up toward the great prophetic revelation of the Body of Christ in unity and fullness: even one Body, fully matured 'unto the measure of the stature of the fullness of Christ!' " [8]

— Frank Bartleman

"This reformation, or 'recovery,' aspect of God's moving through the centuries is unmistakable .... " [9]

— Arthur Wallis

"In the midst of all the decay and confusion around us, both in the world and the Church, may God help us to look heavenward and catch sight of His great purpose — even a Church in the purity, power, and principles of New Testament Christianity!" [10]

— Arthur Wallis

"... a 'restoration' or 'regeneration' is necessary to preserve and increase the Church." [11]

— Pope Gregory XVI, in 1832

"A leading interpreter of the free churches, Franklin H. Littall, makes restoration of the beliefs and practices of the early church the key to the 'Anabaptist View of the Church.' " [12]

"... a powerful motivation for John Wesley's labors was the desire to restore the forms and power of early Christianity." [13]

— Donald F. Durnbaugh

"Events in the history of the churches in the time of the Apostles have been selected and recorded in the book of *The Acts* in such a way as to provide a permanent pattern for the churches. Departure from this pattern has had disastrous consequences, and all revival and restoration have been due to some return to the pattern and principles contained in the Scriptures." [14]

— E. H. Broadbent

"The Church then will have turned 360 degrees: from the birth on the Day of Pentecost, to the falling away (2 Thessalonians 2:3), to the slow restoration, to the final wave, right up to the time when there will be a deluge of the Holy Spirit's power upon the whole Church — Roman Catholic and Protestant. The same unity that was in the upper room of the New Testament Church will be found among Christians in every nation. Mass healings will take place worldwide, demons will be cast out, miracles will become the norm." [15]

— Maxwell Whyte

56

We, at this time in history, are moving into the final period of restoration. It will soon be completed. Jesus will soon return for "a glorious Church" (Ephesians 5:27). What a glorious day to be alive! We will look at this process of decline and restoration in more depth in the next six chapters.

CHART 2 — THE DECLINE AND RESTORATION
OF NEW TESTAMENT CHRISTIANITY

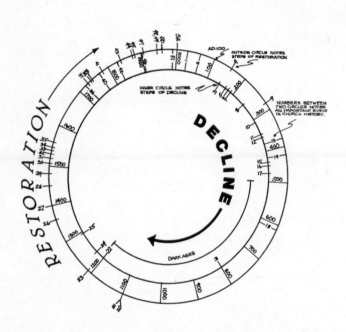

Table 1 — The Decline and Restoration of New Testament Christianity

	Step of Decline*	Im. Event in Church History	Step of Restoration*
1. A.D.30-65 — Apostolic New Testament Church.		x	
2. 60-305 — Roman persecutions (Paul and Peter martyred about 68 A.D.) keep Church pure.		x	
3. 150 — Gifts and ministries of the Holy Spirit cease to operate on any large scale.	x		
4. 156-400 — Montanus — early restoration movement.			x
5. 160 — Local church led by one man (pastor) rather than by a group (elders).	x		
6. 180-300 — Church hierarchy developed and local church loses autonomy.	x		
7. 185 — Baptism of infants begun.	x		
8. 230-350 — Church buildings erected.	x		
9. 280 — Hermit Anthony in Egypt — Christian communities seeking deeper Christian life.			x
10. 313 — Constantine embraces Christianity and decrees Roman persecutions cease.	x		
11. mid 300's — Radical Christians persecuted by Church.	x		

*Note: Steps of decline are explained in Chapter 7; steps of restoration are explained in Chapters 8-11.

	Step of Decline*	Im. Event in Church History	Step of Restoration*
12. 385 — Priscillian and others beheaded in Spain for preaching as a "layman."	x		
13. late 300's — Bible as we know it today was accepted.		x	
14. 432-800 — Northern Europe evangelized with fairly pure Gospel.		x	
15. early 400's—Augustine—salvation only through Roman Catholic Church.	x		
16. 450 — Roman papacy established.	x		
17. 476 — Fall of Rome. Pope controls kings.	x		
18. 600-1350 — Nestorian missionaries continue to spread Gospel in East.		x	
19. 800 — Charlemagne crowned emperor of Holy Roman Empire by Pope.	x		
20. 1100 — Albigenses and Waldenses.			x
21. 1100-1500 — Mystics desire deeper life.			x
22. 1200-1600—Inquisitions—dissenters are killed.	x		
23. 1210 — Francis of Assisi begins apostolic bands.			x
24. 1229 — Bible forbidden in native language of people.	x		
25. 1299 — Submission to the Roman Pope necessary for salvation.	x		
26. 1374-1384 — Wyclife and Lollards preach reform throughout England.			x

| | Step of Im. Event in Step of |
| | Decline Church History Restoration |

Event in Church History	Step of Decline	Step of Restoration
27. 1400-1415 — Hus and the Bohemian Brethren — reformation in eastern Europe.		x
28. 1456 — John Gutenburg prints first Bible.		x
29. 1491-1498 — Savonarola — reformation in Italy.		x
30. 1516 — Erasmus publishes Greek New Testament.		x
31. 1517 — Martin Luther — justification by faith, authority of the Bible, priesthood of all believers.		x
32. 1519-1650 — Reformation spreads.		x
33. 1525 — Anabaptist — baptism for believers only.		x
34. 1530-1650 — Restoration of evangelical theology.		x
35. 1100-Today — Restoration of New Testament Church government and practice.		x
36. 1727-1780 — First Great Awakening	x	
37. 1730-1760 — Zinzendorf and Moravians — early thrust of Protestant missionaries.		x
38. 1738-1790 — Wesleys — witness of the Holy Spirit and holiness.		x
39. 1739-Today — Mass evangelism		x
40. 1792-1842 — Second Great Awakening	x	
41. 1793 — William Carey — modern missions movement.		x

	Step of Decline	Im. Event in Church History	Step of Restoration
42. 1857-1859 — Third Great Awakening.		x	
43. 1850-Today—Women's ministry			x
44. 1865-1910 — Salvation Army — social implication of the Gospel.			x
45. 1880 — A.B. Simpson — physical healing.			x
46. 1900-1930 — Fourth Great Awakening.		x	
47. 1906 — Pentecostal movement — gifts of the Spirit.			x
48. 1935-Today—Scripture memory.			x
49. 1935-Today — Follow up.			x
50. 1960-Today — Personal evangelism.			x
51. 1988(?)-2000(?) — A soon-coming, mighty, world-wide, end-time revival.			x
52. 2000(?) — Complete restoration of the Church to apostolic, New Testament Christianity.			x

6

THE EARLY CHURCH

This writer believes that the early Church, as described in *The Acts,* is God's standard for the entire Church Age. This is God's standard of purity, spiritual authority and power, purposes, principles and patterns, and fruitfulness.

"In the New Testament we have a clear picture of the early Church. It wasn't a perfect Church because it was composed of human beings, and they are never perfect. However, the early Church was perfect in constitution, perfect in the revelation of God's mind, received through His holy apostles and prophets. They had complete light and thus had no need to progress into fuller revelation in the ensuing centuries.

"Through the apostles, the early Church received in that first century a complete revelation of the mind of God. This revelation is, of course, contained in our New Testament. But also, as they walked in the light of this revelation, not only the revelation but they themselves became a model of God's intention." [1]

— Arthur Wallis

Anything less than Acts Christianity is sub-standard! So, let's take a look at the early Church. The following is a summary of the characteristics and patterns of this early Church as recorded in the first half (Chapters 1-14) of the *Acts of the Apostles,* which could also be entitled, *The Acts of the Holy Spirit Through the Early Christians.* You might like to complete this study on your own for the rest of *Acts* (Chapters 15-28).

1. Started on the foundation of a resurrected Christ: Acts 1:3-11.
2. Endued with Holy Spirit power: 1:4-8, 2:2-4, 4:8, 4:31, 4:33, 6:8, 6:10, 7:55, 11:28, 13:9.

3. Given a task to perform: 1:8, 5:20.
4. Worshiped an ascended Christ: 1:9-11.
5. Awaited His future return: 1:11.
6. Helped, instructed by the angels: 1:10-11, 5:19, 8:26, 12:7-11, 12:23.
7. Gathered together: 1:13-15, 2:1, 2:44, 2:46, 4:23, 5:12, 12:12.
8. Unified: 1:14, 2:46, 4:32, 5:12.
9. Prayed: 1:14, 1:24, 2:42, 3:1, 4:24, 6:6, 8:15, 12:5, 12:12.
10. Recognized the place of women: 1:14, 8:12, 9:2.
11. Had recognized leaders: 1:15, 1:25-26, 2:14, 2:42, 4:33, 5:3, 6:3-6, 8:14, 12:17, 13:1.
12. Knew the Scriptures (Old Testament): 1:16-20, 2:16-35, 3:21-25, 4:11, 4:24-26, 7:2-53, 8:30-33, 13:33-41.
13. Recognized apostles (the Twelve plus others): 1:25, 14:14.
14. Open to the Holy Spirit coming any way He chose to come: 2:2-21.
15. Bold: 2:14, 3:4-6, 3:12, 4:13, 4:19-20, 4:29, 4:31, 5:29, 5:42, 9:27-28, 14:3.
16. Witnessed / Preached — out where the people were: 2:14-40, 3:4-26, 4:8-12, 4:31, 4:33, 5:21-25, 5:31, 5:42, 6:7, 6:10, 8:4-5, 8:25, 8:30-35, 8:40, 9:20, 9:28, 10:19-42, 13:5. Preached the following:
    a. Jewish heritage: 2:16, 2:25-30, 2:34-36, 3:13, 5:30, 7:2-53, 13:16-41.
    b. About the Holy Spirit: 2:17-19, 2:33, 2:38-39.
    c. End-times: 2:20.
    d. Salvation: 2:21, 2:40, 4:12, 13:26.
    e. Jesus: 2:22-23, 8:5, 8:35, 9:20, 10:36, 11:20.
    f. The cross: 2:23, 2:36, 3:18, 4:10, 5:30, 13:28-29.
    g. The resurrection: 2:24-32, 3:15, 3:26, 4:2, 4:10, 4:33, 10:40, 13:30-37.
    h. Jesus is Lord: 2:34-36, 4:33, 9:17, 10:36.
    i. Jesus is Messiah: 2:36, 3:20, 5:42, 9:22.
    j. Repentance: 2:38, 3:19, 3:26, 5:31, 8:22.
    k. Water baptism: 2:38.
    l. Forgiveness of sins: 2:38, 3:19, 5:31, 10:43, 13:38.
    m. Wholeness: 3:16, 4:10, 14:9-10.
    n. The Name of Jesus Christ: 3:16, 4:10, 8:12.
    o. The Kingdom of God: 8:12.
    p. The Good News: 8:12, 8:25, 8:40, 13:32, 14:7, 14:15, 14:21.

q. Jesus is the Son of God: 9:20.
r. The Word of God: 13:5.
s. Eternal life: 13:46-48.
17. Grew in numbers: 2:41, 2:47, 4:4, 5:14, 6:1, 6:7, 8:12, 9:31, 9:35, 9:42, 10:44, 11:21, 11:24, 12:24.
18. Baptized (in water) their converts: 2:41, 8:12, 8:16, 8:36-39, 9:18, 10:48.
19. Gave themselves to:
    a. Apostles' teaching: 2:42.
    b. Fellowship: 2:42, 2:46.
    c. Breaking of bread: 2:42, 2:46.
    d. Prayer: 2:42.
20. Discipled their converts: 2:42, 10:48, 11:23, 11:26, 14:22.
21. Evidenced signs and wonders (miracles, healings, deliverances): 2:43, 3:6-7, 4:16, 4:30, 5:12, 5:15-16, 6:8, 8:13, 9:17-18, 9:34, 9:37-41, 13:11, 14:3, 14:9-10.
22. Shared possessions with each other: 2:44-45, 4:32-37, 6:1, 11:29.
23. Had joy: 2:46, 5:41, 8:8, 8:39, 11:23, 13:52.
24. Lived lives of simplicity: 2:46.
25. Praised God: 2:47, 3:8.
26. Were respected by the people: 2:47, 5:13.
27. Exercised authority of Jesus' name: 3:6, 3:16, etc.
28. Were persecuted: 4:3, 4:17-21, 5:18, 5:40, 6:12, 8:1-3, 9:1-2, 9:16, 11:19, 12:1-4, 14:19.
29. Had grace: 4:33, 6:8, 11:23.
30. Were holy: 5:1-11, 8:18-24.
31. Feared God: 5:11, 9:31.
32. Obeyed God: 5:29, 5:32, 8:27-30, 9:17, 10:23.
33. Had leaders who:
    a. Gave themselves to the Word: 6:2, 6:4.
    b. Gave themselves to prayer: 6:4, 10:9, 14:23.
    c. Had a good reputation: 6:3, 11:24.
    d. Were full of the Spirit: 6:3, 6:5, 7:55, 11:24.
    e. Were wise: 6:3, 6:10.
    f. Were men of faith: 6:5, 11:24.
34. Practiced laying on of hands: 6:6, 8:17, 9:27, 13:3, 14:3.
35. Were martyred: 7:60, 12:2.
36. Led their converts to be filled with the Holy Spirit: 8:15-17, 9:17.
37. Heard God's voice: 8:29, 9:10, 10:13-20, 13:2.
38. Were caught away: 8:39-40.

39. Had the gifts of the Spirit in operation: 10:46.
40. Had prophets: 11:27, 13:1.
41. Had elders: 11:30, 14:23.
42. Met in homes: 2:46, 12:12.
43. Had teachers: 13:1.
44. Fasted: 13:2-3, 14:23.
45. Sent out a missionary team: 13:1-5.
46. Planted churches: 13:1, 14:23, 14:27.
47. Were Spirit-filled: 13:52.

Let's summarize these notes and describe the early Church as recorded in the first half of *Acts*. It was a Church that was vividly aware of Jesus' death, resurrection, ascension, and future return. It was a Church that was mightily endued with the Holy Spirit to witness and preach the Gospel boldly and to see signs and wonders take place. They were a fasting, praying Church. Their message was Jesus — the fulfillment of Jewish prophecy, crucified, resurrected, the Son of God, the Messiah, the Lord of all — and that through Him there was forgiveness of sins, wholeness, and eternal life. They knew and often quoted the Scriptures. They experienced much spiritual authority over sickness and demon powers through Jesus' Name. They often met together in their various homes and together in larger places. They were of one heart and mind. Many were added to their number. They baptized their converts, led them to be filled with the Holy Spirit, and discipled them. They gave themselves to the apostles teaching, fellowship, breaking of bread, and prayer. They heard God's voice and obeyed. They were respected by the people. There were recognized leaders and ministries — apostles, prophets, evangelists, teachers, elders, deacons. They practiced laying on of hands. Sin was quickly dealt with by the leaders and by God. They were assisted by angels. There was a place of ministry for women. They lived lives of joy, simplicity, and praise. The first missionary team was sent out to evangelize and plant churches. They were persecuted, and even martyred. What a Church!

7

THE DECLINE FROM NEW TESTAMENT CHRISTIANITY

The decline of the Church from the purity, spiritual authority and power, purposes, principles and patterns, and fruitfulness of the early Church came quickly. By the mid-90's, when John's Revelation was written, the churches had declined to the place that the Spirit's message to five of the seven churches of Asia was a call to "repent." The church at Ephesus had left its first love (Revelation 2:1-7); the church at Pergamum had tolerated false teaching (Revelation 2:12-17); the church at Thyatira had tolerated a false prophetess (Revelation 2:18-29); the church at Sardis was becoming spiritually dead (Revelation 3:1-6); and the church at Laodicea was lukewarm, conceited, unaware of its condition of need, and "wretched, miserable, poor, blind, and naked" (Revelation 3:14-22). All this was within 65 years (A.D. 30-95)!

The decline continued. Dr. Elgin S. Moyer, of Moody Bible Institute, states:

"Already, in the latter part of the Second Century, the Church, especially in the West, was manifesting marked tendencies toward laxity in discipline, formality in worship, dogmatization in doctrine, worldliness in ethical standards, and secularization in its life in general. Between this time and the early part of the Fourth Century the finer, purer, other worldly traits of the early Christian Church were gradually being overshadowed by the grosser, unholy, worldly tendencies that were creeping into the Church from both State and society." [1]

A.D.150 — The Gifts and Ministries of the Spirit (#3)

By A.D. 150, the ministry gifts of the apostles and the prophets were no longer seen on any large scale. The reception of a life-changing enduement with power by the infilling of the Holy Spirit, imparted through the laying on of hands, had ceased on any large scale. The operation of the gifts of the Spirit as recorded in 1 Corinthians 12:4-11 had also ceased to operate on any large-scale.[2] The exception was the Montanists, which was the first large-scale attempt at Restoration. We will look at them in Chapter 8.

A.D. 160-300 — Church Government (#5, 6)

The oversight and shepherding of each of the early churches was shared by a group of men called elders (Acts 14:23, 20:17, 1 Timothy 5:17, Titus 1:5, 1 Peter 5:1-3, etc.). Thus, the authority and responsibility was shared. The elders were an encouragement to one another and a check-and-balance to each other. They were local men, not brought in from the outside. (This writer would understand that Timothy and Titus were not pastors sent long-term to shepherd the churches in Ephesus and Crete. They were apostles, co-laborers with Paul, who were sent by him to complete foundation-laying, i.e., teaching foundational truths and appointing elders.) There was no clergy-laity distinction — just local men whom the Holy Spirit had raised up as overseer-shepherds of the flock. By about A.D. 160, this pattern had given way to each church having one leader, called pastor. Thus, the authority and responsibility now rested with one man.[3]

From A.D. 180 to 330, this change in the organizational pattern of the churches went further. The pastor came to be seen in a different category from the rest of the believers, thus the beginnings of the clergy-laity distinction. With this, the responsibility for the Church and the work of the Kingdom was increasingly seen as belonging to the "clergy" rather than to the whole Church.

Also, one pastor in a given city became the leading pastor of that area, was given the title of bishop, and began to take authority over all of the churches in that area. Thus, we begin to see a loss of the autonomy of the local congregation as it came under the direction of someone outside of that body rather than under the Holy Spirit's direction directly to that group. We also see the beginnings of what eventually became the Roman Catholic hierarchy where men ruled over men, and authority was exercised from Rome all the way down to the individual believer everywhere in the world, rather than each believer being personally under the rulership of the risen Christ, through the Holy Spirit.[4]

A.D. 185 — Infant Baptism (#7)

This writer's understanding of Scripture is that the early Christians baptized only those who had repented of their sins and had put their faith in Jesus Christ. There appears to be no practice of infant baptism. Baptism was by immersion and in the authority of Jesus' Name (Mark 16:16, Acts 2:37-41, 8:12, 8:35-38, 10:47-48). By 185, we see the beginnings of infant baptism. With that practice came the development of the teaching that a baby, once baptized by sprinkling, is saved. Thus the teaching that salvation was by baptism, rather than by repentance and faith in Jesus Christ, was introduced.[5]

A.D.230-350 — Church Buildings (#8)

The early Christians met in homes (Acts 2:46, Romans 16:5, 1 Corinthians 16:19, Colossians 4:15, etc.). (There is the exception of the School of Tyrannus mentioned in Acts 19:9.) There were no expensive building programs and no facilities to maintain. When the group grew too large for one home, they would simply divide and begin meeting in two homes. What simplicity! What mobility! What practicality!

By A.D. 230, concurrent with the development of the clergy, church buildings began to be erected. What began as **ordinary believers,** gathering together in **ordinary places** (their homes) to **share with each other their common life in Christ,** became "special" people conducting "special" services in "special" buildings. This practice of erecting "special" church buildings greatly increased after Constantine embraced Christianity in 312.[6] (More will be said relative to today's practice of having church buildings in Chapter 11.)

A.D.312 — Constantine (#10-12)

Most Church historians list ten major persecutions during the early centuries of the Church's existence, under each of the following Roman emperors: Nero (who reigned 54-68); Domitian (81-96); Trajan (98-117); Marcus Aurelius (161-180); Septimus Severus

(195-211); Maximinus (235-238); Decius (249-251); Valerian (253-260); Aurelian (270-275); and Diocletian (284-305).[7] The Church was kept somewhat pure by the pressure of these persecutions. But all of this changed in A.D. 312.

Constantine, upon his father's death in 306, was proclaimed emperor of Britain, Gaul (France), and Spain. He invaded Italy and was marching toward Rome when he received word that his opponent, Maxentius, was relying on pagan magic for power. Constantine was praying and had a vision of a cross of light in the sky which bore the inscription, "Conquer by this." A short time later he had a dream in which God appeared to him with the same sign and commanded him to make a likeness of it and to conquer with it. The historian Eusebius states that Constantine made a spear overlaid with gold. A cross was formed by a transverse bar upon which there was also a monogram of the letters, "Chi" and "Rho," for the name of Christ. He also had a banner of the cross before him as he went to battle, and his soldiers had a similar cross on their shields. The decisive battle was at Miliviar Bridge near Rome. Constantine was victor, took possession of the capital, and immediately outlawed all persecution of the Christians.

It looked like a victory for Christianity. The persecution ceased. The cross replaced pagan gods on the coins. The Christian clergy was exempt from the military. Constantine used state funds to erect many church buildings. Sunday was made a holiday. He gave his children a Christian education. Whether Constantine was ever genuinely converted to Jesus Christ is not known.[8]

It was not long until many were flocking to be affiliated with the Christian Church — to obtain official favor and even wealth. Soon the world was permeating the Church, instead of the Church permeating the world.

By 385 Priscillian, a lay preacher and reformer in Spain, was beheaded, with six of his followers, because of his genuine commitment to Christ and for preaching as a layman. So, persecution by the State had been replaced by the persecution of Christians by the Church![9]

A.D. 354-430 — Augustine of Hippo —
Salvation Only Through the Roman Catholic Church (#15)

Augustine was born in Tagaste, a town of Numidia in North Africa, A.D. 354. His mother was a genuine Christian; and in 386, at the age of thirty-three, Augustine came to know the Savior for himself. He sold his possessions and gave the proceeds to the poor. He chose to live a very simple life, ate sparingly, dressed simply, and lived communally with friends. He gave himself to prayer and the ministry of the Word, founded a seminary, and devoted much time to helping the poor. He was, indeed, a man of God. But he also developed the doctrine that salvation is available by means of the sacraments, as administered by the one, true Church, the Roman Catholic Church. Thus, there was no salvation outside of the Roman Church.[10]

A.D. 341-461 — The Papacy (#16)

A number of things led to the establishing of the office of the Pope, with headquarters in Rome. In 341 the Council of Antioch ordered that in each province the bishop in the chief city should have precedence over the other bishops in the province. He was given the title archbishop. Especially prominent were the archbishops of Jerusalem, Antioch, Alexandria, Constantinople, and Rome, particularly the latter two. Leo, the Great, was the bishop of Rome from 440 to 461. Based on Matthew 16:18-19, John 21:15-17, and Luke 22:31-32, he decreed that Peter was the first Pope, that the bishop of Rome was the successor of Peter, and therefore, the supreme head of the Church.[11]

A.D. 500-1200 — Papal Power and the Dark Ages (#17, 19)

As the structure of the Roman Empire weakened and disintegrated, the Church stepped in to fill the void, markedly increasing its authority, especially the authority of the Pope.

One Pope who ruled with great authority was Gregory the Great, who was Pope from 590-604. He believed that the world as well as the Church should be ruled by the Pope, as Christ's successor. He extended the authority and influence of the papacy in every way that he could.[12]

In 771 Charlemagne became ruler of parts of the present-day Germany, France, and Italy. He dreamed of a reestablished Roman Empire. On Christmas Day, 800, he was crowned Emperor of The Holy Roman Empire by Pope Leo III; thus the precedent was established that the Pope gave final approval as to the choice of secular rulers.

In 1073 Cardinal Hildebrand of Rome was named Pope. He took the name Gregory VIII. He believed that all the Christian states should form a world empire, with the Pope at its head, as God's representative on earth. To resist his authority was to resist God.

With this increase of worldly power by the papacy, came immorality, materialism, and declining concern about spiritual matters. The late 800's through the 1100's in southern and central Europe were marked by a disintegration of organized society, invasion by Moslems and Scandinavians, and gross immorality in the papacy. As Latourette states, "With such conditions in Rome, the Popes could not wield the influence in European affairs or in the Church of the West that had been exerted by some of their great predecessors. Certainly they could not give the moral and religious leadership that would lift the Church and the Christianity of the West from the slough into which they had fallen."[13]

Innocent III, who reigned as Pope from 1198-1216, brought the papacy to the very pinnacle of its power and prestige. He was fully convinced that the papacy was theocracy, established by God for the good of the Church and the salvation of the world, and that he was entrusted not only with the dominion of the Church but also with the rule of the whole world. To the papal title, Vicar of Christ, he added the title, Vicar of God. He wielded two swords, one for the spiritual, and one for the temporal. Being under the authority of God, he considered himself superior to all men, having authority to set aside the decisions of bishops and provincial councils, and to make or depose kings at will. The rulers of England, Germany, France, Spain, Italy, Sweden, Denmark, Portugal, Poland, Bohemia, Hungary, and Palestine all yielded to his authority.[14]

A.D. 1200-1600 — The Inquisitions (#22)

Throughout all of Church history there were always those individuals and groups who were more spiritual and who were closer to the Christianity of the New Testament than was the established Church. These, considered radical Christians by the established Church, were often persecuted. That was true of the Montanists in the mid-100's, and each group thereafter. Priscillian and his companions who were martyred in A.D. 385 have already been mentioned.

Basil was part of a group called Bogomili, or Friends of God, which had sprung up and multiplied in the Balkan Peninsula (today's Bulgaria, Greece, and Turkey). He was a physician, but also spent much time teaching and preaching. He received an invitation from the Emperor to come to the palace in Constantinople to tell him about his relationship with Christ. Basil was entertained at the table of the Emperor where he spoke openly to the "anxious inquirer." Suddenly the Emperor drew aside a curtain and revealed a shorthand writer who had taken down the entire conversation. Basil was put in chains and cast into prison where he remained for some years. Finally, when he continued to refuse to recant his teachings, he was publicly burned in the Hippodrome in Constantinople.

Another example of persecution was Pierre de Brueys. He showed from Scripture that none should be baptized until they could decide for themselves, that one can worship anywhere and not just in church buildings, that the bread and wine are not changed into the body and blood of Christ, and that it is useless to pray for the dead. He was martyred by being burned alive in 1126.

The rise of the Albigenes and the Waldenses were seen as large movements of "heretics" dangerous to the Church. Dominic was a man zealous for propogating "the orthodox faith" (Roman Catholicism), and devoted to the Roman Church and the hierarchy. In 1215 he founded the Order of Preachers, or Dominican Order, to oppose the teaching of the Albigenses.[15] The persecution of dissenters was made a permanent institution at the Council of Toulouse in 1229. By 1240 heresy had been made punishable by death in every country of Europe except England.

These inquisitions were greatly advanced by the founding of the Jesuits. As early as 1522 Ignatius Loyola began to dream of forming a military company for the defense and promotion of the Roman Catholic Church. His dream became a reality on August 15, 1534, when Loyola and six companions took vows of poverty and chastity. They later took vows of missions and obedience and gave themselves in total obedience to all superior authority. The Society of Jesus, or Jesuit Order, grew. The best, strongest, bravest men were picked —men who were willing to brave any danger and go wherever and whenever they were sent. "Their only fatherland was the Church of Rome, and their only patriotism was the service of its interests." [16]

In 1542 six cardinals were appointed as Inquisitors-General with full power to discover and eradicate heresy wherever it was found. From 1200-1600 tens of thousands of dissenting believers were martyred in the name of Christ by the Roman Catholic Church because they refused to bow to the authority of the Roman Church.[17]

A.D. 1229 — Bible Forbidden (#24)

In a further attempt to eradicate the growing number of sincere Christians who were attempting to adhere to a faith more in keeping with the New Testament, the Council of Toulouse formalized the Inquisitions. It also decided, in 1229, to forbid the Bible to "the laity."[18]

A.D. 1299 — Submission to Pope Necessary for Salvation (#25)

In 1299 Pope Boniface VIII issued a bull declaring "that it is altogether necessary to salvation for every human creature to be subject to the Roman Pontiff." [19]

The major period of the decline of the Church ended between 1150 and 1550 with the growing trend toward restoration, recovery, and reformation, and the emergence of the Albigenses, Waldenses, Lollards, Lutherans, Calvinists, Anabaptists, and Anglicans.

8

THE PROCESS OF RESTORATION THROUGHOUT CHURCH HISTORY

The early, apostolic, New Testament Church soon began to fall away from the purity, spiritual authority and power, purposes, principles and patterns, and fruitfulness that God had intended. But God is a God of restoration. He has purposed to have a "glorious Church, without spot or wrinkle" (Ephesians 5:27), a people who are "to attain to a mature man, to the measure of the stature which belongs to the fullness of Christ" (Ephesians 4:13). He is committed to restoring His Church to the Christianity of the New Testament — in purity; in spiritual authority and power; in purposes; in principles and patterns; and in fruitfulness. The Holy Spirit, early in Church history, began the process of restoration.

A.D. 156-400 — Montanus (#4)

One of the early movements of restoration began about 156 with the appearance on the scene of Montanus of Phrygia of Asia. He appeared at a time when much of the Church had become cold and formal; the gifts of the Spirit had largely ceased to operate; and there was lax discipline. Montanus called for holy living, greater Church discipline, and preached the return of Christ. He was assisted by two prophetesses. The spiritual gifts of speaking in tongues and prophecy were in operation. There were itinerant preachers supported by the believers. The movement spread widely to Greece, Italy, Gaul

(France), and North Africa. The most noted convert from the organized Church to Montanism was the scholar Tertullian, in North Africa, in the early 200's. This movement continued into the 400's.[1]

A.D. 280-550 — Christian Communities (#9)

The decline of spirituality in the churches provoked some to efforts of reform, just as it had the Montanists. For others the solution was to withdraw from the Church and find a deeper walk with God in another setting. At first there were those who withdrew completely and became Christian hermits. Notable among these was Anthony in Egypt, who was born about 250. One day he heard Jesus' words, "If thou wilt be perfect, go and sell what thou hast and give to the poor." He immediately sold and gave away inherited land to the village, sold his possessions, and gave the proceeds to the poor. He moved outside the village, and later to a fort on a mountain, where he gave himself to prayer and fasting for twenty years. The Emperor Constantine wrote him for counsel. Anthony died in A.D. 356 at the age of 105. His example was contagious, and soon hundreds were imitating him.

These hermits, living in a cave or a hut, were sometimes close enough to one another to make fellowship possible, which led to the next step, the development of a Christian community, or monastery. One of the early pioneers of monasteries was Pachomius, who also lived in southern Egypt, from 285 to 346. In the monastery, a number of Christians could live together and seek God in a spiritual setting. They lived lives of chastity, poverty, and discipline, and gave themselves to a strict schedule of work, fasting and prayer, Bible study, memory, and meditation. Monasteries for women also developed. In time, the separated life of the monastery became the way of life for thousands throughout much of Europe, North Africa, and as far east as Mesopotamia. It was in a monastery in Bethlehem that Jerome translated the Latin version of the Bible around 400. In the fifth and sixth centuries practically every Church leader had received his early Christian discipline at one of the monasteries. One of the most famous was founded by Benedict in A.D. 529, eighty-five miles southeast of Rome. For centuries, and even down to modern times, monasteries have provided a deepening effect upon the Christian Church, although they sometimes tend to promote a righteousness by works.[2]

A.D. 432-800 — Christianity in British Isles and Northern Europe (#14)

While the Western Church in southern Europe was departing from

New Testament Christianity, there was a movement in northern Europe, unattached to Rome, that was more true to the New Testament.

During the Dark Ages, Ireland stood out as a beacon. From the sixth to the eighth centuries, it was the most advanced nation in western Europe. Free from the disastrous invasions of the barbarians, the Church kept the lamp of learning burning when the lights were going out all over Europe. During the sixth and seventh centuries, the Irish Church became one of the greatest missionary churches of all times. Patrick came from Scotland to Ireland in the 400's. In 563 the Irish Church sent Colombia (521-596) to Scotland. He was a man of zeal, piety and prayer, and performed many miracles. On the island of Iona he built a monastery which became a strategic center for the training of missionaries. For over two hundred years, missionaries went out from the monasteries of Ireland and Scotland to all parts of the British Isles and Europe. They had no official connection with the Roman Church.[3] We will read more about this in Chapter 16.

A.D. 500-1350 — The Nestorian Church (#18)

The Church in the East — Turkey, Egypt, Syria, Mesopotamia, Parthia, Arabia, Persia, and India — was separated from the Western Church by the use of a different language, Aramaic, rather than Greek and Latin, and by different political circumstances, which led to a distrust of the Romans. Being thus shut off from the influence of the Roman Church, the eastern churches kept their simple and Scriptural character longer than that of the West. Even in the Third Century there was no definite organization of the separate churches into one system.[4]

In time this simplicity did give way to a federation of the churches in the East. In 428 Nestorius was appointed bishop of Constantinople. He opposed the growing tendency to call Mary, "the Mother of God," and to make her an object of worship. (He was also accused of heresy relative to the nature of Christ. Whether his teaching at this point was false or not is not clear.) The pressure against Nestorius was such that he finally fled to Egypt. A number of his followers took refuge in Persia. Here in Persia, Christianity spread quickly, free from the influence of Rome and Constantinople.

As Islam spread throughout the region in the 600's and early 700's, many of these eastern Christians were scattered. When order was restored, however, they became prominent as doctors and as teachers

77

of philosophy, science, and literature.

Nestorian missionaries were soon taking the Gospel to many parts of the continent of Asia — India, Russia, Tibet, China, Korea, Japan, and southeast Asia. From the seventh to the thirteenth centuries, the Church in Persia and Syria was as important in the East as the Roman and Greek Churches were in the West.

A.D.1100 — The Albigenses and Waldenses (#20)

The Reformation (or restoration) did not begin with Martin Luther in 1517. It began with the Montanists in the late 100's! Then there were the Nestorian Christians in Asia and the Irish Christians in northwestern Europe who were remaining closer to New Testament Christianity than was the declining Roman Church. There were other small revival and restoration groups all through the centuries — Priscillian in Spain in the mid-300's, groups in Asia Minor (today's Turkey) and near Mount Ararat from the 300's to the 800's. As E. H. Broadbent states:

> "Even in the first three centuries there were numerous bodies of Christians who protested against the growing laxity and world-liness in the Church, and against its departure from the teachings of Scripture. Movements of revival have never ceased to be repeated, and even when no connection between one and another is visible, the underlying cause is the same — a desire to return to the practice of some New Testament truth. In the early centuries Asia Minor and Armenia were frequently the scene of such revivings, as well as being the refuge of churches that had from the first, in varying degree, maintained purity of doctrine and godliness of life . . . . These churches, carrying out the New Testament principles in a large measure, though no doubt in varying degree in different places . . . .[5]

In the region known today as Bulgaria and western Turkey there were the Friends of God in the 1000-1100's. In the late 1100's and early 1200's in Bosnia (now part of Yugoslavia) there was a large movement. As Broadbent states:

> "The country ceased to be Catholic and experienced a time of prosperity that has remained proverbial ever since. There were no priests, or rather the priesthood of all believers was acknowledged. The churches were guided by elders who were chosen by lot, several in each church, an overseer (called

78

grandfather), and ministering brethren called leaders or elders. Meetings could be held in any house and the regular meeting places were quite plain, no bells, no altar, only a table, on which might be a white cloth and a copy of the Gospels. A part of the earnings of the brethren was set aside for the relief of sick believers and of the poor and for the support of those who traveled to preach the Gospel among the unconverted." [6]

But the two largest groups that became the greatest threat to the Roman Catholic system were the Albigenses and the Waldenses. The Cathari,[7] or "pure ones," began to appear in Europe around A.D. 1000. They had no church buildings, gathered for Bible reading, sermons, and foot washing, and had a common meal together. In southern France they were called the Albigenses, from the district of Albi where they lived. By the end of the 1100's, they were in thousands of cities in Spain, France, and Italy with a total following of four million. Some of them devoted themselves entirely to traveling and ministering the Word. In 1209 Pope Innocent III sent an army to exterminate them. As the army approached the town of La Minorue, they found 140 of these simple believers engaged in prayer, awaiting their doom. They were given a choice to convert to the Catholic faith or be burned. They answered that they owed no papal or priestly authority, only that of Christ and His Word. A large fire was lit, and the believers, without hesitation, all entered the flames and were martyred. It was just twenty years later at the Council of Toulouse in 1229 that the Bible was forbidden to the laity, and the Inquisitions were formally instituted.[8]

The Waldenses sought to adhere strictly to the Scriptures and to revive the simple practices of the Apostolic Age. They first appeared in southern France. Although they derived their name from Peter Waldo (1140-1218), people of their beliefs existed prior to A.D. 800. They soon spread to Spain, Italy, Germany, Austria, and Bohemia.

Peter Waldo was a wealthy merchant and banker in Lyons. Upon being impressed with the brevity and insecurity of life, he inquired of a priest what he must do to secure heaven. The priest, quoting from Matthew 19:21, said, "If you would be perfect, go, sell what you possess and give to the poor, and you will have treasure in heaven; and come, follow Me." (The same Scripture had influenced Anthony in Egypt nine centuries earlier.) Waldo in 1176 paid his creditors, provided for his wife and children, and gave the rest to the poor. He then enlisted two priests to translate portions of the Bible into French.

Waldo then made a diligent study of the New Testament, memorizing long passages. He undertook to imitate Christ, traveling about without purse and preaching in cities and countryside. Soon others had joined him.

The Waldenses were a humble and simple folk. They were described as, "dressing simple, industrious, labouring with their hands, chaste, temperate in eating and drinking, refusing to frequent taverns and dances, sober and truthful in speech, avoiding anger, and regarding the accumulation of wealth as evil." [9] Called the Poor Men of Lyons, they went out preaching two by two. They memorized large portions of Scripture in the local language. Some, in fact, memorized all of the New Testament and portions of the Old Testament.[10] They increasingly came to believe that no teaching except Christ's was binding. They taught:

> "That the Church of Rome was not the head of the Catholic Church, but corrupt. They held that women and laymen could preach, that masses and prayers for the dead were without warrant, that purgatory is the troubles which come to us in this life, and that to be efficacious prayer need not be confined to churches. They criticized prayers in Latin on the ground that they were not understood by the people, and derided church music and the canonical hours. They declared that while priests and bishops who lived as had the apostles were to be obeyed, sacraments administered by unworthy priests were invalid and that a layman was as competent as a priest to hear confessions. They taught that every lie is a deadly sin, that oaths, even in law courts, are contrary to Christ's commands, and believed that all taking of human life is against God's law. They observed the Eucharist together and held that, if necessary, any layman might administer it. Their only forms of prayer were the 'Our Father' and grace at meals. They had their own clergy, with bishops, priests, and deacons, and a head of their fellowship." [11]

They were excommunicated by the Archbishop of Lyons and also by Pope Lucius III in 1184 for their unauthorized preaching. They were indeed "the reformers before the Reformation."[12] They became one of the prime targets of the Inquisition, but some of their descendants still exist in the valleys of the Italian Alps and in other parts of the world.

A.D. 1100-1500 — The Mystics (#21)

There have always been those individuals known as mystics, who have sought God with all of their hearts and have spent many hours a day in prayer, drawing near to and receiving from Him. But in the 1100's and succeeding centuries their numbers were increasing.

One of these mystics was Bernard of Clairvaux. His life was spent largely in a monastery, which he founded in 1115 at the age of twenty-five. It was the Cisterian order and was located at Clairvaux in France. He was deeply moved by the love of Christ and was deeply committed to Him. His life was one of deep contemplation as he attempted to live a life of silence and prayer. He wrote of "longing for the Bridgegroom's presence." But Bernard had a practical side to him and was not able to give himself wholly to prayer because of his love for the Church and the needs of men. He, in fact, became a leading figure in the Western Church and exerted great influence through his writings and preaching, even helping to heal a schism which had developed by the almost simultaneous election of two popes, and helping to promote the Second Crusade. But he was first and foremost a mystic who raised the spiritual level of the entire Roman Catholic Church and attracted thousands to the way of mysticism.[13]

There were many other mystics and monastic orders with mystical tendencies. The orders included the Carthusians which started in 1084 by Bruno and included the founding of many centers of hermits. They were men of great austerity, giving themselves to reading, praying, fasting, laboring, and the copying of Scriptures. There were also the similar orders of Grandmont and Fontevrault and other less known orders, most of them in France.

There were also some wonderful women among the mystics. One of the most well known was Hildegarde (1098-1179). She entered a Benedictine monastery at age eight and spent her life in monasteries. She often had visions, exercised the gift of prophecy, and spoke of the end of the world. She also carried on an active correspondence with popes, emperors, and princes.[14]

There was also Bridget of Sweden (1303-1373), the wife of a prominent noble and the mother of eight. She had many revelations, exercised the gift of prophecy, founded an order for women, and once rebuked the King of Sweden for oppressive taxation and injustice to the poor.[15] Catherine of Siena (1347-1380), starting at the age of twelve, spent six years in private in a room set apart by her parents. She later exercised the gifts of healings, and counseled hundreds, including the Pope, and died at the age of thirty-three.[16]

In the 1300-1500's other mystics arose throughout much of Europe — France, England, Italy, Germany, Spain, the Low Countries (today's Holland and Belgium) -- including the Brethren of the Free Spirit, the Friends of God, the Brothers and Sisters of the Common Life, Thomas a Kempis, and Teresa of Avila.[17] Truly, God was getting the attention of a growing number of people and drawing them into deep communion with Himself.

A.D. 1210 — Francis of Assisi — Begins Apostolic Bands (#23)

Francisco Bernardone was born in Assisi, Italy, the son of a rich cloth merchant. In 1209, at the age of twenty-seven, he heard the call, "Preach, the Kingdom of heaven is at hand, heal the sick, cleanse the lepers, cast out demons, provide neither silver nor gold in your purses." He immediately made this Scripture the rule of his life. A year later, Francis and eleven companions journeyed to Rome to seek papal permission to pursue their ministry, which was reluctantly granted. Thus began the restoration of the early apostolic bands. These associates of Francis sold all they had and went out barefooted, two by two, preaching the Kingdom of God, singing, calling men to repentance, praying for the sick, and helping the poor. They sought to imitate Jesus and obey Him in every way. They slept in hay lofts and ate whatever was offered to them. This order was called the Brothers Minor. A second order for women, the Poor Ladies, came into being. A third order, the Order of Penitants, was founded in 1221. Members of this order were allowed to stay in the world, work, and hold property; but they were to live simply, give alms, and be loyal members of the Catholic Church. Francis of Assisi was a man of purity of purpose and humility of spirit. Some historians believe that he more than any other person saved the medieval Church from complete collapse.[18]

Also founded in the early 1200's were the Dominicans, or Order of Preachers. They founded a number of houses, each being a school to train preachers who were to become missionaries to the masses.[19] Both the Franciscans and the Dominicans were intensely missionary and were soon found throughout Europe, and in Africa and Asia, and later in North and South America. They sought to bring nominal Christians to a deeper faith and to win non-Christians.[20]

Thus we see the beginning of the restoration of itinerant bands of missionaries, which would later be multiplied by hundreds of Protestant missionary societies.

A.D.1374-1384 — Wyclife and the Lollards — Reformation in England (#26)

John Wyclife spent most his adult life as a leading professor at Oxford University in England. In the last ten years of his life he became very outspoken in his radical views concerning the papacy and other Church matters. He insisted that Christ alone was the head of the Church and that the pope was antichrist. He held that every person held an equal place in the eyes of God and that the mediating priesthood and the sacrificial masses were not essential. Wyclife challenged the whole range of medieval beliefs and practices including pardons, indulgences, absolutions, pilgrimages, the worship of images, the adoration of the saints, and the distinction between venial and mortal sins. He concluded that where the Bible and the Church do not agree, we must obey the Bible; and where conscience and human authority are in conflict, we must obey conscience. To further his views, Wyclife led a group of scholars at Oxford to translate the Bible from Latin into the English vernacular of his day. And like Francis of Assisi, over 150 years earlier, he sent men out to preach and to distribute the Bibles and reformation tracts. They were called "poor priests" or Lollards. Wyclife was the first of the Protestant reformers. He died in 1384 "having lit a fire which shall never be put out." In 1406 the English Parliament took a stand against the Lollards, and in 1428 Wyclife's remains were dug up and burned.[21]

A.D. 1400-1415 — John Hus — Reformation in Eastern Europe (#27)

In 1382 Bohemia (western Czechoslovakia today) and England were more closely linked together by the marriage of Anne of Luxemburg, sister of the King of Bohemia, to King Richard II of England. Students began to travel back and forth between Oxford and Prague, and so did the writings of Wyclife! One of those most greatly influenced was John Hus, a professor at the University of Prague. He was soon translating Wyclife's writings into Bohemian. Hus became a powerful preacher in the most influential churches in Prague and in 1409 also became leader of the national Bohemian party at the University. He was soon an outspoken national leader for church reform and for the political and religious rights of the people. His teachings were similar to Wyclife's. He was soon branded a heretic by the clergy and was excommunicated by the Pope. In 1412 Hus left Prague to preach from place to place. All of Bohemia was astir. Hus was arrested and on July 6, 1415, was burned at the stake. His last words were, "Lord, into Thy hands I commend my spirit." Hus became a national hero, and his followers became known as the Bohemian Brethren, and were the spiritual ancestors to the Moravians. [22] They later, in 1467, became a more clearly defined body known as Unitas Fratrum, or the Unity of Brethren.[23]

A.D. 1456 — Bible Printed by Moveable Type (#28)

In the mid-1400's John Gutenberg of Mainz, Germany, invented the process of printing using letters that could be reused. One of the first books printed was the Bible in 1456.[24] This accelerated the Reformation by providing the means for the Bible and other religious writings to be more easily printed.

A.D. 1491-1498 — Savanarola — Reformation in Italy (#29)

As in England and Bohemia, God had His prophet for Florence, Italy. Savanarola (1452-1498) spent his early years in a Dominican monastery. In 1481 he transferred to a monastery of reformed Dominicans in Florence. About 1491 he began to preach against the sins of the day, especially those of the clergy, and called for repentance before God's judgment fell upon the city. His preaching caused a great transformation of the city: women began to dress plainly, merchants became honest, there was much reading of the Bible and giving to the poor. In 1497 the Pope (Alexander VI) excommunicated Savanarola; and on May 23, 1498, he and two of his associates were hanged and their bodies burned. In time the people of Florence returned to their old ways, but God's prophet had spoken.[25]

Wyclife, Hus, and Savanarola were not the only forerunners to the Protestant Reformation under Martin Luther. Others included: John Pupper of Goch (1400-1475), John of Wesel (1410-1481), John Sessel Gansvoort (1420-1489), the Flagellants, and the Brotherhood of the Cross.[26] The tide of those committed to a return to the Christianity of the Bible was rising. It was soon to become a tidal wave that developed into five basic Protestant traditions: Lutheran, Reform, Anabaptist, Arminian, and Anglican.

A.D. 1516 — A New Edition of the Greek New Testament (#30)

Desiderius Erasmus (1466-1536) was a Dutch scholar who greatly longed for the reformation of the Church. He spent much time studying the Scriptures in their original languages and in 1516 produced a new edition of the Greek New Testament, which would soon greatly assist others who translated his Greek New Testament into English, German, and the other languages of the day. Although not desiring a break with the Roman Church, Erasmus greatly influenced Luther, Zwingli, and other reformers.[27]

A.D.1517 — The Reformation Under Luther (#31)

The growing unrest in the Roman Catholic Church that was accelerated by Wyclife, Hus, Savanarola, and many others came to a head and found a spokesman in Martin Luther. This revolt from medieval Christianity and a longing for a restoration of New Testament Christianity centered on four basic questions: How is a person saved? Where does religious authority lie? What is the Church? What is the essence of the Christian life?

What many had been saying for over a hundred years, and some had been saying for several hundred years, came to a head all over northern Europe. The answers became so clear: man is saved by his faith in Jesus Christ and His sacrifice alone, not in any good works that he can do; spiritual authority rests in the Scriptures alone, not in the decrees of popes and religious councils; the Church is composed of all who believe in Jesus as Lord and Savior; water baptism and the Lord's Supper are for all who believe; all believers have direct access to God through Christ; and the Christian life is a life of having a personal walk with God, not the performance of certain prescribed rituals. Luther stated it this way, "Justification by faith, the authority of the Scriptures, and the priesthood of believers."

Martin Luther was born in Eisleben, a town in central Germany, on November 10, 1483, and was the oldest of seven children. His parents were hard-working peasants. His mother was pious but superstitious and taught her children to pray to God and to "the dear saints." In 1501, at age eighteen, Luther entered the famous University of Erfurt, where he distinguished himself as an extraordinary student. By 1505 he had earned a Bachelor and Master's degree and began his study of law. One day he was caught in a thunderstorm, was knocked to the ground by a bolt of lightning, and cried out to the patron saint of miners, "St. Anne, save me, and I'll become a monk." Two weeks later he entered the Augustinian monastery at Erfurt.

Luther was a very dedicated and disciplined monk. He spent much time in fasting and prayer and mortified his body by often sleeping without a blanket in the winter. But he saw himself as a miserable, doomed sinner; and he could not find peace with God. He had prayed for years for the privilege of owning a Bible and at the monastery was able to begin its diligent study. He was especially drawn to Paul's letters of *Galatians* and *Romans,* and increasingly the light dawned on him that *"the just shall live by faith"* (Romans 1:17).

A visit to Rome in 1510, where he saw the sale of indulgences and much idolatry, left Luther disillusioned. In 1512 he became Professor of Theology at the University of Wittenberg, and by 1516 he had become a very popular teacher and preacher, with students flocking to him from all over Germany. Luther was increasingly concerned over the Church's sale of indulgences, a practice which enriched the papacy by allowing people to purchase release out of purgatory for the souls of the departed. In 1517 Dominican John Tetzel was selling indulgences throughout Germany to gain revenue to complete St. Peter's Basilica in Rome. Tetzel boasted, "As soon as the coin in the coffer rings, the soul from purgatory springs." Luther had had enough! He drew up 95 propositions for theological debate, and according to university custom, posted them on the church door at Wittenberg. That act was the spark that ignited the Reformation.

Within a short time, German Dominicans denounced Luther to Rome for his "dangerous doctrines." In 1520 the Pope ordered Luther's writings burned; and on December 10, in retaliation, Luther publicly burned all of the papal books and documents in his possession. In January, 1521, Luther was excommunicated from the Church. He now became a German problem; and young Charles V, the Emperor, summoned Luther to a meeting at Worms in April. He was asked to repudiate his views. Luther responded that he could not unless shown by Scripture to be in error. He concluded, "My conscience is captive to the Word of God. I will not recant anything. To do so is neither right nor safe. Here I stand. I cannot do otherwise. God help me. Amen."

A single individual had pitted his understanding and integrity against established theology and institutions which were the bulwark of society. The Emperor declared Luther an outlaw, but he was saved from arrest and prison by the Prince of Saxony, Duke Frederick, who gave Luther lodging at Wartburg Castle. There he disguised himself as a minor nobleman, and, in the next nine months, translated Erasmus' entire Greek New Testament into German.

Luther never intended to break from the Roman Church, or to establish a new one, but the revolt against Rome spread from town to town across much of Germany. Statues were removed from churches. Luther began writing guidance to the clergy and congregations with regard to the conducting of services. Much was made of music, especially congregational singing. The main focus of the service changed from the sacrificial mass to the preaching of the Scriptures. Communion was made available to all. Priests and nuns began to marry. Luther himself married a former nun, Katherine von Bara, in 1525, and they had six children. In 1530 a summit of Reformation leaders met in Augsburg to draw up a common statement of faith. Luther was still an outlaw and could not attend, but he was represented by Philip Melanchthon. Luther completed his translation of the Old Testament into German in 1534, and continued to give leadership to the movement through his writings until he died on February 18, 1546. Lutheranism quickly spread and became the dominant religion not only in Germany, but also in Denmark, Norway, Sweden, Finland, and Iceland. It also spread to eastern and southern Europe; but Roman Catholicism soon regained the upper hand there.[28]

A.D. 1519-1650 — The Reformation Spreads (#32)

The reformation spread in Switzerland through Zwingli, Farel and Calvin. Zwingli (1484-1531) became pastor of the Great Minster Church in Zurich in 1519 and sought to bring a reformation to the church until 1531 when he was killed on the battlefield helping to defend Zurich against attacking Catholics. Meanwhile, William Farel (1489-1565) was in Geneva furthering the reformation. In 1535 the city voted to become Protestant rather than Roman Catholic. He laid the groundwork for John Calvin (1509-1564) who resided there during the periods 1536-1538 and 1541-1564. Calvin became Geneva's leading spiritual force, and saw it become the leading center of Protestant thought and influence, from which the reformation spread to France, Holland, England, and Scotland. In France, the Protestants were called Huguenots. In the Netherlands, the Dutch Reformed Church came into being.

In England the Reformation was preceded by the teachings of the theologian, William of Occam (1280-1349) and Wyclife (1320-

1384) and his Lollards. It was further helped by Tyndale's translation of the New Testament in 1526, and Miles Coverdale's translation of the first complete Bible into English in 1535. England had long chafed at the spiritual and political dominance of the Pope and the break finally came in 1534 when King Henry VIII made himself the head of the Church of England. Henry wanted to divorce his wife, Catherine, who had not born him a son to be heir to the throne, and to marry Anne Boleyn. The Pope refused to grant the divorce, so the King declared the English Church no longer subject to the Pope. The Reformation did not go as far in England as it had in Germany: Henry's concept was a reformed Catholic Church, national in character, and under royal control. But the Reformation was carried further in the late 1500's and early 1600's by some in the Church of England called Puritans, who championed the King James Bible in 1611, and by those who left the Church of England and became Congregational, Baptist, or Quaker.

In Scotland the Reformation was led by John Knox (1515-1572). Influenced by the Genevan Reformation, it resulted in the establishment of the Scotch-Presbyterian Church in 1560.

In all of these reform movements — Lutheranism in northern Europe, Calvinism in Switzerland and France, the Reformed Church in Holland, the Church of England in England, and Presbyterianism in Scotland — there were many differences in degree of reformation. But in every case there were the three cardinal doctrines of the Reformation: salvation by faith in Christ, not in man's good works; the authority of the Scriptures superceding the authority of the Church; and the priesthood of believers, where one can go directly to God through Christ without the advocacy of a priest. With the restoration of these three important truths, a major step had been taken in the restoration of the Church to New Testament Christianity. But there was much more to come, as we will see in the next chapters.[29]

9

THE PROCESS OF RESTORATION THROUGHOUT CHURCH HISTORY (CONTINUED)

A.D. 1525-1550 — The Anabaptists — Restoration of Water Baptism For Believers Only[1] (#33)

There were some who felt that Luther, Calvin, and the other reformers did not go far enough in their reformation of the Church. These desired a complete return to the Christianity of the First Century and were especially concerned about the nature of the Church and its relationship with civil government.

The situation that brought matters into focus occurred in Zurich, Switzerland, on January 21, 1525. On that day, the Zurich city council had ordered Conrad Grebel and Felix Manz to stop holding Bible classes and to have their followers' babies baptized or face banishment from the territory. Grebel and several others met at the Manz home to discuss the matter. After a time of discussion and prayer, George Blaurock, a former priest, stepped over to Conrad Grebel and asked to be baptized upon his confession of personal faith in Jesus Christ. This he did, and the Anabaptist movement was born. Grebel, Manz, and others were soon arrested, tried by the civil authorities in Zurich, and sentenced to life imprisonment. They escaped and continued to spread their views but were recaptured. Manz was executed by drowning on January 25, 1527. Grebel had died a few months earlier. Thus, the

Reformation movement led by Luther and Calvin was now persecuting others who had taken the reformation, or restoration, further.

The Anabaptists' name means "rebaptizer" and was considered a re-baptism by those who taught that the baptism of infants was valid. They rejected the validity of infant baptism and baptized only those who were old enough to decide personally to follow Jesus. Their goal was the restoration of New Testament Christianity in its entirety. They wanted no part in the state or national Churches. They understood the Church to be independent, voluntary groups of believers. They viewed the Lord's Supper as a remembrance of Christ's death, not as a ceremony in which the body and blood of Christ were present. Their worship times were marked by simplicity. They further believed that Christians should separate from the world as much as possible, should not participate in war, and should live simple and frugal lives. Most of them also practiced foot washing, and some practiced community of goods.

The Anabaptists spread quickly to much of northern and eastern Europe, but not without severe persecution. Thousands were martyred by fire, water, and the sword. By the mid-1500's three groups existed: the Mennonites in northern Germany and Holland; the Hutterites in Moravia, Hungary, and south Russia; and the Swiss Brethren in Switzerland. They were also the forerunners of the United Brethren and the Brethren in Christ churches and profoundly influenced the Baptists, the Congregationalists, and the Friends.

A.D. 1530-1650 — The Restoration of Evangelical Theology[2] (#34)

Accompanying the general thrust of the Reformation was the restoration to the Church of evangelical theology. There were, in fact, five streams of evangelical theology that emerged. From Luther and Melanchthon came Lutheran theology with an emphasis on faith and the grace of God, most simply stated in the *Augsburg Confession* written in 1530 by Melanchthon and approved by Luther.

From Calvin and his associates came Reform theology, or Calvinism, with its emphasis on the sovereign will of God. Calvin's most widely read writings were *Institutes of the Christian Religion* and an abstract from it, *The Geneva Cathechism.* The five main points of Calvinism, as developed by his successors, include "(1) Total depravity, that is, man's whole nature is affected by the Fall, and he is without merit or ability to save himself. (2) Unconditional election, that is, election is determined solely by the sovereign will of God. (3) Limited redemption or atonement, that is, Christ died for the elect only. (4) Irresistible regenerating grace, that is, all the elect will be saved. (5) Perseverance of the elect or regenerate, that is, God's elect are eternally secure." [3] Presbyterian theology and its *Westminster Confession of Faith*, drawn up in 1646, was also a modification of Calvin's theology. There are still Christian groups today that hold to all five points, but there are also a number of groups that have developed a modified Calvinism that only holds to points 1, 2, and 5, and some to 4.

The Anglican theology developed as an evangelical modification of Catholic theology. It is best expressed in the *Thirty-Nine Articles of Religion* approved by the Church of England in 1563 and sanctioned by Parliament in 1571.[4]

In 1539 Menno Simons published *Foundation of the Christian Doctrine* which became the common statement of doctrine and practice of the various Anabaptist groups.

In Holland the teachings of Jacob Arminius (1560-1609) produced yet another stream of evangelical theology known as Arminianism. Arminius rejected the strong Calvinism theology of the Dutch Reformed Church and developed his own five points which state that: (1) Christ died for all men, (2) salvation is by faith alone, (3) those who believe are saved, (4) those who reject God's grace are lost, and (5) God does not elect particular individuals for their outcome. Arminian theology was largely adopted by Methodism and the various Holiness and Pentecostal groups.[5]

A.D. 1100-Today — The Restoration of New Testament Church Government and Practice (#35)

With the restoration of true conversion, justification by faith, and an evangelical presentation of Christianity, as given in the Bible, it was now God's time to restore a more Biblical form of Church government and practice.

One can characterize New Testament Church government and practice as follows:

1. *Voluntary association.* A New Testament Church is made by a group of born-again Christians who have freely chosen to associate together to glorify God, edify one another, and extend Christ's Kingdom.
2. *Separation of Church and state.* There is to be no government control of these groups of believers.
3. *The autonomy of the Churches.* Each of the New Testament churches is to be a self-governing group. There is no Biblical

basis for any hierarchy to exist above the local church. Based on the New Testament example, there is a place for input from the founding apostle, other apostles, and prophets; but there is no Biblical basis for denominational hierarchies. (It would be this writer's view that Paul and others, in Acts 15, went to Jerusalem to consider the circumcision issue because it was from Jerusalem that this teaching had come. They were not going "to Headquarters.")

4. *Plurality of leadership.* The leadership authority and responsibility in each of the groups is to be shared by a group of men called elders (Acts 14:23, 20:17, 1 Timothy 5:17-22, Titus 1:5, James 5:14, 1 Peter 5:1-5). Elders are also called overseers (Acts 20:28, Philippians 1:1, 1 Timothy 3:1-2, Titus 1:7), leaders (Hebrews 13:17, 24), and shepherds or pastors (Ephesians 4:11). The modern-day practice of a one-man leader, called pastor, assisted by a group of laymen, called elders, has no Biblical basis. "Pastors" and "elders" are the same group in Scripture. They are assisted by another group, called deacons, who serve the church in practical ways (Acts 6:1-7, Philippians 1:1, 1 Timothy 3:8, etc.).

5. *Meeting in homes.* The early Christians gathered together in their homes, or wherever they could, without erecting elaborate, expensive buildings (Acts 2:46, 1 Corinthians 16:19, Colossians 4:15, etc.).

6. *An open gathering where the Holy Spirit can use many to minister.* In the First Century Church the gatherings of the Christians were not centered around the ministry of a single person, but were open meetings where the Holy Spirit could use various people as He chose (Romans 12:4-8, 1 Corinthians 12, 1 Corinthians 14:26, 1 Peter 4:10, etc.).

7. *Evangelism.* They desired to share the Good News throughout the week, in every way possible, with as many as possible.

8. *A simple, giving lifestyle.* The early Christians lived a simple lifestyle that allowed them to bless others (Acts 4:32-37, 20:35, Galatians 2:10, 6:10, Ephesians 4:28, 1 John 3:17-18, etc.).

1100-1300 — Albigenses and Waldenses[6]

We find many of the preceding principles and practices being recovered as early as the 1100's. In southern France we find Pierre de Brueys teaching from the Scriptures, "that none should be baptized until they had attained to the full use of their reason; that it was useless to build buildings, as God accepts sincere worship wherever offered ..."

These and others who were called Albigenses, Waldenses, and other names said that "they owned no papal or priestly authority, only that of Christ and His Word." Peter Waldo and his "poor men of Lyons" in the late 1100's sold all that they had and gave to the poor and lived very humble and modest lives.

1525-1550 — Anabaptists

We have already noted that the Anabaptists rejected infant baptism and wanted no part of state or national Churches. They understood the Church to be voluntary groups of believers, whose gathering times for worship were to be marked by simplicity.

1600's — Baptists[7]

There are probably more different groups of Baptists in the world today than any other religious group. They generally hold to water baptism by immersion for believers, the autonomy of the local church, and the separation of Church and state. The first Baptist Churches began to appear in England and on the European Continent in the early 1600's, and sometimes link their heritage to the Anabaptists. They became very numerous in England and the United States in the 1700's and 1800's.

1600's — Separatists[8]

The Puritans desired to stay in the Church of England, but to purify it of all traces of its early Roman connection. Other believers, in England wanted to separate from the Church of England completely. In their views, each self-governing congregation was supposed to be made up only of believers, with Christ as their only head. They were called Separatists, or Independents, and were the spiritual ancestors of the Congregationalists.

Mid-1600's — The Quakers[9]

In the mid-1600's in England we see George Fox (1624-1691) and his Society of Friends, or Quakers as they were commonly called, adhering to many of these same principles — simple lifestyle, autonomy of the local churches, and the separation of Church and state. They often met in homes or wherever they could. We are especially indebted to them for their open meetings where the Holy Spirit was allowed to move, and anyone "so moved upon" could speak to the group.

Mid-1600's — Labadie (1610-1674)[10]

Jean de Labadie was born in Bordeaux in 1610. He was educated by the Jesuits and ordained a priest in 1635. However, he believed that

God called him to reform the Church to the pattern of the first assembly in Jerusalem. He left the Jesuits and began to teach. Large numbers came to his lectures. He would expound several chapters of Scripture at a time. Eventually, he saw that each congregation was to be independent and directly under Christ. He set out to plant apostolic churches. In time, community of goods was practiced; and some of the gatherings were marked by speaking in tongues, prophecy, and dancing in the Spirit.

1670-1725 — Pietism [11]

Within the Lutheran Church there arose a movement in the late 1600's, led by Philip Spener (1635-1705) and August Francke (1663-1727), that called for purity and simplicity of living. Spener gathered those interested into small groups called "little churches within the Church" for the reading of the Scriptures and for mutual assistance in spiritual growth. They called for moderation in food, drink, and dress.

1830 — "Plymouth" Brethren in England[12]

In the early 1800's, in various parts of the British Isles, there were those believers who were feeling a burden to get away from denominationalism, the dryness of the Church of England, and a one-man ministry, and return to the practices of the Early Church. Several similar groups came into being: one in Dublin, Ireland; one in Plymouth, England; and one in Bristol, England, where George Muller, known for his Christian orphanages, was one of the leaders. John N. Darby (1800-1882) was an early influence in these groups, who called themselves simply "brethren," although others were soon calling them Plymouth Brethren. These Brethren did not believe in a separately consecrated building for worship but gathered in their homes, a warehouse, or wherever they could, to edify one another and to partake of the Lord's Supper. They also did not believe in a separate ordained ministry but believed that the Holy Spirit would raise up in their midst those gifts and ministries that were necessary to meet their needs and elders of His choice to give oversight. Although beginning primarily among the upper class, they were soon ministering to the middle and lower classes, and some of their number were also going out to plant churches on every continent. The Brethren were a clear attempt in modern times to return to the government and practices of the Early Church. In recent years some of them have departed from some of their original concepts and now have church buildings, an order of service, and a pastor.

1830 — Disciples of Christ[13]

As the Brethren were coming into being in England, there were also those in the United States who desired to return to a form of church life more in keeping with the New Testament. Barton Stone (1772-1844) of Presbyterian background was one of the early ones. He was very active in Kentucky in the revivals and camp meetings that were in prominence at that time. In 1804 he left the Presbyterian pastorate and chose simply to be called a Christian. Others left too, baptized one another by immersion, and called themselves "the Church of Christ."

Thomas Campbell (1763-1854) migrated from Ireland, where he had been a Presbyterian pastor, to western Pennsylvania. He was soon allowing any Christian to partake of the Lord's Supper, and, when confronted by his presbytery, withdrew. Others also withdrew and started "the Christian Association of Washington" (Pennsylvania) and adopted the slogan "where the Scriptures speak, we speak; where the Scriptures are silent, we are silent." In 1809 Campbell was joined by his son, Alexander (1788-1866). There were soon many who were following them under the name of Disciples.

Stone and the Campbells merged their groups around 1830 and formed the Disciples of Christ or The Churches of Christ. They believed that the church is a group of believers, that each group is autonomous, that there should be baptism by immersion for believers only, and that there should be a group of leaders called elders. Thus, they were another attempt in modern times to return to New Testament church government and practices. It is sad that they began with a desire to see unity in the Body of Christ under the name Christian, but have in recent years become somewhat separatist in their attitude toward other Christians.

So, for over eight centuries since the 1100's, God has been speaking to various Christians in many parts of the world, and in every century, of the need to return to the simple church government and practices of the Early Church. We will see more of this in Chapter 11.

1727-1780 — The First Great Awakening (#36)

Each of the items that God has restored throughout Church history have been restored on the crest of a wave of revival. We shall correlate restoration with the four great evangelical awakenings of modern times.

On the crest of the First Great Awakening we see the beginning of the restoration of missions (#37), the beginning of the restoration of the Person and work of the Holy Spirit (#38), and the restoration of mass evangelism (#39).

1739-The Present — Restoration of Mass Evangelism[14] (#39)

Taking the Gospel out to the masses was practiced in a limited way by the "poor men of Lyons" in France in the late 1100's and in the early 1200's by St. Francis and his Franciscans. But it was through John Wesley and George Whitefield that mass evangelism began to be restored in a broad way to the Body of Christ.

In February of 1739 George Whitefield began preaching in the open fields to the miners, and invited John Wesley to join him in this new approach to evangelism. Soon Whitefield and Wesley were preaching to great outdoor crowds of thousands throughout England, and many were turning to Christ. Whitefield also made seven preaching tours of the Thirteen American Colonies between 1738 and 1770. As the Methodist movement spread to the United States, so did the outdoor preaching.

A further development of mass evangelism were the outdoor camp meetings that were part of the Second Great Awakening. At one of these in the summer of 1801 at Cane Ridge, Kentucky, some 25,000 people came by wagon, horse, and foot to hear the Gospel and get saved.

Great city-wide mass evangelism crusades were developed by Charles G. Finney (1792-1875), Dwight L. Moody (1837-1899), and in the twentieth century by R. A. Torrey, Gypsy Smith, Billy Sunday, Aimee Semple McPherson, Oral Roberts, Billy Graham, T. L. Osborn, and a host of others. With the advent of television and satellites, these crusades have further been used to reach thousands more with the Gospel of Jesus Christ. Certainly God has restored mass evangelism to His Church in recent centuries.

1730-Today — Restoration of World Evangelization (#37, 41)

Jesus had given a commission to His followers to take the Gospel to every person in every nation in every generation until the end of the Age (Matthew 28:18-20, Mark 16:15, Luke 24:45-49,John 20:21, Acts 1:8). The Early Church took this Commission seriously — they were intensely evangelistic. They were accused of "upsetting the inhabited earth" (Acts 17:6). By A.D. 300 it is estimated that there were 50,000 Christians in Rome and 50 to 100 million throughout the Roman Empire. By A.D. 1000 the Church stretched from China to Spain and from northern Europe to northern Africa. The Roman Catholic Church, primarily through the Franciscan, Dominican, Augustinian, and Jesuit Orders, continued to spread Catholic Christianity to parts of Africa, Asia, and North and South America during

A.D. 1300-1700. However, the early Protestant movements were too involved consolidating their gains and developing their reformed theology and church organizations and practices, to give much thought to the Great Commission. But beginning in the 1600's and mushrooming in the 1800's, the Protestant Church was soon to awaken to a great thrust of world evangelization.[15]

Early Attempts

Several early, unsuccessful attempts at missionary activity occurred in the 1500's and 1600's. In 1555 Calvin sent a group to work in Brazil, but they were all killed. In 1622 a seminary was established in India, but it only lasted twelve years. In 1661 George Fox sent three Friends missionaries to China, but they never reached their destination. In 1664, Baron Justinian von Weltz, an Austrian Lutheran, issued a call for the training and sending of missionaries; but a disobedient church would not heed his call and finally he set sail himself for Dutch Guiana (Surinam), where he died an early death.[16]

Halle University

In 1694 the Lutheran Pietists, led by Philip Spener (1635-1705) and August Francke (1663-1727), opened the Halle University in Germany, and in 1705 sent Bartholomew Ziegenbalg and Heinrich Plutschau to India. They were the first of many to go from Halle to several parts of the world.[17]

Moravians (#37)

One of those who studied at Halle was Nicholaus Ludwig, Count of Zinzendorf (1700-1760). Zinzendorf was a devoted Christian who claimed, "I have one passion, it is He (Jesus Christ) and He alone." In 1722 Zinzendorf offered his estate as a home to about 300 Bohemian Brethren refugees from Moravia. They built a village and called it Herrnhut (The Lord's Watch). In 1727 revival came to Herrnhut, and in the same year they started an around-the-clock prayer chain that lasted for over 100 years.

In 1730 during a visit to Copenhagen, Zinzendorf met a Negro from the West Indies and two Eskimos from Greenland, each pleading with him to send missionaries. Upon return to Herrnhut he placed the challenge before the group. The response was immediate and enthusiastic. In 1732, the first went to the Virgin Islands. By 1760, over two hundred Moravian missionaries entered ten nations in North America, the Caribbean, and Africa. They were provided with their travel to their destination, but once they arrived they were to be self-supporting, usually by a trade they had learned. Most of them lived and died in the land of their adoption. Before long, the Moravians had three members on the mission field for every one at home; and within 200 years had sent out 3,000 missionaries.[18]

1792-1842 — The Second Great Awakening (#40)

The Second Great Awakening provided the impetus for the great Protestant mission movement. This mission movement began through the Moravians (#37) earlier in the century (1732-1760), but came into its full fruition through William Carey and others (#41) as a result of the Second Great Awakening.

There was also a further restoration of New Testament Church government and practice (#35) with the emergence of the "Plymouth" Brethren and the Disciples of Christ, both around 1830.

1730-Today — Restoration of World Evangelization (continued)

William Carey[19]

The Moravians were one of the greatest missionary movements the Christian Church has ever known. However, missions did not "catch on" throughout the Protestant movement until the late 1790's and early 1800's.

In 1723 Robert Millar wrote *A History of the Propagation of Christianity and the Overthrow of Paganism,* in which he advocated intercession as the primary means of converting the heathen. Within twenty years prayer groups were to be found all over the British Isles interceding for the conversion of the heathen. In 1746 Christians of the Thirteen American Colonies agreed to enter into a seven-year prayer pact with those of England, praying for the spread of the Gospel throughout the world. In 1783 all Baptist Churches in Northamptonshire, England, area began to intercede on the first Monday of each month for the heathen world. Their joint resolution read;

> "Let the whole interest of the Redeemer be affectionately remembered, and the spread of the Gospel to the most distant parts of the habitable globe be the object of your most fervent requests. We shall rejoice if any other Christian societies of our own or other denominations will unite with us, and we do now invite them to join most cordially heart and hand in the attempt. Who can tell what the consequences of such a united effort in prayer may be?"

It was into this growing concern for world evangelization that William Carey (1764-1834) entered. He had apprenticed himself to the shoemaker at Hackleton at age fourteen. He was converted at eighteen, at which time he left the Church of England. Later he became a Baptist, was ordained at age 26, mended shoes and taught school on weekdays, and preached on Sundays. In his spare time he taught himself Latin, Greek, Hebrew, Italian, French, and Dutch! It was the reading of *The Last Voyage of Captain Cook* that first aroused his interest in missionary work. Subsequently he learned all he could of David Brainerd, the Danish-Halle Mission, John Eliot, and the Moravians. And on the wall of his cobbler shop was a world map where he wrote every bit of mission information he could find.

In early 1792 at a meeting of Baptist ministers in Northamptonshire, he proposed that they discuss the implications of the Great Commission. One of them retorted: "Young man, sit down. When God pleases to convert the heathen, He will do it without your aid or mine." Carey would not be stopped. A few months later he published *An Inquiry Into the Obligations of Christians to Use Means for the Conversion of the Heathens.* Some place that 87-page booklet alongside Luther's *Ninety-Five Theses* with regard to its influence on the Church. On May 30, 1792, he again spoke to the Baptist ministers, taking Isaiah 54:2-3 as his text, and during which time he stated the now-famous phrase, "Expect great things from God; attempt great things for God." Before the meeting was over, Carey had persuaded them to include in the minutes a resolution that they would present a definite plan at the next meeting for the formation of a "Baptist Society for Propagating the Gospel Among the Heathen."

The next meeting was on October 2. Nothing was said about the matter all day. But in the evening a smaller group of thirteen gathered with Carey to discuss the matter. As the brethren were seeming to waver and hope was all but gone, Carey took from his pocket a booklet entitled, *Periodical Account of Moravian Missions;* and with tears in his eyes and a tremor in his voice said, "If you had read this and know how these men overcame all obstacles for Christ's sake, you would go forward in faith." The men finally agreed to form "The Particular Baptist Society for Propagating the Gospel Among the Heathen." The mission was to be supported by individual subscriptions. Anyone subscribing ten pounds at once, or ten shillings and a sixpence annually, was considered a member.

It was one thing to get the mission society formed — quite another to get to the field! Carey's father thought he was mad, and his wife initially refused to accompany him. But on June 13, 1793, William Carey, accompanied by a reluctant wife, two companions, and four children, set sail for India where he spent the next forty years.

Following Carey's example, in the next twenty-five years, twelve major agencies for missions came into being in Europe and the United States. William Carey was indeed "the father of modern missions."

Further Developments[20]

This initial wave of modern mission activity was followed by a second great wave that included those with a burden to reach inland Asia and Africa (1850-1900), a host of single women missionaries (1890-1910), the student volunteer thrust (1890-1910), Pentecostal missionaries that started going out around 1910, and all that has happened in recent years. More will be said about this in Chapters 14 through 18. We have truly seen the restoration of world evangelization since 1730.

1857-1859 — The Third Great Awakening (#42)

As a result of the Third Great Awakening we see a restoration of the women's place in the work of the Lord (#43), a restoration of the social implications of the Gospel (#44), and the beginnings of the restoration of healing (#45).

1850-Today — Restoration of Women's Place in the Church (#43)

Women played an important role in the Old Testament. Miriam was part of the triad of leadership, along with Moses and Aaron, over the nation Israel (Micah 6:4). She also led the women in dancing (Exodus 15:20). Women became Nazarites (Numbers 6:2). Women influenced Moses' decision (Numbers 27:1-11). Deborah was a prophetess, judging Israel, giving decisions of judgment to the people, and having "the word of the Lord" for the leader of the army (Judges 4:4-10, 14). A little slave girl had a word for the captain of the army (2 Kings 5:1). God chose Huldah, the prophetess, to have "the word of the Lord" for the kings (2 Kings 22:8-20), even though Zephaniah and Jeremiah were probably in Jerusalem at the time. Psalms 68:11 mentions a great host of women evangelists. Esther was chosen by God to become queen and save the Hebrew nation from extinction.

In the New Testament, Anna, a prophetess, spent night and day fasting and praying in the Temple, and spoke to the people of the Messiah (Luke 2:36-38). There were several women who traveled with Jesus and the Twelve (Luke 8:1-3). Jesus always treated women with great kindness and dignity. The angel at the empty tomb told women to take the word of Jesus' resurrection to the Eleven, and Jesus appeared to women first before He appeared to the Eleven (Matthew 28:1-10, Mark 16:1-11, Luke 24:1-12, John 20:1-18). There were women among those who were waiting in the upper room for the Day of Pentecost (Acts 1:14).

It is God's plan for women to play an important role in the life of the Church. On the Day of Pentecost, Peter, quoting the prophet Joel, says that the Holy Spirit is to be poured out on men and women alike so that they can prophesy, and presumably to empower them for ministry and for the fulfillment of the Great Commission (Acts 2:17-18). (1 Corinthians 14:34-36 and 1 Timothy 2:11-15, which are used by some to restrict the ministry of women, are viewed by this writer as dealing with local situations whereas Acts 2:17-18 is foundational to the Church Age and puts women on an equal footing with men in the outpouring of the Spirit and the subsequent Church Age.)

Women played a large and varied role in the Early Church. Dorcas had a sewing ministry (Acts 9:36-39). Lydia had a ministry of hospitality (Acts 16:14-15, 40). Priscilla, along with her husband Aquila, taught Apollos (Acts 18:24-26). Paul also calls them his fellow-workers in Christ, who risked their lives for him; and the church met in their home in Rome (Romans 16:3-5). Philip had four virgin daughters who were prophetesses (Acts 21:9). Women were persecuted for the Gospel (Acts 22:4). Phoebe was deaconess of the Church at Cenchrea and carried *The Letter to the Romans* to Rome (Romans 16:1-2). There is even the possibility that Junia, mentioned in Romans 16:7, was a female apostle. Women are called to full-time ministry (1 Corinthians 7:34). Women prayed and prophesied (1 Corinthians 11:5), which included public edifying, exhorting, and comforting (1 Corinthians 14:3). Euodia and Syntyche were among Paul's fellow-workers (Philippians 4:1-3). The older women taught the younger (Titus 2:3-5). John's second letter indicates a woman had a prominent place among a group of believers (2 John 1). But the place of final authority rests with men, i.e., the elders — 1 Timothy 3:1-5.

The prominent place of women in the life of the Church did not seem to last very long; although in the latter part of the Second Century, Montanus was assisted by two women prophetesses.[21] In the early 300's, monasteries for women began to emerge. We see women beginning to play a little fuller role as mystics and spoke for God in the 1100's to 1300's (as noted in Chapter 8). In the early 1400's we see Joan of Arc (1412-1431) believing that she was led by God to inspire the French troops and save Orleans, France, from the invading English army.[22]

But the real restoration of the place of women in the Church did not begin until the 1800's, and is still taking place today. Prominent in giving leadership to the prayer, revival, and holiness emphases in the

1840-1870 period was a Methodist woman, Phoebe Palmer. She also was quite active in helping to pioneer a number of urban, social welfare projects in New York City and elsewhere.[23] Women played an important role in the Salvation Army, founded in 1878 by William Booth in England. His wife, Catherine, worked closely with him in leadership; his daughter, Evangeline, succeeded him as General; and women were officers right beside men.[24] The General once made the statement, "Some of my best men are women."

Wives played an active role with their husbands in the Moravian missionary thrust in the 1700's. Both of Hudson Taylor's wives were great partners. In the 1820's, single women began to trickle to the mission field, and by the late 1800's and early 1900's that trickle had become a tidal wave. By 1900 there were over forty women's missionary societies in the United States alone, and by 1910 women outnumbered men in Protestant missions.

In 1917 Aimee Semple McPherson (1890-1944), after struggling with whether or not women could preach, began her tent preaching. In 1923 Angelus Temple was opened in Los Angeles, and in 1927 the International Church of the Foursquare Gospel was incorporated.[25]

In recent decades we have seen women increasingly assume a proper place of ministry in the church. Dr. Cho, pastor of the largest church in the world, in Seoul, Korea, has women leading many of the house groups. What would modern Christianity be like without Corrie ten Boom, Vonette Bright, Joy Dawson, Kathryn Kuhlman, Catherine Marshall, Henrietta Mears, Eugenia Price, Rosalind Rinker, Mother Teresa, Iverna Thompkins, and a host of others!

1865-1910 — Restoration of the Social Implications of the Gospel (#44)

Jesus said (Matthew 25:35-46) His followers were to feed the hungry, give drink to the thirsty, care for the stranger, clothe the naked, and visit the sick and imprisoned; and in so doing to the least of society we are doing it to Him. Paul's letters teach to "do good to all men" (Galatians 6:10), to "please his neighbor for his good, to his edification" (Romans 15:2), and "at this present time your abundance being a supply for their want" (2 Corinthians 8:14).

The early Christians practiced Christian charity. Adolf Harnack, in his *The Mission and Expansion of Christianity in the First Three Centuries,* lists ten major areas where charity was practiced:

"...alms in general, support of teachers and officials, support of widows and orphans, support of the sick and infirm, the care of

102

prisoners and convicts in the mines, the care of poor people needing burial, the care of slaves, providing disaster relief, furnishing, employment, and, finally, extending hospitality." [26]

There were those in early restoration days who cared for the needs of society: the poor men of Lyons in the late 1100's, the Franciscans in the 1200's, and other individuals and groups through the centuries; but it was William Booth (1829-1912) and his Salvation Army that God especially used to restore this dimension to the reformed Church. Booth was converted at fifteen. For awhile, he was with the Methodists, but became an independent evangelist, and in 1864 went to London's East Side to preach the Gospel and minister to the poorest of people. His street preaching, often accompanied by drums and other musical instruments, met with phenomenal success. Within eleven years there were thirty-two stations promoting evangelism and social service among London's destitute. First called the East London Revival Society, and then the East London Christian Mission, the work was finally named the Salvation Army and organized along army lines in 1878. Booth's book, *In Darkest England and the Way Out,* published in 1890, stated that in one year in London over two thousand people had committed suicide, 30,000 were living in prostitution, 160,000 had been convicted of drunkenness, and over 900,000 were paupers.

The Army sought to minister physically as well as spiritually to the lowest of the underprivileged. By 1888 there were one thousand Salvation Army Corps throughout Britain and many who had been sent to other nations. Today the Salvation Army is a symbol of Christianity ministering to the needy around the world. [27]

Within the Church of England there was a small group of men, including J. F. D. Maurice (1805-1872) and Charles Kingsley (1819-1875), who from 1848 to 1854, developed a Christian Socialist movement, attacked the extreme competition in society, and believed that the Christian faith stood for a society that would enable men to work together, instead of against one another. In 1889 the Christian Social Union was formed "to apply the moral truths of Christianity to the social and economic difficulties of the age." [28]

In the late 1800's Christians gave some of the leadership in developing labor unions in order to promote better working conditions in the factories. One of the leading spokesmen was Roman Catholic Pope Leo XIII. It's interesting that Karl Marx (1818-1883) and Engels (1820-1895) were also concerned about the condition of society, and in 1848 in London issued their *Communist Manifesto.*

Marx had been reared as a Christian but had become bitter against Christianity and the Church. [29]

In the United States concern for social issues among Christians greatly increased after 1865. Many were focusing on the issues of poverty, working-men's rights, the liquor traffic, slum housing, and racial bitterness. There was a growing conviction among evangelicals that society must be reconstructed through the power of a sanctifying Gospel, and all the evils of cruelty, slavery, poverty, and greed be done away.[30]

Leading the fight against slavery were Christians, including evangelists Charles G. Finney and Elder Jacob Knapp, who preached against it in their revival meetings; Orange Scott, who along with others left the Methodist Church over the issue of slavery, and formed the Wesleyan Methodist Church in 1843; and the Quakers who helped many slaves escape to the North through their "underground railroad." [31]

Those of a more liberal theological stance who championed "the Social Gospel," and sought to inspire Christians to bring all society as well as individuals into conformity with the teachings of Jesus included Washington Gladden (1836-1918), a professor of church history at Rochester Theological Seminary. Rauschenbusch's book, *Christianity and the Social Crisis*, published in 1907, brought him nation-wide recognition as the outstanding spokesman for the Social Gospel.[32] In their attempt to emphasize the social dimension of the Gospel, some of these men lost the individual, saving dimension of the Gospel. Many evangelicals reacted to the liberal's over-emphasis on the social Gospel by emphasizing personal salvation to the exclusion of its social implications. By the early 1900's Christianity in the United States was divided between the liberals, who emphasized the social Gospel only, and the fundamentalists, who emphasized personal salvation only.

This section would not be complete without mentioning the nursing profession that was begun by Florence Nightingale (1820-1910), a Christian, and the Red Cross which was begun by Henri Dunant, a Protestant layman of Geneva, both in the 1850's.[33] The restoration of the social implications of the Gospel continues today (see Chapter 10), but the initial restoration period occurred between 1865-1910.

1750-Today — The Person and Ministry of the Holy Spirit

The Holy Spirit — His Person, power, fruit, and gifts — played a very prominent role in the First Century Church. *The Acts of the Apostles* could just as accurately be called *The Acts of the Holy Spirit.*

By A.D. 150 the infilling of the Holy Spirit and the operation of the gifts of the Spirit had ceased to operate on any large scale except among the Montanists.[34] The Holy Spirit certainly continued to have a role in the life of the Church, even through the Dark Ages, since any spiritual life or power is due to His presence and ministry. Every revival throughout all of Church history is due to His outpouring. However, it was not until the 1800's that the full and rightful place of importance of the Holy Spirit began to be restored and recognized by the Church.

The Infilling of the Holy Spirit (#38)

The Methodist doctrine, which developed in the mid and late 1700's, included teaching several important aspects of the Person and ministry of the Holy Spirit. Their concept of salvation included the new birth which one could know assuredly by "the witness of the Spirit." They also taught a deeper experience, subsequent to the new birth, called Christian perfection or entire sanctification. The Methodist and holiness groups in the late 1800's began to call this experience "the baptism of the Holy Spirit." At this time the heart was cleansed of the "old man" and filled with the Holy Spirit, thus enabling the recipient to live a holy life.[35] Their teaching was later perpetuated by The Wesleyan Church, The Church of the Nazarene, and other holiness denominations. The term "baptism of the Holy Spirit" was later also used by Pentecostals to refer to the infilling of the Holy Spirit, but they taught that "speaking in tongues" was the "initial, physical evidence" of that infilling.

In 1875 at Keswick, England, a conference was begun for the deepening of spiritual life. In time, a Keswick teaching developed, similar to Methodism, that taught a "baptism of the Holy Spirit" or an "infilling of the Holy Spirit" which Christians were encouraged to seek. This "infilling" was received at the time that one surrendered to Jesus Christ as the absolute Lord of his life. This was taught widely by well-known Christian leaders of the late 1800's —including Andrew Murray, F.B. Meyer, A.J. Gordon, Oswald Chambers, and many others. The Keswick conferences and teaching have made a major contribution to the understanding of the Person and ministry of the Holy Spirit in Christendom.[36]

There are, in fact, three present-day schools of theological teaching on the person and work of the Holy Spirit that we would all do well to study: the Methodist, or holiness teaching; the Keswick teaching; and the Pentecostal or charismatic teaching.

Healing (#45)

Jesus spent His time preaching, teaching, healing, and delivering people from demons. Physical healing, by anointing with oil is taught in James 5:14-16, has been the practice of some Christians all through the ages. But it was not until the late 1800's and into the 1900's that the healing ministry began to be restored to its rightful place. (Since healing is one of the gifts of the Holy Spirit, it is included in this section.)

A.B. Simpson began advocating healing as being available in the atonement of Jesus Christ in the 1880's.[37] From 1900 to 1930 there was a great wave of healing through the ministries of Alexander Dowie, F.F. Bosworth, John G. Lake, Smith Wigglesworth, Aimee Semple McPherson, Charles S. Price, and a host of others. This has been further reinforced since 1947 by the healing ministry that has flowed through William Branham, Gordon Lindsay, Oral Roberts, T.L. Osborne, Tommy Hicks, Kathryn Kuhlman, Francis MacNutt, and many others.[38] Also, since about 1970 there has been an emphasis on the healing of the emotions, or hurts caused by traumatic experiences and the abusive actions of others.

1900-1930 — The Fourth Great Awakening (#46)

On the crest of the wave of the Fourth Great Awakening was a further release of healing (#45) and the restoration of all of the other gifts of the Spirit (#47).

The Gifts of the Spirit (#47)

Prophecy, healings, speaking in tongues, the casting out of demons, and all of the other gifts of the Spirit have operated from time to time throughout the Church's history. It was not until the late 1800's that they have begun to be restored more widely to the Church. We have already looked at healing.

In 1832 Edward Irving (1792-1834) founded the Catholic Apostolic Church, based on his understanding that apostles, prophets, speaking in tongues, and healing were being restored to the Church.[39]

The gift of tongues operated in various places in the 1800's and in Topeka, Kansas, in 1901 as described on page 23. In 1902 Lewi Pethrus of Sweden "spoke strange words which surprised me a great deal."[40] In 1906 many of the spiritual gifts were in operation at the Azusa Street meetings (see Chapter 3). From there the Pentecostal movement developed and spread throughout North America and around the world. By 1920 a number of Pentecostal denominations had emerged, all of them emphasizing the gifts of the Spirit.

Since about 1950 the restoration of the operation of the gifts of the Spirit has spread through the charismatic renewal to much of Christendom worldwide. There are now an estimated 150 million Pentecostal-Charismatic Christians in the world. To this needs to be added many others who believe in the gifts of the Spirit but who would not call themselves "charismatic." An example of the latter would be Fuller Theological Seminary where a class entitled, "Signs, Wonders, and Church Growth," is offered. Many non-charismatics are changing their views in these days. Dr. Donald A. McGavran, known world-wide as the "dean of Church growth," recently stated:

"I do not come from a Church background that emphasizes healing. In fact, we have been a bit critical of it. Yet in my research I have discovered the winning of the lost has come in great numbers where men and women were healed in Christ's name. Amazing church growth has resulted." [41]

Truly, God is restoring the Person and ministry of the Holy Spirit to His Church in modern times.

1935-Today — Scripture Memory (#48)

It is difficult to trace the memorization of the Bible throughout Church history. We do know that Jesus and the early disciples knew the Old Testament. Jesus often quoted it in His teaching. Peter, on the Day of Pentecost, quoted a number of Old Testament passages.

In modern times, there was the beginning of a restoration of Scripture memory through Dawson Trotman and The Navigators, beginning in the late 1930's. The principles and practices of the Navigators were picked up by many other individuals and groups. In recent years there has been the teaching of Jerry Lucas that has helped thousands to memorize Scripture by putting it into picture form.[42]

1935-Today — Follow-up and Discipling (#49)

Jesus said that our task included teaching to our converts all that He had taught us — Matthew 28:20. The First Century Christians took that aspect of the Great Commission seriously as shown in Acts 14:21-22, 15:36; Colossians 1:28; 1 Thessalonians 2:10-12; 2 Timothy 2:2, etc.

This task of following up the decision of a new Christian to follow Jesus had often been neglected by the Church until modern times. In the 1930's we saw Dawson Trotman, founder of the Navigators, beginning to develop the art of follow-up. His concepts were picked up and popularized by Billy Graham and his team in the 1950's. They were further developed and applied to the local church in the 1960's by Waylon Moore in his book, *New Testament Follow-Up*. Since that time many have developed various concepts and procedures of follow-up and discipling as the Holy Spirit has continued to restore this important aspect to the life of the Church.

1960-Today — Personal Evangelism (#50)

We see the early Christians propagating the Gospel in two ways. First, they shared the Gospel with groups of people, as on the Day of Pentecost, in an approach that has come to be called "mass evangelism." They also shared the Gospel with individuals in an approach that we call "personal evangelism." Mass evangelism began to be restored in 1739 through George Whitefield and John Wesley. Personal evangelism is only in recent years being restored to the Church.

At the turn of this century there were only two books on personal evangelism, one by Charles Trumbull and one by R.A. Torrey. Both taught personal evangelism methods to be used in the context of counseling seekers at a mass evangelism crusade. In 1922, J.E. Conant wrote his book, *Every-Member Evangelism*. The Navigators used personal evangelism extensively in their work, beginning in the mid-1930's. In the 40's and 50's there was Youth For Christ, Christian Business Men's Committee, Horace Dean's ministry, and Fred Jordan's Soul Clinic.

But the real restoration began about 1960 through the ministries and writings of many: Bill Bright and Campus Crusade for Christ, Christians in Action, Gene Edwards, the Jesus People, James Kennedy, Charles Kingsley, Nate Krupp, C.S. Lovett, Hubert Mitchell, Youth With A Mission, Dick Whipple, and many others. Today personal evangelism is considered to be a normal part of the life of many Christians.

For centuries God has been restoring New Testament Christianity to His Church. The restoration is being completed in our day. The next two chapters outline some of the exciting things that God is doing today.

10

TODAY-THE COMPLETION
OF THE RESTORATION

What a privilege it is for us who are alive today: God, in this hour, is completing the restoration of His Church. Jesus will come back for a Church that is fully restored to the purity, spiritual authority and power, purposes, principles and patterns, and fruitfulness of the early Church as recorded in *The Acts*. It may take five years — or twenty-five — but the restoration will be completed!

So what are some of the things that are happening in the Body of Christ today, that indicate that the restoration is still in progress, and that there will soon be a fully-restored Church to await the return of our Lord? Let's take a look!

Deeper Meaning and Application of the Gospel

Sin, the Ten Commandments, and Repentance

Twenty years ago when the Gospel was preached there was little said about sin and the need to repent. It was just, "receive Christ." Dr. J. Edwin Orr, noted evangelical statesman, recently wrote the following:

"Thirty years ago, the notorious gangster Mickey Cohen attended a meeting in Beverly Hills addressed by Billy Graham. He expressed some interest in the message, so several of us talked with him, including Dr. Graham, but he made no commitment until some time later when another friend urged him — with Revelation 3:20 as a warrant — to invite Jesus Christ into his life.

"This he professed to do, but his life subsequently gave no evidence of repentance, 'the mighty change of mind, heart, and life.' Mr. Cohen rebuked our friend, telling him, 'You did not tell me that I would have to give up my work!' He meant his rackets. 'You did not tell me that I would have to give up my friends!' He meant his gangster associates. He had heard that so-and-so was a Christian cowboy, so-and-so was a Christian actress, so-and-so was a Christian senator, and he really thought that he could be a Christian gangster.

"Recently, people were intrigued by the announcement that a notorious pornographer professed to be 'born again.' But he has given no evidence of repentance, and it has been forgotten that the only evidence of the New Birth is the new life. His first editorial said he now followed the spirit of Jesus and Buddha.

"The fact is, repentance is a missing note in much modern evangelism. The appeal is not for repentance, but for enlistment.

"This has become a national scandal. Evangelistic enterprises are claiming the response of multitudes. A national poll has announced that 50 million Americans state they are 'born again,' but a national newspaper observes that this evangelical awakening (so-called) seems to have little effect upon the morals of the country, as murder, robbery, rape, pornography, and other social evils abound. The fault is in the message. Holy Scripture calls upon new recruits of the Christian Church to repent." [1]

There is today growing recognition that the Ten Commandments are God's moral/ethical standard for mankind. When we break them, we sin. In order to be reconciled to God, we must repent. We must have a change of mind and heart, be sorry, and turn from our sins, resulting in a change of lifestyle that is in accordance with the will and Word of God.

Wholeness or Total Salvation

When this writer was converted to Jesus Christ in 1957, his concept of "salvation" was "the new birth." Certainly that is the most important aspect of salvation, for it is the new birth that translates us from "the kingdom of darkness" into "the kingdom of light." But there is a broader dimension to salvation. The Greek word "soteria" can be translated "salvation, deliverance, wholeness, soundness." It is God's desire to do more than forgive sin: He wants to make people whole — physically, mentally, emotionally, and spiritually. So there is

110

a broader "package" of salvation, designed to make people whole, that includes:

1. Hearing the Gospel — Romans 10:14
   - bad news first — fact of sin — breaking of God's law — 1 John 3:4, James 2:10-11, Romans 3:9-23, Galatians 24.
   - n the Good News — John 3:16, Romans 5:8, 1 John 0.
   - on of sin — John 16:7-11, 2 Corinthians 7:10.
   - e — Luke 13:3, Acts 3:19, Acts 20:21.
   - us Christ as Lord and Savior — Acts 16:31, John 8:34-38.
   - Leviticus 6:4-5, Luke 19:8-9.
   - — Mark 16:15-16, Matthew 28:19-20, Acts 9, 16:30-34, Romans 6:1-11.
   - nce from demonic activity — Luke 4:18, Matthew , Acts 5:3.
8. Healing —
   a. renewing the mind — Romans 8:6, 12:2, Ephesians 4:23, Philippians 4:8, 1 Corinthians 2:16.
   b. inner, emotional — Psalms 34:18, 86:11, 147:3, Isaiah 53:4-5, 61:1, Jeremiah 30:17 (including self-acceptance, experiencing the Father's love, etc.).
   c. physical — Isaiah 53:4-5, Matthew 8:15-17.
9. Baptism, or filling, with the Holy Spirit — Acts 8:14-18, 19:1-7, etc.
10. The operation of the gifts of the Spirit — 1 Corinthians 12:7-11, 1 Peter 4:10.
11. A life of continual growth and ministry —
    a. a life of victory — John 16:33, Romans 8:31-39, Revelation 2:7, 11, 17, 26, 3:5, 12, 21.
    b. trials and suffering, to make us Christ-like — Romans 5:3-5, 1 Peter 1:6-8.
    c. a walk of faith, to learn His sufficiency — Philippians 4:11-19.
    d. ministry — to God, against the devil, to our families, to other believers, to the world.

e. walking in new light that God gives you — 2 Peter 3:18,
1 John 1:7.

Today God is making this broader "package" of salvation ("total
salvation") real to many, and bringing them to a place of "wholeness."
Jesus will return for an army of victorious, whole people.

The Word

There is today a return to the Word of God. In theological circles
there is a growing consideration of the doctrine of Biblical inerrancy.
There is also a growing emphasis today on the expository preaching of
God's Word in the Christian churches of the world. God's people are
no longer content with a message that contains a verse or two. They
want the Word of God explained and preached, verse by verse, and
book by book.

There is a return to the Bible today in the personal lives of people.
There has probably never been a generation throughout Church
history when there has been so much emphasis on the Word as there is
today. Everywhere one goes today there is a growing emphasis on
Bible reading, study, memory, meditation, and application. This is
evident in personal lives and in tens of thousands of Bible study groups
that are in progress in almost every city on earth.

Knowing God Intimately

God's people are no longer satisfied with just being saved and being
involved in church activities. There is a growing hunger to know God;
to know the Father, to know the Son, to know the Holy Spirit; to know
God intimately; to know His person, His character, and His ways. (An
outline of the outstanding characteristics of God in each book of the
Bible can be found in Appendix 5.)

Who We Are in Christ

God's people are coming to understand all the great spiritual
privileges, blessings, authority, and power that is theirs because they
are sons of God and joint-heirs with Jesus Christ.

Being Conformed To His Image

Romans 8:28-29 says that we are predestined to become like Jesus,
and that the Father is causing all things to work toward that supreme
objective. 2 Corinthians 3:18 likewise talks about our being trans-
formed into the image of Jesus. What a privilege: to become more and

more like Jesus! That's what the word "Christian" (Acts 11:26) means — "little Christ." That's God's plan for each of us! He does it through trials (Romans 5:3-5, 8:17-18, James 1:2-4, 1 Peter 1:6-8, etc.). God is allowing His people in many parts of the world —China, Russia, Eastern Europe, parts of Africa, Southeast Asia, Central America, etc. — to go through great trials in order to conform them to the image of Christ. They are responding! God will have a company of people who are like His Son here on earth for Jesus when He comes back.

The Presence and Power of God

Holy Spirit Power

As we move toward the end of this Age, and the completion of the restoration, God will pour out His Spirit world-wide as has never before been seen. The entire earth will experience what happened in Jerusalem on the Day of Pentecost. (See Chapter 4.) With this "latter rain" (Joel 2:23) of the Spirit will come a season of many great miracles of healing, etc., just as took place in *The Acts.* Many who are listening to God are sensing this. Alan Langstaff recently wrote:

"In 1978, I began to sense that God was about to do something new. There's a new day coming for the move of the Spirit in the church.
— the miraculous will become more commonplace.
— unusual miracles will take place among God's people.
— the glory of God will be manifested in the people of God." [2]

Dick Mills recently wrote:

"All over the world people sensitive to the movings of the Lord believe that a new wave of God's glory and power will be coming in. What a joy it is to hear Spirit-filled saints around the world — Singapore, Scotland, Latin America, Europe, Africa, Australia, New Zealand — talking about the next wave of the Spirit.... I'm believing that the last chapter of the Church Age is still to be written. The world hasn't seen anything yet compared to what they will see ... A greater display of the miraculous is going to occur. The generation alive at the coming of the Lord will have no excuse for their unbelief. We can expect the Church Age, which began with a burst of the supernatural evidences, to end full circle at the Second Coming. The Church will once

113

again have apostolic purity, power, and productivity. When Jesus returns, the Church will go out in a burst of power and glory!" [3]

Of course, we must also have discernment with reference to satanic counterfeit supernatural happenings.

A Revelation of the Father

The Protestant Reformation included, as part of its theology, a revelation of the Son, the Lord Jesus Christ. Beginning with the Methodists and moving on to Keswick, Holiness, and Pentecostal/Charismatic teaching and experience, we have had a restoration of the Person and ministry of the blessed Holy Spirit. In recent years, God has been giving to His people a renewed revelation of God, as Father. We are coming to understand and experience His great mercy, His unending love, His absolute faithfulness, His glorious holiness. What a joy it is to get to know the Father!

Angels

As the restoration comes full circle, and as God's power is being poured out, we will continue to see more and more activity of angels. Angels will increasingly be assisting God's people as it says in Hebrews 1:14 and as we see in the Early Church, recorded in *The Acts.*

Ministry

God is revealing a whole new concept of Christian ministry that is restoring to us the understanding and practice of the Early Church, as recorded in the *New Testament.*

Ministry Is For All

Christian ministry is not something that is just for certain people. Ministry, in the New Testament sense, is for all! Every person in the Body of Christ is important to God — and should be important to us. God has equipped every Christian with gifts that enable him to minister in some particular way. His ministry, however apparently insignificant, is very important (Romans 12:1-8, 1 Corinthians 12:1-27, 1 Peter 4:10).

Ministry to God

Our first place of ministry is to God (Acts 13:2). This is a ministry of thanksgiving, praise, and worship. That's the main theme of the Psalms. Today, God is restoring Spirit-anointed praise and worship to His people around the world.

Our other ministry to God is intercession — laboring with Him by interceding for those concerns that He lays on our hearts. (Intercession is a ministry both to and for God and on the behalf of those for whom we pray (Ezekiel 22:30).) God is restoring intercession to His church today. He is raising up many intercessors. (For further information you are encouraged to write the addresses given in Appendix 3.)

Ministry Against the Devil

Matthew 12:29 talks about "binding the strong man" before you can take his property. Today God is restoring warfare to His Church. Many are learning how to do battle with the forces of darkness. This is closely related to praise, worship, and intercession.

Ministry to Our Families

The family was the first, and is the most important unit of society (Genesis 1-2). The Church and nations are only as strong as the families of which they are made. God is restoring the importance and Biblical pattern of marriage and the family. Beginning with Larry Christenson's book *The Christian Family,* in 1970, much has been said in recent years about the importance of marriage and the Christian home and family. Weekend retreats (sponsored by Marriage Encounter and other similar groups) where married couples can improve their marriage, are gaining popularity. God has spoken to many full-time Christian workers that family has priority above ministry. In the United States, marriage is on the comeback: in 1982, 2.5 million couples married — more than in any previous year. And the divorce rate is dropping, too. For the first time in twenty-two years, the divorce rate declined in 1982, a three percent drop from 1981, and the first drop since 1962.[4]

How important it is for parents to center their marriage and family life around Christ. And how important it is for the father to gather his family each day for a time of Bible reading, sharing, and prayer.

Part of the renewed emphasis on the family is also seen in the commitment on the part of Christians to Christian education. In the United States alone, there are approximately one million youngsters enrolled in nearly 20,000 evangelical Christian schools, with three new Christian schools being started every day.[5] This is simply a return to our early, national roots. Education in America in the early days was Christian. The *New England Primer* opened with the Lord's Prayer, the Apostles' Creed, the Ten Commandments, and a list of the books of the *Bible*. William McGuffey's *Readers* stressed religion, morality, and knowledge, in that order. Between 1836 and 1920, 120 million copies were used in schools.[6] Estimates are that today up to three million children are being taught at home.[7] One must add to this the hundreds of Bible schools and Christian colleges and universities that exist around the world.

Ministry to One Another

In recent years God has been emphasizing the importance of personal relationships and ministering to one another. Some of the key passages include:

1. Conversing with one another — Luke 24:17, 32.
2. Loving one another — John 13:34-35.
3. Sharing with one another — Acts 4:32.
4. Being devoted to one another — Romans 12:10.
5. Not judging one another — Romans 14:13, 19.
6. Accepting one another — Romans 15:7.
7. Caring for one another — 1 Corinthians 12:25.
8. Bearing one another's burdens — Galatians 6:2.
9. Submitting to one another — Ephesians 5:21.
10. Regarding one another with importance — Philippians 2:3-4.
11. Admonishing one another — Colossians 3:16.
12. Encouraging one another — 1 Thessalonians 5:11.
13. Living in peace with one another — 1 Thessalonians 5:13.
14. Seeking that which is good for one another — 1 Thessalonians 5:15.
15. Stimulating one another to love and good works — Hebrews 10:24-25.
16. Confessing our sins to one another and praying for one another — James 5:16.
17. Serving one another — 1 Peter 4:10.

116

18. Having humility toward one another — 1 Peter 5:5.
19. Having fellowship with one another — 1 John 1:7.

This is a major reason for being a part of Christ's Body, that we might minister to one another that which is lacking.

Ministry to the World

There is a growing realization among God's people that He has left us here on earth for a purpose: to be His ministering servants to the world. We are to take the Gospel to the whole world; to be a prophetic voice to every area of society; and to minister to the hurting, the hungry, and the needy of the world.

1. *Evangelism.* Jesus gave to His church a commission to go into all the world and take the Gospel to every person in every nation; and to baptize and disciple those who respond to this Gospel (Matthew 28:18-20, Mark 16:14-20, Luke 24:47-49, John 20:21, Acts 1:4-8). Today the Church is responding to Jesus' command as never before. In fact, the evangelization of the world is such a major part of the life of the Church, and what God is doing today, that an entire section of this book is devoted to it (Chapters 15 through 18.).

2. *Being a prophetic voice to society.* Jesus said that Christians are "the salt of the earth" and "the light of the world" (Matthew 5:13-16). We are to be a prophetic voice, a guiding light, a changing influence in society. The Church of Jesus Christ is to be God's voice here on earth — explaining the will and ways of God and calling all of society to walk therein. Dr. Carl F. H. Henry recently said, "Our Christian duty includes a public proclamation of the standards by which the Coming King will judge all men and nations." [8]

The Western world for centuries was built on a Judeo-Christian foundation that God and His will were central. In recent decades that has all changed. Most of society is now only concerned about man and his every whim. This must be changed! We must return to a Judeo-Christian world-view that puts God in the center of all of life. **We must advocate and work for the Lordship of Jesus Christ in every area of society** — in the homes; in the schools; in government, including the laws, the courts, the foreign policy; in commerce and industry; in the media; in the arts; and most certainly in the Church. We must rise up and do something about pornography, abortion, homosexuality, lotteries, a coming nuclear holocaust, the injustices, and the humanism

117

that prevails. And we must do it now, while our freedoms still allow us the opportunity.

Three excellent books that elaborate on the need for the Church to rise to her prophetic voice ministry are: *A Christian Manifesto* by Francis A. Schaeffer; *A Time for Anger,* by Franky Schaeffer; and *The Second American Revolution,* by John W. Whitehead. (See the Bibliography for details.) There is also a new magazine entitled "Transformation," that is to be "an international dialogue on evangelical social ethics," and is available through P.O. Box 1308-EQ, Fort Lee, New Jersey 07024. It is encouraging to see several organizations of Christian lawyers which have emerged in recent years with the purpose of protecting religious liberty and to voice concern about the divorce of American law from its Christian roots.[9] (A list of these is given in Appendix 6.)

3. *Ministering mercy and compassion.* As recorded in Matthew 25:31-46, Jesus said that we are to feed the hungry, give drink to the thirsty, invite the stranger in, clothe the naked, and visit the sick and imprisoned. Ministering to them as if we are ministering to Him. The number of poor, hungry, homeless, needy people is increasing all over the world. God is burdening His people to be increasingly involved in various ministries of mercy and compassion to the poor, the needy, the refugee, the downtrodden — next door and around the world. A list of organizations specializing in relief and development ministries is given in Appendix 9-M.

11

TODAY — THE COMPLETION OF THE RESTORATION (CONTINUED)

Church Life and Structures for Ministry

God is doing much today to restore the gifts, ministries, structures, and patterns of life that we see in the Early Church in order to prepare the way for a mighty, end-time move of the Holy Spirit. In this section we are going to look at these.

Defining "Church"

A study of patterns of church life and ministry needs to begin with a look at the word "church." The word "church" is used several ways in our culture: the building on the corner that we go to on Sunday, the organization that hires the pastor, a denomination, etc. To understand God's plan, we need to see how the Bible uses the word. The word "church" and "churches" in our English Bible is a translation of the Greek word "ekklesia." It is from the Greek words "ek," which is translated "out," and "kaleo," which is translated "to call;" thus the composite: "the called out" ones. So the word "church" means "the called out ones," those who have been called out of the world by the Holy Spirit, into a saving relationship with God, the Father, through the atoning death, burial, and resurrection of the Lord Jesus Christ. There is also the sense of being called to assemble, or to gather together.

This Greek word "ekklesia" appears 114 times in the New Testament. Twice it is translated (in the New American Standard translation) "congregation," and refers to an assembly of the children of Israel — Acts 7:38, Hebrews 2:12. Three times it is translated "assembly," and is referring to groups of people other than Christians, who are assembled together — Acts 19:32, 39, 41. The remaining 109 times it is translated "church" seventy-four times, and "churches" thirty-five times. In every case it is referring to believers, those who have been "called out" of the world into a relationship with God.

It is very interesting and important to see how these words "church" and "churches" are used. Thirteen times they refer to all believers everywhere in the world, or the Church universal. Thirty times they refer to all of the believers in a given city. With the possible exception of 2 Corinthians 8:24, all of the believers in a city were always referred to as a unit, one church, the church of Jerusalem, Corinth, Ephesus, etc. It is not always clear whether or not these believers all met together in one place. Sometimes the word refers to a specific group of Christians who regularly met together, usually in homes. (Further details on all of this can be found in Appendix 7.) The word never refers to a denomination or an organization; and it never refers to a building. This writer concludes that the early Christians saw themselves functioning in three arenas — as part of a group that gathered together on a regular basis, usually in someone's home; as part of all the believers in their city; and as part of God's family, world-wide.

So what about today? Every Christian needs to be deeply committed to a group of believers that regularly comes together (in a home, "church" building, cathedral, school, barn, forest, hut, etc.). He also needs to be vitally concerned about what's happening with all of the believers of his village, town, or city, and should be praying and working to see all of these believers functioning as one body. He also should be aware and concerned about the Lord's Church world-wide, not just those believers world-wide that are part of his denomination. (More on all of this will be discussed in Chapters 12 and 13.)

The Traveling Ministries

So we have God's "called-out ones," being part of the "church of (that city)." We might call that "the resident church." But there was also another entity that was part of God's Church: those who were involved in a traveling ministry.

Let's first look at Philip, the evangelist. He was first selected to be part of the Seven, to take care of the food distribution (Acts 6:1-6). When the persecution came to Jerusalem, he was scattered to the city of Samaria where God greatly used him (Acts 8:1-13). For a time the apostles Peter and John came to work with him (Acts 8:14-25). He was then directed by an angel to go to Gaza where he witnessed to the Ethiopian eunuch (Acts 8:26-39). Then he was snatched away by the Spirit to Azotus where he preached in all the cities until he came to Caesarea (Acts 8:40). Finally, we see Philip at his home in Caesarea (Acts 21:8-9), where he was considered an "evangelist." There is no record of Philip ever being "sent out" by any church group or anyone else, although he may have been. But there he is, chosen by God to have a traveling ministry of evangelism, wherever God would lead him.

There were the prophets. We see Agabus and others coming from Jerusalem to Antioch to tell of a coming famine (Acts 11:27-28). There is no indication in Scripture who sent them: was it the apostles, the elders at Jerusalem, the church, God? Next we see Judas and Silas, also prophets, chosen by the apostles, the elders, and the whole church, to accompany Paul and Barnabas to Antioch (Acts 15:22-31). While there, they had a message of encouragement for the church (Acts 15:32). Then they were sent back to their place of origin (Acts 15:33). We next see Agabus coming to Caesarea with a word for Paul (Acts 21:10-11). So there were prophets who sometimes traveled from place to place. They were sometimes sent out officially by the church: apostles, elders, and/or the whole church; and it appears that sometimes they were sent out by the Spirit Himself.

Finally we have the apostles, the "sent ones." There are those who believe that there were only twelve apostles and that apostles were only for the Early Church. It is true that there were the Twelve that Jesus originally picked to be His constant companions. They were called "apostles" (Matthew 10:2, Mark 6:30, Luke 6:13, etc.), and they have a very special place in God's plan (Matthew 19:28, Revelation 21:14, etc.). But there is also the continuing function, or ministry, of apostles throughout the Church Age (Ephesians 4:11-16). They, along with prophets, are used of God to lay the foundation for new works, i.e., local churches, new ministries, etc. (Ephesians 2:20). Those who were apostles, in addition to the Twelve, in the New Testament, included: Matthias (Acts 1:26), Paul (Romans 1:1, etc.), Andronicus, Junias, others (Romans 16:7), brethren (2 Corinthians 8:23), James, the Lord's brother (Galatians 1:19), Silvanus (Silas) and Timothy (1 Thessalonians 1:1, with 2:6), Barnabas (Acts 14:4, 14:14), a number (1 Corinthians 15:7, with 15:5), Apollos and Sosthenes (1 Corinthians 4:9, with 1:1 and 4:6), Epaphroditus (Philippians 2:25), and Titus (clearly seen by what he did). Some see Matthias as Judas' replacement (Acts 1:15-26) while others see Paul as God's choice, due to Paul's prominence in Scripture. The important point is that apostles are a very important, basic part of God's plan for the entire Church Age. In Chapters 8-11 of *The Acts* we see the travels of the Apostle Peter. In Acts 11:22-26, 29-30, we see the Apostle Barnabas. In Acts 13-28 we see the travels and work of the Apostles Paul, Barnabas, and others who worked with them. (A complete resume of all the travels of the traveling ministries recorded in *The Acts* is given in Appendix 8.)

In Acts 13:1-4 we see Barnabas and Saul (Paul) specifically "set apart" by the Holy Spirit "for the work to which I have called them." After this initial setting apart, it seems that they were primarily accountable to God. There are those who teach that all traveling ministries are to be submitted to a local church, and use Paul as their example. It appears to this writer that when Paul and Barnabas were sent out from the church at Antioch, they were "set apart, separated, bordered off" (Acts 13:2) to become a new spiritual unit, and were no longer under the local church's control. In Acts 16:6-10, Paul was directed by the Holy Spirit and a vision to go into Macedonia rather than Asia. He did not submit this decision to the church at Antioch or to a mission board anywhere. Once "set apart" by the Holy Spirit, and released by the Antioch church, this apostolic team was accountable to the Lord Himself. But they were deeply committed to relationships and fellowshipped and shared with the brethren whenever they were in Antioch (Acts 14:26-28), and submitted themselves to one another for mutual correction (Galatians 2:1, 2). Let's all be very open to the Lord and to one another as we continue to learn God's ways in this matter.

So we have the Church of our Lord Jesus Christ, (or the Body of

Christ), formed and functioning in two separate entities or structures: the resident churches and the traveling ministries. But there was much cooperation, flowing of people from one to the other, and blessing one another. (Dr. Ralph D. Winter, of the U.S. Center for World Mission, has much to say about the continuing of these two structures throughout Church history in his booklet, *The Two Structures of God's Redemptive Mission.*)

This writer believes that all of this will be fully restored before Jesus returns. Believers will once again return to meeting in homes. All of the believers of a given city will function as the Body of Christ in that city. There will be a concern for the Church world-wide. There will be a full restoration of the traveling ministries of apostles, prophets, and evangelists. Church buildings and denominations will become less and less important. All of this may sound very radical. Time will tell. These are days when Christian leaders must lay aside tradition and prejudice and seek to hear what the Holy Spirit is saying.

Unity

One of the Biblical principles that relates to church life and structures for ministry is unity. In John 17:21-23, Jesus prayed that His Church would be "perfected in unity" in order that "the world may know that Thou didst send Me." All of God's people functioning as one is a very important part of God's plan, so important, that a separate section of this book is devoted to this theme (see Chapters 12 and 13).

Authority

Hebrews 13:17 reads, "Obey your leaders, and submit to them; for they keep watch over your souls, as those who will give an account." In 1 Peter 2:13 we find, "Submit yourselves for the Lord's sake to every human institution." The centurion who came to Jesus claimed to be "a man under authority." So to whom is the believer to submit, and to what degree is he to be "under authority"? In these days, God is restoring a Biblical understanding of authority to His people. There are four levels of God's authority and there are four areas of human authority.[1]

God's authority:
1. The absolute authority of God as Sovereign over the entire Universe. Even those angels, nations and individuals that

123

have not yet recognized or bowed to God's authority are under it! (Genesis 1:1, 1 Chronicles 29:12, Psalms 47:8, Daniel 4:35, Luke 8:28.)

2. The authority of Jesus as Head of the Church. The first place of submission for every Christian is to the Lord Himself. (Matthew 28:18, Ephesians 1:19-23, Hosea 3:8, Revelation 19:11-16, 22:12-14).

3. The authority of the Scripture as written truth. The next place of submission for every Christian is to God's Word. It is the standard by which we are to live, and by which we will be judged. (2 Timothy 3:16-17, Psalms 119:142, 151, John 8:31-32, Acts 17:11).

4. The authority of conscience. Our next place of submission is to what our heart tells us to do. (Romans 2:15, 14:5, 14:13, 14:23, 1 Corinthians 8:12.)

Human Authority:

We are also to submit to the human authorities that God has placed over us in each of the four basic arenas of life:

1. The home — Exodus 20:12, 1 Corinthians 11:3, Ephesians 5:21-33, 6:1-4, 1 Peter 3:1-7.

2. The Church — Acts 20:17, Ephesians 4:7-16, Hebrews 13:17, 1 Peter 5:1-5.

3. The government — Romans 13:1-7, 1 Timothy 2:1-2, 1 Peter 2:13-17.

4. The place of employment — Jeremiah 22:13, Ephesians 6:5-9, 2 Thessalonians 3:10, 1 Peter 2:18.

In these days, God is restoring authority to His Church. As is the case whenever God is restoring something, some go overboard. So in the matter of authority, there have been abuses. But increasingly, God is raising up those with the spirit of servant-leadership. Each of us needs to know who we are related to in the Body of Christ. This submission is not an unquestioned obedience, but a voluntary, reciprocal deference of equals. This is clearly seen in Ephesians 5:21. These relationships of authority and submission grow out of personal relationships that God graciously establishes.

As the city church continues to develop, God will raise up His authority in each locality. It will flow through the apostles, prophets, teachers, and elders of His choosing. His servant-leaders will become evident; and God's people will joyfully relate to them. Likewise, the traveling ministries (apostles, prophets, and evangelists) will come to see their place of submission: apostles being submitted directly to the Lord and to one another; and traveling prophets and evangelists submitted to the apostles. And there is a sense in which all of us are to be submitted to another and to the whole Church.

When a traveling ministry comes into a local area where God's authority is clearly functioning, the resident church and the traveling ministries will need to seek God to see how they are to submit to one another. For example, if a recognized apostle comes to a location where the Body of Christ exists, does he submit to the local spiritual authorities (elders), or do they submit to him, or both? There is much that God has yet to say to the Body of Christ today about true, Biblical authority and how it is to function. God's authority, flowing through His servant-leaders will be a major issue in the next few years. And God will make it clear as we listen to Him.

Shared Leadership

Leadership, or oversight, and ministry were usually shared in the Bible. Moses was yoked with Aaron and Miriam (Micah 6:4). Jesus sent the Twelve and the seventy out in pairs (Luke 9 and 10). Paul was teamed up with various co-workers at different times — Barnabas, Silas, Timothy, Titus, John Mark, Luke, etc. When Paul and Barnabas appointed elders in the churches, they appointed elders (plural) in each church (singular) (Acts 14:23).

Throughout Church history there have been many "loners," doing their "own thing," individuals concerned about "my church" or "my ministry." God is changing that in these days. He is restoring team-work, co-laboring, partnership, shared leadership and ministry, to His Church. A growing number of churches are moving into a shared plurality of eldership type of government. His people are learning to share in the authority and responsibility of His Kingdom.

Fellowship — the Shared Life

Acts 2:42 tells us that the early Christians gave themselves to (1) the apostles' teaching, (2) fellowship, (3) the breaking of bread, and (4) prayer. Most Christians today are familiar with teaching and prayer. The breaking of bread probably refers to the Lord's Supper

(Matthew 26:26-29, 1 Corinthians 11:20-26), although it was sometimes closely associated with having a meal together (Matthew 26:26, Acts 2:46). But what is "fellowship"?

The English word "fellowship" is translated from the Greek word "koinonia." It has a much deeper meaning than having a cup of tea or coffee together or just having light conversation together. Koinonia means "sharing" or "participating." Christian fellowship is to "share" our lives with one another: confessing our sins to one another (James 5:16), having meals together (Acts 2:46), sharing our finances and possessions with each other (Acts 2:44, 4:32-37, Romans 12:13, Philippians 4:15, 1 Timothy 6:18, etc.), encouraging one another (1 Thessalonians 5:11, Hebrews 10:24-25), preaching the Gospel together (Philippians 1:5), etc.

Increasingly, the Holy Spirit is speaking the true meaning of the word "fellowship" to God's people, and they are responding by sharing their lives with one another at very deep and intimate levels in Bible study-sharing groups, in ministry teams, in Christian communities, etc. True fellowship is being restored to the Church.

Gathering in Homes

The early Christians gathered together mainly in their homes (Acts 2:46, 5:42, 11:12-14, 12:12, 16:40, Romans 16:5, 16:23, 1 Corinthians 16:19, Colossians 4:14, Philemon 2). There were no, or very few, "church" buildings erected for Christians to meet in until the early 300's. For three hundred years the Christian Church was home-centered: just believers coming together in their homes to worship (Acts 13:2) and praise God (Acts 2:47), pray (Acts 12:5), read the Scriptures (1 Timothy 4:13), encourage one another (Hebrews 10:24-25), sing (Ephesians 5:19, Colossians 3:16), listen to the apostles' teaching (Acts 2:42), have a meal together (Acts 2:46), have the Lord's Supper (1 Corinthians 11:22), etc. When the group grew too large for one home, one could assume they simply began to meet in two. What a simple way to expand: no expensive building programs, fund-raising, or facilities to maintain. Think of the money saved that was used to fulfill the Great Commission and to minister to the poor.

Today God is restoring these simple home-centered meetings to His Church. In the Soviet Union, China, and other "closed" nations, secret house-churches are the way of life for most of the Christians. In many pioneer mission situations, the converts are won in their homes through door-to-door evangelism or home Bible study groups. The young believers are then discipled in home-centered meetings. In some places a "church" building is eventually erected, but in other places the times of coming together are kept in the homes. In large, crowded cities, like Hong Kong and Singapore, many of the churches are house-churches. There is, in fact, a growing house-church movement world-wide. Even in suburban North America, one of the most popular Christian activities is house-meetings, during the week or on Sunday evening. This writer believes that God is leading His Church more and more back to the home. We will see this trend continue to accelerate world-wide. In fact, we could see the church buildings closing quite quickly in many nations through a change in non-profit tax laws, or an energy crisis, a political upheaval, an economic collapse, war, or end-time persecution (see Chapters 19-20). This writer believes that Jesus will find His Church primarily meeting in homes when He returns.

Body Ministry

There were three kinds of meetings in the early Church. There was the preaching meeting, out where the lost were, centered around the preaching of an apostle or evangelist, for the purpose of evangelizing the people (Acts 2:14-41, 8:5-8). There was the gathering together of new believers for basic teaching, given by the apostles, prophets, and teachers (Acts 2:42, Hebrews 5:11-6:3). After the initial teaching, the believers soon gathered together, not in a one-person-centered meeting, but rather to minister to one another. Paul's clearest, most extensive teaching on the gathering of believers (1 Corinthians 12-14) brings this out so clearly. We are to come together as a body (1 Corinthians 12:12-27) and allow the various gifts and ministries to function and flow (1 Corinthians 12:1-11, 28-31; 14:1-33), in an atmosphere of love (1 Corinthians 13), for the purpose of edifying all (1 Corinthians 12:7, 14:3-5, 12, 26). In summarizing these three chapters (12-14), Paul states in 1 Corinthians 14:26, "What is the outcome then, brethren? When you assemble, each one has a psalm, has a teaching, has a revelation, has a tongue, has an interpretation. Let all things be done for edification." This is the Biblical pattern: each one ministering what God has given him to minister, for the edification of the body. In this type of gathering, there is still room for the ministry of the apostles, prophets, evangelists, pastors, and teachers.

127

Today most of our Christian meetings are still centered around one person, the "pastor." He has to provide all of the ministry, which God never intended. It also means that the gathered-ones cannot benefit from one another's ministry. But God is changing this. Here and there, God's people are receiving a revelation of the truth of 1 Corinthians 14:26, and are moving toward the body "building itself up in love" (Ephesians 4:16). This type of every-believer ministry flows quite naturally in a smaller, home-centered gathering. But even in large church meetings, some are allowing an open time for anyone to minister. Some are even allowing the entire service to be open to the Holy Spirit's direction; that He might use anyone, anytime, in any way that He chooses! Of course, the flow of ministry needs to be judged by those in leadership (1 Corinthians 14:29). Are we willing to stop controlling everything and start allowing the Holy Spirit to be in charge?

Training for Ministry - Coaches

If the body is to "build itself up in love" (Ephesians 4:16), and the Christian gatherings are to be open to the ministry of all (1 Corinthians 14:26), what are the pastors and other leaders to do? They are to be coaches! Ephesians 4:7-16 states that God has given to His Church apostles, prophets, evangelists, pastors, and teachers to equip, perfect, encourage, "coach" the believers as they discover and function in their gifts and ministries. The "called ones" exist to train and coach the whole church into their many ministries. So it's not the congregation sitting by while a few minister center-stage. Instead, it's a few coaching in the background, and all ministering! This was the case in the Early Church. There were no special Bible schools and seminaries, except the one mentioned in Acts 19:9. Jesus trained the Twelve simply by their being with Him. Paul did the same (Acts 20:4). The training was practical, on-the-job training. Today God is restoring these concepts to His Church. When Jesus returns, each believer will know what his gifts and ministries are, and will be functioning in them. The "called ones" will be fulfilling their coaching role. What a day it will be!

The Laying on of Hands

A practice of the Early Church was the laying on of hands. It was not an empty form. Things happened when hands were laid on a person and the prayer of faith was prayed: blessing was imparted through the laying on of hands (Matthew 19:13-15, Mark 10:16), as was healing (Mark 5:23, 6:2-5, 7:32, 8:23-25, 16:18, Luke 4:40, Acts 9:10-18, 28:8), deliverance (Luke 13:10-13), and the baptism with the Holy Spirit (Acts 8:14-19, 9:12-17, 19:6). Signs and wonders occurred through the laying on of hands (Acts 5:12, 14:3, 19:11), spiritual gifts were imparted (1 Timothy 4:14, 2 Timothy 1:6), and people were set apart for special ministries (Acts 6:6, 13:3). It was considered a basic practice (Hebrews 6:1-2). In recent years, God has been restoring the New Testament practice of laying on of hands to His Church.

Truth

Jesus said that when the Holy Spirit comes, He will teach the Church all things, guide into all truth, and bring all things to remembrance (John 14:26, 16:13). As we continue to move toward the end of the Age, there may be yet other truths that the Holy Spirit will restore to His Church. We need to continually ask God to keep us open and flexible.

1988(?)-2000(?) — A Soon Coming, Mighty, World-wide, End Time Revival Resulting in the Complete Restoration of the Church to Apostolic, New Testament Christianity (#51, 52)

The completion of the restoration of the Church to God's full, original intentions will all be completed as a result of a soon-coming, mighty, world-wide, end-time revival (see Chapter 4). Many are praying for this last, great revival. God is certainly getting His Church ready. It could break forth very soon. With it will come the full restoration of the Church to New Testament purity, spiritual authority and power, purposes, principles and patterns, and fruitfulness. We will see the Body of Christ come into unity. We will see the world evangelized. And it will bring on world-wide persecution. What a glorious day to be alive!

ConcludingThoughts

Why is God Restoring New Testament Christianity to His Church?
1. God desires to have a beautiful, clean, prepared Bride (the Church), ready to meet the Bridegroom (Jesus) when He comes (Ephesians 5:27, Revelation 19:6-7).

129

2. God is preparing and equipping the Church for her final thrust of world evangelization (see Chapters 14-18).
3. God is preparing the Church for coming persecution (see Chapters 19-20).

As We Begin to Grasp the Concept of Restoration, What Should Be Our Attitude?

1. We should be extremely thankful for what God has done in the past, and for the price that others have paid to see the Restoration come as far as it has.
2. We must not be content with what God did in the past. We should be diligently seeking Him for what He wants to restore today — in our lives, our families, our churches, and in His Body around the world.
3. We must compare all that is being said and done today, and in the future, with His Word. That which is of Him will be in accordance with His Word.
4. We should not be exclusive or critical toward fellow Christians who seem to have less or more understanding than we do. We need to keep our eyes on Jesus (Hebrews 12:1-2, John 21:21-22)! He will make it all clear as we sit at His feet.

PERSONAL ASSIGNMENT — RESTORATION

Questions to Answer

1. Explain the restoration concept of Church history.

2. List three things that were restored to the Church between A.D. 1200 and 1950.

3. What are three things that God is restoring today?

Questions for Meditation and Application

1. What do you think of this whole concept of restoration?

2. What are some things that God may want to restore next in your life?

3. What are some things that God may want to restore next in your local church? What part are you to play in this?

Assignment

1. Begin to pray regularly for the restoration of God's purity, authority and power, purposes, principles and patterns, and fruit-fulness to your life, family, church, and to His Church world-wide.

2. Seek God about what He would have you do to further the process of restoration in His Church.

PART III — UNITY

'Behold, how good and how pleasant it is for brothers to dwell together in unity!...there the Lord commanded the blessing."

— Psalms 133:1, 3

"I do not ask in behalf of these alone, but for those also who believe in Me through their word; that they may all be one; even as Thou, Father, art in Me, and I in Thee, that they also may be in Us; that the world may believe that Thou didst send Me. And the glory which Thou hast given Me I have given to them; that they may be one, just as We are one; I in them, and Thou in Me, that they may be perfected in unity, that the world may know that Thou didst send Me, and didst love them, even as Thou didst love Me."

— John 17:20-23

"Disunity in the Body of Christ is the scandal of the ages." [1]
— Paul Billheimer

"Love — and the unity it attests to —is the mark Christ gave Christians to wear before the world. Only with this mark may the world know that Christians are indeed Christians, and that Jesus was sent by the Father." [2]

— Francis Schaeffer

12

BASIC DEFINITIONS AND CONCEPTS

Definition of Unity

The dictionary defines unity: "state of being one; oneness; the fact or state of being united or combined into one; oneness of mind, feeling, as among a number of persons; concord, harmony, agreement, a relation of all the parts or elements of a work constituting a harmonious whole and reproducing a single general effect." [1]

Biblical Basis for Unity

The Bible has much to say about Christian unity. The following are some of the most important passages, followed by a brief summary of the author's understanding of what the verse says about unity.

Psalms 133:1-3 — "Behold, how good and how pleasant it is for brothers to dwell together in unity! It is like the precious oil upon the head, coming down upon the beard, even Aaron's beard, coming down upon the edge of his robes. It is like the dew of Hermon, coming down upon the mountains of Zion; for there the Lord commanded the blessing — life forever."

It is where brothers dwell in unity that God gives His blessings.

Matthew 18:19 — "Again I say to you, that if two of you agree on earth about anything that they may ask, it shall be done for them by My Father who is in heaven."

There is tremendous prayer power that flows out of unity.

John 10:16 — "And I have other sheep, which are not of this fold; I must bring them also, and they shall hear My voice; and they shall become one flock with one shepherd."

All of God's people make up one flock, with Jesus as our Shepherd.

John 13:34-35 — "A new commandment I give to you, that you love one another, even as I have loved you, that you also love one another. By this all men will know that you are My disciples, if you have love for one another."

The world will know that we are Jesus' disciples when we love (lay our lives down for) one another, as He did for us.

John 17:20-23 — "I do not ask in behalf of these alone, but for those also who believe in Me through their word; that they may all be one; even as Thou, Father, art in Me, and I in Thee, that they also may be in Us; that the world may believe that Thou didst send Me. And the glory which Thou hast given Me I have given to them; that they may be one, just as We are one; I in them, and Thou in Me, that they may be perfected in unity, that the world may know that Thou didst send Me, and didst love them, even as Thou didst love Me."

Jesus prayed that His Church would be "one," "perfected into a unit" (NASB marginal reading), "perfected in unity," just as the Father and the Son are One. The world will believe that the Father sent the Son when it sees this unity.

Acts 1:14 — "These all with one mind were continually devoting themselves to prayer, along with the women, and Mary the mother of Jesus, and with His brothers."

The early Christians were of one mind, even before the Holy Spirit was poured out.

Acts 2:1 — "And when the day of Pentecost had come, they were all together in one place."

They were all together in one place.

Acts 4:32 — "And the congregation of those who believed were of one heart and soul; and not one of them claimed that anything belonging to him was his own; but all things were common property to them."

They were of one heart and soul, with a oneness of heart toward their possessions, sharing with those in need.

Romans 12:4-5 — "For just as we have many members in one body and all the members do not have the same function, so we, who are many, are one body in Christ, and individually members one of another."

All Christians are members of one body. There is to be both unity and diversity. We are united to one another.

Romans 15:6 — "that with one accord you may with one voice glorify the God and Father of our Lord Jesus Christ."

Christians are to be of one accord and glorifying God with one voice.

1 Corinthians 1:10-17 — "Now I exhort you, brethren, by the name of our Lord Jesus Christ, that you all agree, and there be no divisions among you, but you be made complete in the same mind and in the same judgment. For I have been informed concerning you, my brethren, by Chloe's people, that there are quarrels among you. Now I mean this, that each one of you is saying, 'I am of Paul,' and 'I of Apollos,' and 'I of Cephas,' and 'I of Christ.' Has Christ been divided? Paul was not crucified for you, was he? Or were you baptized in the name of Paul? I thank God that I baptized none of you except Crispus and Gaius, that no man should say you were baptized in my name. Now I did baptize also the household of Stephanas; beyond that, I do not know whether I baptized any other. For Christ did not send me to baptize, but to preach the gospel, not in cleverness of speech, that the cross of Christ should not be made void."

Christ's Church is not to be divided over leaders or over practices.

1 Corinthians 12:12-13 — "For even as the body is one and yet has many members, and all the members of the body, though they are many, are one body, so also is Christ. For by one Spirit we were all baptized into one body, whether Jews or Greeks, whether slaves or free, and we were all made to drink of one Spirit."

Christians are baptized, or placed, "into one Body," the Body of Christ, by the Holy Spirit, at the time of their conversion.

Galatians 3:28 — "There is neither Jew nor Greek, there is neither slave nor free man, there is neither male nor female; for you are all one in Christ Jesus."

All Christians are one in Christ, regardless of differences of national or ethnic background, social status, or sex.

Ephesians 2:14-16 — "For He Himself is our peace, who made both groups into one, and broke down the barrier of the dividing wall, by abolishing in His flesh the enmity, which is the Law of commandments contained in ordinances, that in Himself He might make the two into one new man, thus establishing peace, and might reconcile them both in one body to God through the cross, by it having put to death the enmity.

Jesus died to reconcile all that believe into one body.

Ephesians 4:1-6, 11-16 — "I, therefore, the prisoner of the Lord, entreat you to walk in a manner worthy of the calling with which you have been called, with all humility and gentleness, with patience, showing forbearance to one another in love, being diligent to preserve the unity of the Spirit in the bond of peace. There is one body and one Spirit, just as also you are called in one hope of your calling; one Lord, one faith, one baptism, one God and Father of all who is over all and through all and in all.... And He gave some as apostles, and some as prophets, and some as evangelists, and some as pastors and teachers, for the equipping of the saints for the work of service, to the building up of the body of Christ; until we all attain to the unity of the faith, and of the knowledge of the Son of God, to a mature man, to the measure of the stature which belongs to the fullness of Christ. As a result, we are no longer to be children, tossed here and there by waves, and carried about by every wind of doctrine, by the trickery of men, by craftiness in deceitful scheming; but speaking the truth in love, we are to grow up in all aspects into Him who is the head, even Christ, from whom the whole body, being fitted and held together by that which every joint supplies, according to the proper working of each individual part, causes the growth of the body for the building up of itself in love."

All Christians are part of one Body (vs. 4), and have the same Holy Spirit, hope, Lord (Jesus Christ), faith , baptism, and Father (vss. 4-6). We are exhorted to "preserve the unity of the Spirit in the bond of peace" by relating to one another with humility, gentleness, patience, forbearance, and love (vss. 1-3). The risen Christ has given to His Church apostles, prophets, evangelists, shepherds, and teachers to bring His Church to "the unity of the faith, and of the true knowledge of the Son of God, to a mature man . . . from which the whole body, being fitted and held together by that which every joint supplies, according to the proper working of each individual part, causes the growth of the body for the building up of itself in love." (vss. 11-16)

Philippians 1:27, 2:1-8 — "Only conduct yourselves in a manner

137

worthy of the gospel of Christ; so that whether I come and see you or remain absent, I may hear of you that you are standing firm in one spirit, with one mind striving together for the faith of the gospel" (1:27). "If there is any encouragement in Christ, if there is any consolation of love, if there is any fellowship of the Spirit, if any affection and compassion, make my joy complete by being of the same mind, maintaining the same love, united in spirit, intent on one purpose. Do nothing from selfishness or empty conceit, but with humility of mind let each of you regard one another as more important than himself; do not merely look out for your own personal interests, but also for the interests of others. Have this attitude in yourselves which was also in Christ Jesus, who although He existed in the form of God, did not regard equality with God a thing to be grasped, but emptied Himself, taking the form of a bond-servant, and being made in the likeness of men. And being found in appearance as a man, He humbled Himself by becoming obedient to the point of death, even death on a cross.

Paul exhorts the Philippian Christians to be united in their thinking, love, spirit, and purpose, working together for the Gospel, by living humble, selfless, Christ-like lives.

Summary

This writer is convinced that Scripture plainly teaches:

1. There is only one Church, the Church of our Lord Jesus Christ, the "called out ones," those who know Jesus as Lord (John 10:16, Romans 12:4-5, 1 Corinthians 12:12-13, Ephesians 2:11-22, 4:4-6, Colossians 3:11).
2. This oneness is not to be just a theological concept, but a practical reality, something that is seen by the world, a witness of Jesus' coming to earth. (John 13:34-35, 17:20-23; Acts 1:14, 2:1, 4:32, 5:12; Romans 15:6, 1 Corinthians 1:10-17, 3:1-7, 2 Corinthians 13:11, Galatians 3:28, Ephesians 4:1-3, 11-16, Philippians 1:27).
3. The pathway to unity is humility, selflessness, gentleness, patience, forbearance, and love (Ephesians 4:1-3, Philippians 2:1-8).
4. It is this Church, functioning as one, that God will bless (Psalms 133:1-3, Matthew 18:19, Acts 1:14, 2:1).

Biblical Basis for Division

Christ's Body has been divided over many things throughout its two thousand years of history. Are these many divisions warranted by Scripture? Is there a Biblical basis for division, and, if there is, what is it?

Scripture clearly teaches that there should be no division in the Body of Christ over leaders — either through whom one came to Christ or under whose leadership one presently functions (1 Corinthians 1:10-16, 3:1-7). There should be no division over the practice of baptism (1 Corinthians 1:13-16). This truth could be enlarged to also include no division over any other practice. There is to be no division over doctrine: the Church should seek to be of one mind (Matthew 18:19, Acts 1:14, 5:12, 1 Corinthians 1:10-11, 2 Corinthians 13:11, Philippians 1:27, 2:2). This will come in time as we learn to submit our views to one another. Believers are not to be divided by racial, national, or cultural differences (Ephesians 2:11-22, Colossians 3:11). There are to be no divisions due to economic or social standing (Colossians 3:11, Galatians 3:28, James 2:1-13). There may be some practical division in the Body initially over cultural differences due to a "people movement" (where a whole "people group" turns to Christ) or the evangelism efforts directed toward a certain group. In time these should disappear and the whole Body function as one. (More on this in Chapter 13.)

However, the Bible does recognize two reasons for distinction in the Body of Christ: function and geography. First, the resident church and the traveling ministries are distinct from one another because of different callings or function. But the traveling ministries are to cooperate with the resident church whenever they are in an area where the resident church exists, and each is continually to bless the other. Second, the resident church of one location is separated by geography from the resident church of another location. The Church of Jerusalem is separate from the Church of Corinth because of geography; they are in separate locations. The resident church in one location is to bless the resident church in another location, too, as the need arises and the Spirit directs (Acts 11:27-30, 1 Corinthians 16:1-3, 2 Corinthians 8 and 9).

What a challenge, yet so clear in Scripture! There are only two Biblical reasons for distinction in the Body of Christ: the traveling ministries are separate from the resident church because of their distinct functions; and the Body of Christ in one location is distinct from that in another location because of geography. But there is to be no division in the Body of Christ over differences of leadership, practice, doctrine, race, nationality, wealth, or social standing. What does all of this mean to us today? That's the subject of the next chapter.

What About Denominations

They exist — over 20,000 of them — and growing at the rate of five new ones each week! Many of these new denominations are non-white, indigenous ones in the Third World.[2] So how did it all begin?

The early Christians considered themselves part of the one, Universal Church. And they saw only one Church in any given city, i.e., the church of Philippi.

As the Roman Catholic Church developed, it tried to preserve the oneness doctrinally and organizationally. This resulted in the teaching that, to be saved, one had to believe the teaching and be a member in good standing of the Catholic Church.

In A.D. 1054, the final break came between the Eastern branch of the Church, with headquarters at Constantinople, and the Western branch of the Church, with headquarters at Rome.[3] Although each claimed to be the true Church, this schism brought to an end, for all practical purposes, the idea of oneness of organization. Even before the Great Schism, there had been various groups of believers that were separate from the main organization. The Montanists in the period A.D. 156-400 were looked on with disfavor by the rest of the Church. The Irish missionaries, who went throughout much of northern Europe in the 500-600's, were not under the domination of Rome. In A.D. 400-1300 the Nestorian Church flourished in central Asia. To these could be added the Novatianists, the Donatsists, the Arianists, the Pelagianists, and other groups that arose within

140

the Church, and sooner or later, were branded as heretics. Some of the teachings of these groups were not always orthodox but how could man decide that they were no longer part of Christ's Church?

Then came the pre-Reformation groups — the Waldenses, the Albigenses, the Lollards, the Husites, and others — all functioning without the blessing of the Roman Church. With the Reformation, and the emerging Church groups — Lutheran, Reformed, Anglican, Presbyterian, Anabaptists — all hope of organizational unity vanished.

So how did all of the denominations come into being? Many throughout all of Church history were part of God's restoration, or reformation process, and because of their adherence to "the new" that God was restoring, they found themselves officially cut off from the established Church of their day: the Montanists, the Lollards, the Lutherans, the Plymouth Brethren, the Pentecostals, etc. Others came into being through great surges of evangelism: the Methodists, the Salvation Army, the Foursquare Church, many of the new Third World denominations. And still others emerged through national, language, and cultural identity. When Baptists, as an example, migrated from northern Europe to the United States, they continued to conduct services in their native language and transplanted themselves as German Baptists, Swedish Baptists, etc.

And then there have been new denominations started because of a difference of interpretation of a certain passage of Scripture or because of a social issue. The Wesleyan Methodist Church came into being as a split from the Methodist Episcopal Church over the issue of slavery. Denominations have begun because two leaders could not work together, sometimes because both were too unyielding and strong in their wills. Luther and Zwingli could not get together because of doctrinal differences and differences of temperament.

God has used the various denominational bodies to preserve and proclaim various doctrinal truths. It is hard to foresee them closing up shop unless forced to by outside pressures, such as that which happened in China in 1949-51 when the Communists took over. But, as strong local churches continue to emerge; and,

141

as the city-church concept continues to develop; and as the traveling ministries continue to come into their full inheritance in God's plan; this writer believes that denominational and other organizational distinctives will become less clear as each receives truth from the others and as all simply flow into functioning as the Body of Christ.

13

PRACTICAL APPLICATION TODAY

The Situation Today in the "Free" World

Disunity among Christians in the free world is an abomination to God! We are divided over everything! We are divided over doctrine. ("Our interpretation of Scripture is the right one.") We are divided over leaders. ("We go to Pastor Smith's church.") We are divided over buildings. ("We worship at Main and Ninth.") We are divided over name and heritage. ("We belong to the _____ denomination.") We are divided over the importance and place of the local church versus para-church ministries. ("They're not part of 'the church'!") We are divided over race and culture. ("They go to the Black church.") We're divided over standards. ("They've become worldly.") We're divided over when to meet. ("They're seventh-dayers.") And the list could go on.

The situation is such that there is scarcely any witness of oneness to the world. The church page in the Saturday newspaper leaves the impression that each group is trying to out-do the others with the best message, or most famous outside speaker or singing group. And on Sunday, the Lord's Day, all resemblance of unity is lost as we all head our separate directions to meet with our particular group. In fact, much of the

143

Sunday morning auto traffic is Christians passing one another, going in opposite directions, to our separate meeting places! God help us!!

Why the Disunity?

What are the reasons for all of the disunity? I suggest the following:

1. *Lack of understanding of the true basis for unity.* Unity is not uniformity. We are one because of our relationship with the Lord Jesus Christ. There is to be great diversity, and at the same time, unity.
2. *Lack of vision, God's priorities.* We far too often lose sight of the things that really count, and focus in on our own little programs, petty problems, and survival.
3. *Too much emphasis on differences.* We place far too much emphasis on our differences — doctrine, heritage, leaders, style of worship, etc.
4. *Too much emphasis on our organization.* We are too busy perpetuating our own organization rather than advancing Christ's Kingdom.
5. *Pride.* We have not died to pride. We are still trying to be "the best" — have the best doctrine, best heritage, best organization, best leaders, best building, best programs, greatest growth, etc., etc.
6. *Competitiveness.* We have allowed the world's competitiveness to follow us into our Christian lives and our Church life.
7. *Insecurity.* Many times our security is based on our relationship with a Christian organization rather than on our relationship with Jesus; thus any talk of unity that seems to jeopardize the future of our organization is perceived as a personal threat.
8. *Lack of communication.* We are unaware of each other, or don't understand one another, or distrust each other because we don't communicate. We haven't sat down, gotten acquainted, and set up channels of communication.
9. *Fear, distrust.* We fear and distrust each other due to a lack of communication, unresolved problems and unhealed

144

personal hurts from the past, personal insecurities, rumors, etc.

10. *Economic problems.* We are afraid if we lose people to another group we won't be able to pay the bills!

11. *Personal ambition.* How much of our disunity is due simply to the personal ambition of an individual (or a denomination) to build his own kingdom.

12. *Satan.* And, of course, the devil is always doing everything he can to cause disunity among God's people.

As tragic as the church's disunity, is the leaders' disunity. In fact, it is one of the major contributing factors. Instead of the spiritual leaders in a given area being primarily submitted to one another, they are submitted to a denominational organization and hierarchy. And, instead of fellowshipping with their fellow leaders in their town, they travel to a district conference to fellowship with those that they agree with (doctrinally, organizationally, etc.). The non-denominational pastors have their fellow non-denominational pastors with whom they fellowship. Commitment, submission, and fellowship is based upon doctrinal and organizational sameness. It should be based upon relationships that develop along geographical location and function. We should be primarily committed to, submitted to, fellowshipping with, and working with those believers whom God has placed geographically close to us, regardless of doctrinal and organizational distinctions, and with those who have the same function or calling: for example, youth work, evangelism, Bible translation work.

Results of Disunity

The fruit of disunity is:

1. *Lack of discipline.* As things are today, if a Christian is disciplined because of immorality (or any other reason), he simply goes and joins the group down the street and resumes his "ministry," while continuing his sin. And, when a false teacher comes to town, if he is rejected by one group, he can usually find another group in the same town that will receive his ministry.

2. *Duplication.* Think of all the time, money, and effort that is

145

wasted due to duplication because we are competing instead of cooperating.
3. *Hold-up to World Evangelization.* Disunity in the Body of Christ is the greatest hold-up to the evangelization of the world. The world will not believe that Jesus has come, and that the Church has His life and truth, until they see Christians laying down our lives for each other (John 13:34-35) and functioning as one (John 17:20-23).

Encouraging Trends

Much that has been previously said in this chapter is somewhat negative and quite discouraging. But true. However, there is another side. There are many encouraging trends: city-wide evangelistic crusades; inter-denominational Bible study and prayer meetings; Christians working together in non-denominational organizations; nation-wide gatherings of leaders; pastors coming together in a given area for prayer; city-wide gatherings of Christians; continent-wide associations; and world-wide congresses on prayer, evangelism, and social action. God is doing much to bring unity to His Body. There are, in fact, so many situations in the Body of Christ world-wide where unity is developing that an entire book could be written just giving these examples. An encouraging trend toward unity in the United States is the Network of Christian Ministries, 5600 Read Blvd., New Orleans, LA 70127.

The Persecuted Church

There is less problem with disunity in the Body of Christ in China, the Soviet Union, and other places. Most denominational and other distinctions have been wiped away by Communist persecution. All that is left are "believers," meeting secretly wherever and whenever they can, coming together to worship their risen Lord and to encourage one another, and evangelizing everywhere they go. What a blessing: there is little competition; just Christ's Body functioning as it should.

What God is After

The various trends toward cooperation and unity will continue until we will see the following take place:

146

1. World Christian leaders will come together on a regular basis to **share their lives** with each other; to seek the Lord as to how they are to **work together** to evangelize the world and see the Church brought to maturity; and to find ways to **eliminate competition** and **duplication.**
2. National Christian leaders will do the same.
3. The Christian leaders in a given locality (city, town, village, island, etc.) will do the same until God's people in that locality are truly functioning as one body.
4. The resident church (city-church and smaller, functioning units) and the traveling ministries will both come into their full inheritance, and will bless and serve one another.
5. Denominational distinctives will increasingly diminish.

What We Can Do

What can we do to see unity come to the Body of Christ? There are many possibilities. The following is a partial list. Ask God what He would have you do.

1. Study the Scriptures to become convinced of God's plan for His Church (see Chapter 12).
2. Learn to accept and make room for the different understandings and practices of one another. We must come to see that unity and diversity are mutually compatible (Romans 12:4-5, 1 Corinthians 12:4-7, Ephesians 4:1-16).
3. Study Church history to understand the present situation.
4. Repent of our attitudes, words, and actions that cause disunity.
5. Choose to never speak slanderous of any other Christian or Christian group.
6. Pray for unity to come to the Body of Christ in your town/city, nation, the world.
7. Be a person of integrity, in life and word, so that others will trust you.
8. Die to your own self, ministry, church, doctrines, standards, and organization.
9. Put Jesus in the center of your life, ministry, and organization. Exalt Him alone. Extend His Kingdom only.
10. Be a person of humility (Philippians 2:1-8).

147

11. Reach out in love and acceptance to all Christians; find ways to get to know your brothers and sisters in Christ, and to let them get to know you.

12. Fully forgive other Christians and Christian groups for all hurts that you may have received from them.

13. Spiritual leaders in a given town/city begin to come together regularly (weekly, bi-weekly, monthly) to get acquainted, share, and pray.

14. Get to know the other Christians in your neighborhood. Start a monthly, neighborhood, interdenominational Bible study-prayer group.

15. Pray for other church groups.

16. Find ways to serve other parts of Christ's Body (Matthew 20:25-28).

17. Find ways to speak highly of other groups.

18. Find ways to work together.

19. Develop avenues of communication with the rest of the Body of Christ.

20. Practice voluntary accountability. Choose to submit your life and ministry to others in your locality.

21. All the church groups in a given area (town, section of city) come together regularly (monthly, quarterly) for a combined gathering (Sunday evening?).

22. All the church groups in a large metropolitan area come together regularly (quarterly, annually) in a large stadium or auditorium.

23. Have city-wide evangelistic crusades and other city-wide cooperative ministries.

24. Be prepared to persevere to see unity develop.

In Conclusion

What will it take to bring unity to Christ's Body in the "free" world: an economic collapse, a political upheaval, nuclear war, a Communist takeover? Or will we lay down our personal and organizational "rights" and become one of our own free will?? Jesus' prayer (John 17:20-23) will be answered. There will be unity for the unsaved world to see. All Christians will learn to love (lay our lives down for) one another. The only questions are: Will we help or impede the process?

What price are we willing to pay to see it happen? Will we allow it to happen under conditions of freedom or will God have to bring it to pass through persecution?

PERSONAL ASSIGNMENT — UNITY

Questions to Answer

1. List three Scriptures that speak of unity.

2. What are the only two Biblical bases for division?

Questions for Meditation and Application

1. In what ways is Christ's Body in your own town/city divided?

2. What are some things that you could do to further the process of unity in your city?

Assignment

1. Begin to pray for unity to come to Christ's Body in your town, nation, the world.

2. Seek God about what He would have you do to further the process of unity in your city and nation.

PART IV

WORLD EVANGELIZATION

"Go therefore and **make disciples of all the nations,** *baptizing them in the name of the Father and the Son and the Holy Spirit, teaching them to observe all that I commanded you; and lo, I am with you always, even to the end of the age."*

— Matthew 28:19-20

"And this took place for two years, so that ALL who lived in Asia HEARD the word of the Lord, both Jews and Greeks."

— Acts 19:10

"In all of history, there has never been a more exciting time than this to be a Christian. A wave of world Christians is carrying the gospel to places it has never before reached. We are indeed in the springtime of missions." [1]

— C. Peter Wagner

"Men were to be His method . . . men who could lead the multitudes . . . One must decide where he wants his ministry to count: in the momentary applause of popular recognition or in the reproduction of his life in a few chosen men who will carry on his work after he has gone." [2]

— Robert E. Coleman

14

DEFINITIONS AND BIBLICAL BASIS

The Great Commission in the Old Testament

Redeeming mankind from the clutches of sin, death, and Satan and reestablishing God's sovereign rule over the earth, has always been in the mind and heart of God. Just as soon as Adam and Eve disobeyed God in the Garden of Eden, because of Satan's trickery, God was there putting into operation His plan of redemption (Genesis 3:15). In Ephesians 1:4, Paul states that we were chosen in Christ before the foundation of the world. God has always seen to it that His plans come to pass, even when that required a universal flood (Genesis 6-10) and the multiplication of languages (Genesis 11). In Genesis 12:1-3, God chose Abram to go forth from his homeland and relatives to a land that God would show him in order that "all the families of the earth" would be blessed. From Abraham came the nation Israel that was to be a special, holy nation (Exodus 19:4-6), with the purpose of telling the other nations about God (Psalm 67, Isaiah 49:6), and giving birth to the Messiah, Jesus (Genesis 49:10, Matthew, chapter 1). Isaiah 40-55 refers to the spread of the Gospel to all mankind. The book of Jonah tells of God sending Jonah to a non-Jewish city, Nineveh, with His message. Some of the other Old Testament passages that reveal the missionary mandate in the Old Testament include Genesis 18:18, 22:18, 26:4, 28:14, Deuteronomy 28:10, 2 Chronicles 6:32-33, Isaiah 56:6-8, Jeremiah 12:14-17, Zechariah 2:11, and Malachi 1:11.

The Great Commission Given by Jesus

After Jesus' death and resurrection, He gave what has come to be called "The Great Commission." Jesus gave this command, or mandate, on four occasions, as recorded in five places in Scripture.

1. *During His appearance to the ten disciples* —in Jerusalem, on the first day of His resurrection, Thomas being absent —John 20:21-23 — "Jesus therefore said to them again, 'Peace be with you; as the Father has sent Me, I also send you.' And when He had said this, He breathed on them, and said to them, 'Receive the Holy Spirit. If you forgive the sins of any their sins have been forgiven them; if you retain the sins of any, they have been retained.' "

2. *During His appearance to the Eleven* — on a mountain in Galilee —Matthew 28:16-20 — "But the eleven disciples proceeded to Galilee, to the mountain which Jesus had designated. And when they saw Him, they worshiped Him; but some were doubtful. And Jesus came up and spoke to them, saying, 'All authority has been given to Me in heaven and on earth. Go therefore and make disciples of all the nations, baptizing them in the name of the Father and the Son and the Holy Spirit, teaching them to observe all that I commanded you; and lo, I am with you always, even to the end of the age.' " Mark 16:15-18 — "And He said to them, 'Go into all the world and preach the gospel to all creation. He who has believed and has been baptized shall be saved; but he who has disbelieved shall be condemned. And these signs will accompany those who have believed: in My name they will cast out demons, they will speak with new tongues; they will pick up serpents, and if they drink any deadly poison, it shall not hurt them; they will lay hands on the sick, and they will recover.' "

3. *With the Eleven at Jerusalem* — Luke 24:44-49 — "Now He said to them, 'These are My words which I spoke to you while I was still with you, that all things which are written about Me in the Law of Moses and the Prophets and the Psalms must be fulfilled.' Then he opened their minds to understand the Scriptures, and He said to them, 'Thus it is written, that the

153

Christ should suffer and rise again from the dead the third day; and that repentance for forgiveness of sins should be proclaimed in His name to all the nations, beginning from Jerusalem. You are witnesses of these things. And behold, I am sending forth the promise of My Father upon you; but you are to stay in the city until you are clothed with power from on high.' "

4. *At the time of His final appearance and ascension* — outside Jerusalem — Mark 16:19-20 — "So then when the Lord Jesus had spoken to them, He was received up into heaven, and sat down at the right hand of God. And they went out and preached everywhere, while the Lord worked with them, and confirmed the word by the signs that followed." Luke 24:50-53 — "And He led them out as far as Bethany, and He lifted up His hands and blessed them. And it came about that while He was blessing them, He parted from them. And they returned to Jerusalem with great joy, and were continually in the temple praising God." Acts 1:4-12 — "And gathering them together, He commanded them not to leave Jerusalem, but to wait for what the Father had promised, 'Which,' He said, 'you heard of from Me; for John baptized with water, but you shall be baptized with the Holy Spirit not many days from now.' And so when they had come together, they were asking Him, saying, 'Lord, is it at this time You are restoring the kingdom to Israel?' He said them, 'It is not for you to know times or epochs which the Father has fixed by His own authority; but you shall receive power when the Holy Spirit has come upon you; and you shall be My witnesses both in Jerusalem, and in all Judea and Samaria, and even to the remotest part of the earth.' And after He had said these things, He was lifted up while they were looking on, and a cloud received Him out of their sight. And as they were gazing intently into the sky while He was departing, behold, two men in white clothing stood beside them; and they also said, 'Men of Galilee, why do you stand looking into the sky? This Jesus who has been taken up from you into heaven, will come in just the same way as you have watched Him go into heaven.' Then they returned to Jerusalem from the mount

called Olivet, which is near Jerusalem, a Sabbath day's journey away."

Let's take a closer look at these five passages of Scripture and see exactly what Jesus was saying.

1. All **authority** for accomplishing the task is available, in Jesus' Name — Matthew 28:18, Mark 16:17, Luke 24:47, John 20:23.
2. All **power** for accomplishing the task is available, through the fullness of the Holy Spirit. One is not to get involved in fulfilling the Great Commission until first he has been endued with that power — Luke 24:49, Acts 1:8.
3. It is **a command to go to every person in every nation with the purpose of proclaiming the Good News** of God's salvation —Matthew 28:19, Mark 16:15, Luke 24:47, John 20:21, Acts 1:8.
4. This Good News is to be responded to by **repentance** (a turning from sin) and **faith** in the Lord Jesus Christ — Mark 16:16, Luke 24:47.
5. Those responding are to be **baptized** in water —Matthew 28:19.
6. They are to be **discipled**/taught all of Jesus' words — Matthew 28:19-20.
7. **Jesus** would be **with those** who are **obedient** to the Great Commission throughout the entire Church Age — Matthew 28:20.

Definitions

1. *Evangelize* — to communicate the Good News of Christ and His salvation to a person (or a group of people) in such a way that he (they) understands, and therefore is able to decide what he (they) is going to do about it.
2. *Disciple* — to teach the will and ways of God to a person (or a group of people) so that he (they) comes into conformity with His will and ways in every area of life.
3. *Unreached People Group* — a group of people, with similar geographical, language, and cultural distinctives, within

which there is no indigenous community of believers able to evangelize them without outside (cross-cultural) assistance.

New Testament Success

What kind of success did the early Church have with taking the Gospel to their world? Tremendous! They had **converts every day** —Acts 2:47, 16:5. They touched the **whole, known civilized world** in approximately twenty years - Acts 17:6. They **totally evangelized some areas:** Acts 19:10 tells of taking the Gospel to all who lived in Asia (the western one-third of today's Turkey), Jew and Gentile, in two years; and 1 Thessalonians 1:8 tells of the young church in Thessalonica taking the Gospel to most of today's Greece ("Macedonia, Achaia, and every other place"). All of this was without our modern means of communication and transportation, without church buildings, without the printing press, without seminaries, and a host of other things that we think we must have to do the job.

Why New Testament Success?

Why did these early followers of Jesus have converts daily; touch the whole, known world; and totally evangelize some areas? The following are offered as some of the reasons. You may be able to add other items to the list.

1. They were **deeply committed** to Jesus (Luke 14:25-35).
2. They were **deeply committed** to **one another** and gave selflessly (Acts 4:32-35, 11:29).
3. They knew their **Bible** (Old Testament). An example is Peter quoting the Old Testament on the Day of Pentecost (Acts 2:17-21, 25-28, 34-35) and Stephen before the Council (Acts 7).
4. They were people of **prayer** (Acts 1:14, 4:31,12:12).
5. They were motivated by **Christ's love** (2 Corinthians 5:14).
6. They were people of **faith** (Acts 6:5, 11:24).
7. They were controlled by the fear (reverential respect) of God, and had **no fear** of men (Acts 4:18-20).
8. They lived a **simple,** mobile **life-style** (Luke 10:4-7, Acts 13:4).
9. They had been **trained on-the-job.** Jesus trained the Twelve that way. So did Paul (Acts 20:4, Philippians 4:9).

10. They understood and exercised the **authority** that they possessed in **Jesus' Name** (Acts 3:6, 16).

11. They were continually empowered by the **Holy Spirit** (Luke 24:49, Acts 1:8, 2:4, 4:8, 4:31, 6:3, etc.).

12. They were **directed** by the Holy **Spirit** (Acts 8:29, 16:6-7).

13. They gave world evangelism **top priority** in their individual and corporate life. They could not "stop speaking" what they had seen and heard (Acts 4:20).

14. They **began** where they were (Jerusalem) (Luke 24:47, Acts 1:8, chapters 2-7).

15. They **preached Christ,** not themselves (Acts 2:22-36, 4:12-23, 8:35).

16. Their preaching was confirmed by **miracles** (Mark 16:20, Acts 5:14-16, 28:8-9).

17. They ministered **wholeness** to the total man (Matthew 10:8, Mark 16:17-18, Acts 3:6, 8:7, 9:33-42, 28:8).

18. They saw the Great Commission as a **personal command** to each of them (Matthew 4:19, John 15:8, 15:16, Acts 5:42, and all of *The Acts*).

19. They evangelized **everywhere** they went (Matthew 10:7-8, Mark 16:20, Acts 8:4).

20. They evangelized as a normal part of their **every day** life (*The Acts*).

21. They shared the Gospel with people **out where** the people were (*The Acts*).

22. They adequately **discipled** their converts (Acts 15:36, 1 Thessalonians 2:7-12, Colossians 1:28).

23. They grew by **multiplication,** not just addition (Acts 6:7, 2 Timothy 2:2).

24. They worked in **teams** (Luke 10:1, Acts 18:5, 20:4).

25. They **understood** the **powers of darkness** (Acts 16:16-18, 1 Thessalonians 2:18).

26. They accepted **persecution** joyfully (Acts 5:40-41, 16:24-25).

27. They gathered their converts into **functioning** New Testament **bodies** (Acts 14:23, Philippians 1:1, 1 Thessalonians 1:1). These bodies were very simple in their mode of operation; they gathered together for their mutual edification

(1 Corinthians 14:26, Hebrew 10:24-25); they met in homes (Acts 2:46, Romans 16:5, Colossians 4:15); their leaders were "laymen" (Acts 14:23).

28. There was **unity** throughout the Body of Christ. All the believers in a given city were part of the church of that city (1 Corinthians 1:2, Philippians 1:1, 1 Thessalonians 1:1). Any tendency away from that unity was clearly spoken to (1 Corinthians 1:10-17, Philippians 1:27, 2:2-4).

29. There was **discipline** in the Church (Acts 5:3-11, 1 Corinthians 5:12).

Can we have that same success today? **Of course we can:** if we have the early Church's purpose, authority and power, principles, and patterns!

15

WORLD EVANGELIZATION THROUGHOUT CHURCH HISTORY

What a great thrill it is to trace the progress that the Christian Church has made in evangelizing the world since the Great Commission was given. In this chapter we will look at the five major waves of world evangelization that have taken place over almost 2,000 years.

First Wave—Evangelizing the Roman Empire-A.D. 30-500[1]

Jesus came to earth "when the proper time had fully come" (Galatians 4:4, Amplified Bible). That "proper time" included a vast Roman Empire that was ready to be evangelized. There was a common language used throughout the Empire: Greek. The Roman authority had brought peace to the Empire of 100 million people. Thus, people were turning their attention to the finer things of life, including the spiritual. Excellent roads and sea ports had been built, making travel easier. The Jewish people were dispersed throughout the Empire, taking with them their synagogues, the Greek (Septuagint) translation of the Old Testament, their worship of the one true God, and their expectation of a coming Messiah.

Into this "proper time" situation, Jesus, the Messiah, was born in Bethlehem. He lived a perfect, sinless life. He taught the ways of God to the multitudes. He trained the Twelve, who would someday take His place. He died on the cross for the sins of the whole world. He was buried. Three days later He came back to life. He was on earth, in a new body, for forty days. He gave to His followers the Great Commission. And He ascended into heaven.

After His ascension, these followers waited in prayer in Jerusalem for the coming of the Holy Spirit. After they were filled with His presence and power, they went out and preached everywhere.

As recorded in *The Acts,* Paul evangelized and planted churches in most of the major cities of the Empire. There is historical evidence that Peter's travels took him to Antioch, Corinth, Babylon, Rome, and as far north as Great Britain. Andrew ministered in Greece, around Ephesus, and in southern Russia. John spent many years as a leader in Asia Minor, residing in Ephesus. Philip, the apostle, probably went as far as France. Bartholomew preached in Armenia, Arabia, Persia, and India. Thomas, likewise, went eastward to Babylon, Persia, and on to India. Matthew went to Egypt and Ethiopia, Mark to Egypt, and on the list could go. And, of course, it was not just the apostles who were spreading the faith. Every Christian was involved, everyday, everywhere he went.

By A.D. 200, Christians were found in all parts of the Roman Empire, and even beyond. Some historians estimate that ten per cent of the population (10 million of 100 million) had become Christians in Rome alone. By A.D. 500, the Christian faith had taken root from parts of India and China to Spain, and from Ireland and England to the Sahara desert, and had become the preferred faith of the large majority of the population of the Roman Empire. These centuries were also a time when the New Testament Canon (which of many writings were accepted as the inspired ones), Christian theology, and church organizations were developing.

The Christians also had a profound effect upon society. The pagan cults diminished. They ministered to the poor; supported widows, orphans, and the disabled, entertained travelers; and sent aid to other churches who were suffering from famine or persecution. Divorce was not allowed, except after the violation of the marriage vow by one of the partners. Abortion and infanticide was forbidden. Christianity also made its impact upon music, art, literature, and upon the laws. It had become "the salt of the earth" and "the light of the world."

Second Wave — Evangelizing Northern Europe
and Central Asia — A.D. 500-1300[2]

During the Dark Ages, Ireland stood out as a beacon. Ireland had initially been evangelized by Patrick of Scotland. Patrick was sold as a slave from Scotland to Ireland at the age of sixteen. Several years later he escaped, studied in France, and returned to Scotland where he had a vision in which Irish people were saying, "We beseech thee, child of God, come and again walk among us." This was his Macedonian call. Against the desire of his parents and friends, he returned to Ireland in A.D. 432. There he gathered people in the open fields and preached Christ to them. 127 whole tribes turned to Christ.[3] He baptized over one hundred thousand and planted over 300 churches. It was said of Patrick that "he found Ireland all heathen and left it all Christian." [4] His message and methods were much closer to New Testament Christianity than to that of the Roman Church, and the Celtic Church did not come under the dominance of Rome until A.D. 664.[5]

The monastic schools in Ireland provided the best education available, and during the 500's and 600's the Church of Ireland became one of the greatest missionary Churches of all times. From the Irish monasteries, missionary teams went out to most of northern Europe. Columba went to Scotland where he evangelized, performed many miracles, and founded churches and monasteries. Columban with twelve companions went from the monastery at Bangor, Ireland, to Gaul (France), Switzerland, and northern Italy. It was said of Columban that he was "always learning, always teaching, always wandering, always preaching." Willibrord and eleven others preached with great power to the Frisians of the low countries (Holland). Boniface of England (680-754) was apostle to the Germans. After the Vikings of Scandinavia invaded Great Britain, France, and Germany, the Church responded by sending men to evangelize these barbarians of the North. Most notable was Anskar, the apostle of the North (801-865). All of this took place over a period of several hundred years (800-1200).

Eastern Europe and Russia were initially evangelized during A.D. 900-1200 by missionaries from the Eastern Church, which was centered in Constantinople. By 1200 most of Europe was nominally Christian. Finally, the Nestorian Church, centered in Persia, took the

Gospel to parts of India, Russia, Tibet, China, Korea, Japan, and Southeast Asia between A.D. 600 and 1350.

Loss to Islam — A.D. 600-1200[6]

While Christianity was making great gains in northern and eastern Europe and parts of Asia, it was losing ground in the Middle East and Africa. Mohammed was born in Mecca, Arabia, in A.D. 570. In 610 he began to teach his new religion of morality and monotheistic faith. He fled to Medina in 622. After his death in 632 his followers unified the warring tribes of Arabia and set out to conquer the rest of the world. Jerusalem fell to their swords in 638, and they swiftly moved across northern Africa and through Spain. They were finally stopped in southern France in 732 by Charles Martel at the Battle of Tours. There was a second Muslim tide of conquest 500 years later. Constantinople fell in A.D. 1453, and much of central Asia, Turkey, Greece, and the Balkan countries became Muslim. What was once strongly Christian — Palestine, Syria, Asia Minor (Turkey), Greece, and northern Africa — was largely lost to Islam.

To counter the advance and conquests of Islam, the Western Church initiated the Crusades. There were seven between A.D. 1095 and 1272. The motives were a mixture of economic, political, religious, and personal. The Crusades were a failure: Jerusalem and Palestine were not recaptured; and the atrocities committed by the Crusaders in the name of Christ have left an indelible scar on the Muslim mind to this very day.

Third Wave — Roman Catholic Missions to the Whole World — 1300-1700[7]

While the Protestant Churches of Europe were fighting for their survival, revising their theology, establishing their organizations, and consolidating their gains, the Roman Catholic Church went out to spread their form of Christianity to the rest of the world.

The Catholic missionary orders — The Franciscans, the Dominicans, and the Augustinians — had come into being in the 1200's, and the Jesuits in 1540. As the Portuguese and Spanish began their overseas explorations, the Roman Catholic missionaries were right there on the same ships, or shortly thereafter. In 1493, Pope Alexander VI issued a Bull assigning Africa and the East Indies to Portugal, and the new world to Spain. The following year Brazil was transferred to Portugal. In 1537, Pope Paul III ordered that the Indians of the new world be brought to Christ "by the preaching of the divine word, and with the example of the good life." In 1628 a central seminary, the College of Propaganda, was established in Rome to train native clergy from all parts of the mission world.

Missionaries were with Vasco de Gama when he arrived in India in 1498. In 1605, Robert de Nobili, an Italian Jesuit, arrived. He adopted Indian dress and diet, and labored in India for 42 years, reaching many Hindus, especially among the upper classes. Matteo Ricci (1552-1610) entered China from Macao and by 1650 there were 250,000 converts. In 1549, Francis Xavier (1506-1552), one of the initial members of the Society of Jesus, landed in Japan. By 1581, there were 200 churches and 150,000 professing Christians, and by 1600 there were 500,000. They were martyred in 1638 when Japan turned anti-Christian. The Philippine Islands were discovered by Magellan in 1521. Missionaries arrived in 1564. Within a century two million had been baptized. The initial thrust into Southeast Asia was by a Frenchman, Alexander de Rhodes (1591-1660). Among his early converts were two hundred Buddhist priests.

In the 1480's and 1490's, Catholic mission work was begun in Africa — in the Congo, Angola, Mozambique, Rhodesia, and Madagascar. But the going was hard and little progress was made. It was the Protestant missionaries that finally penetrated Africa in the 1800's.

In the Americas, Columbus arrived in 1492. He had set out to find a new route to the East and also to propagate the Gospel wherever he went. And there was mission work in Brazil in 1550, Haiti in 1502, Cuba in 1512, Mexico in 1523, Columbia in 1531, and Peru in 1532. By 1555, Roman Catholic missionaries had taken Christianity to the West Indies, Mexico, Central America, and much of South America. Outstanding was Bartholomew de Las Casas (1474-1566), a Dominican, who made seven voyages to Spain to plead the cause of the oppressed Indians of Central and South America. Also, Samuel Fritz (1654-1724), a Jesuit, who spent forty years exploring the Amazon country and was known as "the apostle to the Amazon Indians."

In 1526, Franciscans entered Florida, missions were established in

163

New Mexico in 1542, Texas in 1544, by late 1500's in southern California, and in the early 1600's in Georgia, Virginia, South Carolina, Maine, New York, and Maryland. When Jacques Cartier arrived in Canada in 1534, there were priests in his party.

Some of the Roman Catholic missionary preaching was evangelical, some of it was mixed with Catholic tradition and even pagan practices, but at least the Name of Christ was being spread throughout much of the world during this period of Church history, through this missionary thrust.

Fourth Wave — Protestant Missions
to the Whole World — 1700-1960[8]

Early Attempts — A.D.1555-1715

The concern for reform and renewal of the Church, that had been building for over three centuries, came to a head in 1517 when Luther nailed his 95 theses to the Church door at Wittenburg. But it took nearly three centuries before the Protestants made a major thrust in missions. Initially, they were consumed with their own survival — formulating a clear presentation of Protestant theology, establishing a new organizational framework for their constituents, consolidating their gains, and surviving persecution. And then, too, some of the reformers taught that God would save the elect without any intervention, on the part of man. Calvin wrote: "We are taught that the Kingdom of Christ is neither advanced nor maintained by the industry of men, but is the work of God alone." Others taught that the Great Commission was just for the original apostles. The Protestant countries also were not, at first, the explorers that the Spanish and the Portuguese were. Furthermore, when the Protestants left the Catholic Church, they did not retain the orders, or missionary bands, when they formulated their concepts of organization.

Prior to Luther's Reformation, the Unity of Brethren had sent representatives to Austria, Brandenburg (part of today's East Germany), Poland, Russia, Moldavia (in the Soviet Union near today's Romania), Greece, Palestine, Egypt, and Turkey between the mid and late 1400's. And there were Protestant voices crying out for the cause of world evangelization: men like Erasmus (1466-1536) and Hadrian Saravia (1531-1613). The Anabaptists made the Great Commission the responsibility of every member. The Hutterites organized systematic missions throughout Europe from their bases in Moravia. In 1555, Calvin sent four reformed preachers with a group of French Huguenots to Brazil to found a colony for persecuted Protestants. The leaders abandoned the group and they were finally all killed.

In 1622, the Dutch East India Company established a seminary at the University of Leyden, in Holland, to train chaplains and missionaries for the East Indies. It lasted only twelve years, but twelve missionaries were sent out, although most of them returned after a few years. In 1661, George Fox, founder of the Quakers, sent three men to China, but they never arrived. About 1664, an Austrian Lutheran, Baron Justinian von Weltz, wrote three pamphlets calling for the opening of a training school for missionaries, the forming of a missionary association, and the getting on with the fulfilling of the Great Commission. He was considered a fanatic, and in time he went to Holland, was ordained "an apostle to the Gentiles," and set sail for Dutch Guiana (today's Surinam), where he died an early death before he could see any results.

In North America, The Society for the Propagation of the Gospel in New England was founded in 1649. Its first missionary was John Eliot, who had been ministering to the Indians since 1631. The Society for Promoting Christian Knowledge was organized in 1698 as an agency within the Anglican Church to provide Christian literature for all parts of the world. In 1701, the Society for the Propagation of the Gospel in Foreign Parts was formed to minister to the needs of colonists and to evangelize the indigenous heathen. At the time of the independence of the Thirteen Colonies, the Society had three hundred missionaries in the Colonies.

Another early attempt at Protestant missions came in 1705. Eleven years earlier, Philip Spener (1635-1705), a German Lutheran and leader of the Pietist movement, had founded Halle University. In 1705 Denmark was recruiting men for chaplain and missionary work for their colony at Tranquebar, on the east coast of India. Barthelomew Ziegenbalg and Heinrich Plutschau, both of whom had studied at Halle University, were recruited. They set sail on November 29, 1705, and arrived July 9, 1706. Plutschau served for five years and Ziegenbalg for fifteen. In 1715, while on furlough, Ziegenbalg spoke on missions in Denmark, Germany, and England and spent time at Halle, where he greatly influenced one of the students, Nicolaus Zinzendorf.

The Moravians — 1730-1770

Nicolaus Ludwig von Zinzendorf was born on May 26, 1700. Six weeks later his father died, making him heir to one of Europe's leading families. He was raised by his Aunt Henrietta and his grandmother, Lady Gersdorf, at her estate east of Dresden, in an atmosphere of hymn singing, Bible reading, and prayer. Here as a child Zinzendorf wrote love letters to Jesus, tossing them out of the castle tower window, and by the time he was six had an established devotional life. At ten Zinzendorf went to Halle to become a student at the Pietist Center, where he had close contact with the leader of the movement, August Francke. By age fifteen, he read the New Testament in Greek, and was fluent in Latin and French. He was also spending 6 to 7 a.m. and 8 to 9 p.m. in prayer. While a student his obsession for Christian unity also began to develop.

After completing his studies, Zinzendorf married and spent part of the year as a count in the royal court and part of the year at his estate. In December, 1722, a group of Bohemian Brethren from Moravia, led by Christian David, sought refuge on Zinzendorf's property. By 1725, ninety had settled at Herrnhut, and by 1726 there was a Christian community of three hundred. But there were problems in uniting these followers of Hus, Luther, and Calvin into one body. In May, 1727, the community was formed into small groups to exhort one another and to pray for revival. The volume and intensity of prayer increased throughout the summer and on August 13, there was a mighty outpouring of the Holy Spirit. On August 26, twenty-four brethren and twenty-four sisters covenanted together to continue from one midnight to the next in prayer, each spending one hour. Soon others joined in, and the **hourly intercession continued for over one hundred years.**

In 1730, when Zinzendorf was visiting Copenhagen, he met a Black man from the West Indies, and two Eskimos from Greenland, who pleaded with him to send missionaries to them. In 1732 Leonard Doper and David Nitschmann sailed for St. Thomas in the Virgin Islands to work among the slaves. Soon others were going out: to Greenland (1733), Surinam (1735), Africa (1737), North American Indians (1740), Ceylon (1740), China (1742), Persia (1747), Jamaica (1754), and Antigua (1756). Their philosophy of missions consisted of five simple points: (1) look for the first fruits, those who are ready to respond; (2) preach Christ; (3) go to the neglected peoples; (4) seek to

166

expand Christ's Kingdom; and (5) be self-supporting. What missionaries they were! When they were sent out, they were provided with their fare, although some sold themselves as slaves to get there. Upon reaching their destination they were to be self-supporting. They spent their entire life ministering to their adopted land and were buried there. By 1930 there was still one Moravian missionary for every twelve church members. Thus, the Protestant missionary movement had been born. But it was through William Carey that the missions emphasis was to spread to the rest of the Church.

William Carey — the Modern Missions Movement — 1790-1830

William Carey (1761-1834) has been called "the father of modern missions." (An account of his early years can be found on pages 98-100.) Carey and his party arrived safely in India on November 19, 1793. After seven years Carey could not claim one Indian convert. Carey translated the entire Bible into Bengali, Sanskrit, and Maraki, and some portions into many other Indian languages. His purpose was to build an indigenous church "by means of native preachers" and by providing the Scriptures in the native tongue. By 1818, after twenty-five years, there were 600 baptized converts and several thousand more who attended services and classes. William Carey died in India in 1834. He had made a major contribution toward the evangelization of India and, just as important, had "set the pace" for the rest of Christendom. In the twenty-five years after the appearance of Carey's book, *Enquiry . . .* , and following his example, twelve significant mission agencies came into being in Europe and the United States, including the London Missionary Society (1795), the Scottish and Glasgow Missionary Societies (1796), the Netherlands Missionary Society (1797), the Church Missionary Society (1799), the British and Foreign Bible Society (1804), the American Board of Commissioners for Foreign Missions (1804), the American Baptist Missionary Union (1814), and the American Bible Society (1816).

Meanwhile, God was also at work in the infant United States of America. In 1802, while out plowing on his farm in Connecticut, Samuel Mills was called by God to preach the Gospel. To prepare himself he went to Williams College in Williamstown, Massachusetts. There he gathered together a group who met frequently in a maple grove for prayer and discussion. One day, on their way there, they were caught in a thunderstorm. Taking refuge in a haystack, they had an extraordinary prayer time for the heathen world. They concluded by standing to their feet and saying, "We can do it if we will." They were henceforth known as "the Haystack Group." After graduating, several went on to Andover Seminary. They were joined by Adoniram Judson and soon formed the Society of Inquiry on the Subject of Missions. In 1810 the Board of Commissioners for Foreign Missions was formed and in 1812 the first American missionaries set sail. The party of eight included Adoniram Judson, Samuel Newell, Samuel Nott, their wives, Gordon Hall and Luther Rice. They were commissioned in Salem, Massachusetts, on February 5, 1812; set sail later in the month; and arrived in India in June. En route to India, Judson received a new understanding about baptism, and was baptized by immersion upon arriving in India. This led to the forming of the American Baptist Foreign Mission Society in May 1814. The Judsons stayed in India only a short time and then went on to Burma, arriving July 13, 1813. He labored there for thirty-seven years with only one visit back home.

Protestant missions to Africa began in the Cape Colony with the Moravians in 1737. In the early 1800's Protestant missionaries had established three beachheads: on the west coast at Sierra Leone, the east coast at Ethiopia and Kenya, and the south at Capetown. Robert Moffat, the patriarch of South African missions, spent fifty-three years there. They were followed by David Livingstone and many others.

In 1797, thirty British missionaries were dropped off at Tahiti, Tonga, and Marquesas by the mission ship *Duff.* Robert Morrison arrived in China from Scotland in 1807. In 1820 the first missionaries arrived in Hawaii, having come from New England.

Many times the progress was painfully slow and many of these early missionaries died of disease on the field. Out of the 35 who went to Ghana, Africa, between 1835 and 1870, only two lived more than two years! Still, an initial penetration was made, and the Gospel took root in some of the coastal areas of Asia and Africa, and the Pacific islands.

Moving Inland — 1850-1900

The coastal areas of parts of Asia and Africa had been initially evangelized. It was now time to make a further thrust, penetrating inland. Twenty-one year old J. Hudson Taylor (1832-1905) arrived in Shanghai, China, from England in 1854 to work with the Chinese

Evangelization Society. Within a few months he was making trips into the interior. He decided to become more like the Chinese: he dyed his hair black and wore it in a pigtail and began to wear Chinese clothes. In 1857 he resigned from the Chinese Evangelization Society, in 1858 he married Maria Dyer, and in 1860 they returned to England for an extended furlough to recuperate from health problems and to acquire further education. While in England the burden for the millions of unevangelized Chinese continued to grow, and in 1865 the China Inland Mission was born. It was a new approach to missions: the purpose was to reach inland; it was to be non-denominational; the headquarters was to be in China, not England; the workers were recruited primarily from the working classes, and were often not ordained or seminary trained; all workers were to depend entirely upon God for their needs; and all were expected to wear Chinese clothes. By 1882, China Inland Mission had entered every province of China; and by 1914 it had become the largest foreign missionary organization in the world, reaching a peak of 1,368 workers in 1934.

Likewise in Africa, David Livingstone was moving inland. Arriving at Capetown in 1841, he almost immediately began traveling, always pushing north and east into the interior. Between 1852 and 1873 he made three major expeditions into the interior of Africa. On his third and last expedition he did not see another European for almost seven years. In fact, there were rumors that he had died, so Henry Stanley, a *New York Herald* reporter was sent to find him. He caught up with him near Lake Tanganyika in late 1871, greeting him with the now famous words, "Dr. Livingstone, I presume." Stanley stayed on, traveling with Livingstone for four months, and during that time, was converted from being "the worst infidel in London" to becoming a Christian by watching "the old man carrying out the words, 'leave all and follow Me'."

Soon others were catching the vision to reach those who lived inland. Over forty new agencies took shape, including Livingstone Inland Mission, Sudan Interior Mission, Africa Inland Mission, Heart of Africa Mission, Unevangelized Fields Mission, and Regions Beyond Missionary Union.

Adding Fuel to the Fire — 1875-1960

The great world-wide missions movement was in full swing. God caused five additional developments which "added fuel to the fire."

The first was a wave of single women missionaries. God had always used women — Joan of Arc, Catherine Booth, the Moravian women, but it was frowned upon by much of the Church. In 1823 Betsy Stockton, a Black, went to Hawaii as a missionary. From 1873-1912, Lottie Moon labored as a Southern Baptist missionary in China, evangelizing, planting churches, training leaders, and influencing the Church leaders back home. Amy Carmichael left Northern Ireland in 1893 for fifty-five years of unbroken service in India. By 1900 there were more than forty women's mission societies in the United States alone, and by 1910 women outnumbered men as Protestant missionaries.

The second significant development was the emergence, between 1885 and 1920, of five national organizations in North America that further added much "fuel to the fire." The Student Volunteer Movement for Foreign Missions was organized in 1888 to challenge college students to consider foreign missions seriously for their lifework. The Student Volunteer Movement watchword was "the evangelization of the world in this generation," and students were challenged to take the pledge, "It is my purpose, if God permit, to become a foreign missionary." By 1945, 20,000 students had gone to the field and another 80,000 who took the pledge, were led to stay home and support the work. In 1902, the Missionary Education Movement was formed. It was similar in purpose to the Student Volunteer Movement, but more denominationally oriented.

In 1906 John B. Slemen and seventy-five other "laymen" founded the Laymen's Missionary Movement to challenge laymen to give to missions. By 1916, through over three thousand great city-wide, transdenominational conventions and banquets, nearly a million men caused mission giving in America to quadruple. During 1910-12, a similar campaign, the Religion Forward Movement, brought a social concern emphasis to missions. Their message was "the whole Gospel for the whole world." In 1918, James I. Vance, S. Earl Taylor, and John R. Mott, with 135 representatives of American Protestant mission boards, inaugurated the Interchurch World Movement to "unite the Protestant churches of North America in the performance of their common task." By 1920, one hundred forty mission boards, representing thirty-four Protestant denominations, that included eighty to ninety percent of all American Protestant missions, had affiliated themselves with the movement. One of their successes was a cooperative raising of $200,000,000 for missions.

This period also included the World Missionary Conference at Edinburgh, Scotland, in 1910 when leaders of most of the missionary societies of the world joined together to develop a strategy for the completion of world evangelization. One of the results of this conference was a move toward shifting the authority from the mission agencies to the developing, national churches.

The third significant occurrence was the world-wide Pentecostal movement that emerged between 1900-1920, which brought a great new surge of spiritual power to the Church, and resulted in a wave of Pentecostal missionaries going out to all parts of the world.

The fourth major development that "added fuel to the fire" has taken place in the later years of the Protestant wave of missionary activity. That is the utilization of various modern technologies to advance the cause of Christ.

Beginning in the 1930's Cameron Townsend, Kenneth Pike, and others have worked together to perfect the adaptation of modern research and technology to the task of Bible translation work. By the Fifteenth Century there were only about thirty translations of the Bible. It was William Carey who made Bible translation work an integral part of missionary work. Following his example, most of the pioneer missionaries of the next century were Bible translators, including Robert Morrison (China), Adoniram Judson (Burma), and Hudson Taylor (China). Due to their labors, all or portions of the Bible appeared in five hundred languages during the Nineteenth Century.

Since 1900, major portions of the Bible have been translated into an additional thousand languages, half of these since 1950. Much of this has been done by the wonderful ministry of Wycliffe Bible Translators. Cameron Townsend went to Guatemala in 1917 to sell Bibles for the Los Angeles Bible House. He soon found himself in a remote area with 200,000 Cakchiquel Indians who could not speak Spanish. The question an Indian asked "Uncle Cam" one day, "If your God is so smart why can't He speak my language?," caused Townsend to spend the next thirteen years producing a translation for them. By 1929 he had produced the New Testament. In 1934 he and L.L. Legters founded Camp Wycliffe in Arkansas to train others for Bible translation work. Soon assisting Townsend with the task of training translators was the brilliant linguist, Dr. Kenneth Pike. At the time of Cam Townsend's death in 1982, there were 4,500 translators working in nearly one thousand languages. The Wycliffe philosophy has always simply been "The greatest missionary is the Bible in the Mother tongue."

Using the radio to spread the Gospel was pioneered by Aimee Semple McPherson, Paul Rader, Charles E. Fuller, Dr. Walter A. Maier, and others in North America. And overseas it has been greatly expanded by HCJB, Far Eastern Broadcasting Company, Trans-World Radio and many others. To this, today, can be added the use of Gospel recordings, audio and videotapes, films, television, and satellites — all being used to spread the glorious Gospel of our wonderful Lord Jesus Christ.

Throughout the 1940's God used Walter Herron, Betty Greene, Nate Saint, and a host of others to pioneer missionary aviation. Two of the best known aviation organizations are Missionary Aviation Fellowship, founded in 1944; and Jungle Aviation and Radio Service (JAARS), an arm of Wycliffe Bible Translators, started in 1947.

The fifth occurrence that "added fuel to the fire" was that which took place just after World War II. Thousands of servicemen caught a glimpse of the great needs that existed at "the ends of the earth," and upon their discharge from service, enrolled in Bible schools, formed new mission agencies, and went back overseas to serve Christ by the thousands in the late 1940's and 50's. From 1940-1960 there were about one hundred forty new agencies founded in North America alone and the number of missionaries identified with the Inter-denominational Foreign Missions Association (IFMA) and the Evangelical Foreign Missions Association (EFMA) grew from five thousand to eleven thousand.

Fifth and Final Wave — The Whole Church, From the Whole World, With the Whole Gospel For the Whole Man, To Every Person

Beginning slowly in the 1950's and continuing to gather momentum, we are now in the fifth, and perhaps final, wave of world evangelization. It is not Protestant or Catholic, but the whole Church uniting together to fulfill the Great Commission. The Charismatic renewal of the 1950's through the 1970's, and other factors, are bringing unity to all of the people of God. There are even new mission agencies, like Youth With A Mission, where Roman Catholic and Protestant

172

missionaries are working together. It is no longer the Western Church taking the Gospel to the Third World nations. Instead, it is the whole Church, world-wide, taking the Gospel to the yet unevangelized. There were, in fact, by 1984, over four hundred new Third World agencies and over 18,000 Third World missionaries who had gone out to reach others. This last wave involves taking the "whole Gospel to the whole man": ministering the love, truth, and power of Jesus to the whole man; bringing spiritual, mental, emotional, physical, and social wholeness to the total man. It involves taking the Gospel to every person on the face of the globe, including over 16,000 unreached people groups. It includes planting a church within the reach (geographically, linguistically, and culturally) of every person on earth. We will look at all of this further in the next three chapters.

16

WORLD EVANGELIZATION TODAY — FINISHING THE TASK

The Church of our Lord Jesus Christ is God's vehicle for fulfilling the Great Commission. After an initial thrust of evangelism to the Roman Empire (A.D. 30-500), a wave of evangelism to the rest of Europe and to central Asia (500-1300), A Roman Catholic thrust to the whole world (1300-1700), and a huge wave of Protestant missionary activity (1700-1960), we are now in the midst of the fifth, and perhaps final, great wave of evangelization[1]. We are seeing today a growing wave of evangelism and mission activity that could result in the Great Commission being fulfilled in this generation. We are now witnessing the whole Church (not just Protestant or Catholic), from the whole world (not just Western missionaries going to Third World nations), with the whole Gospel for the whole man, to every person in the whole world. What a tremendous time to be alive!

Population Statistics[2]

The world's population (estimated mid-1986) is five billion people. In the days of Abraham and Moses it was probably less than 100 million. By Jesus' time it was 250-275 million. In 1800, when the Protestant missionary wave was getting started, it was 900 million. The world population became one billion in 1850, two billion in the 1930's, three billion in 1960, four billion in 1975, and five billion 1986. It is increasing by about eighty-one million per year (222,000 per day) and will reach six to seven billion by A.D. 2000. This accelerating growth is vividly seen on Chart 3.

These 5.0 billion are found in approximately 223 countries. (See Appendix 9-A for a list.) They are found residing in approximately

175

24,000 different ethnic groups, and speak approximately 5,500 languages. The fastest growing regions are the already over-populated areas of Africa, Asia, and Latin America. The ten most populated countries are listed in Table 2. The world population and area, broken down by continents, is given in Tables 3 and 4 and shown visually on Chart 4. The population density for each country is seen vividly on Chart 5. The world's largest cities are given in Tables 5 and 6.

Task Yet Remaining

An overview of the task yet remaining includes:

1. Getting the Gospel to every person. Ninety-four percent are still unsaved. **Over one million go into eternity every week around the world without Jesus Christ.** A map showing the distribution of the saved and the lost around the world is given as Chart 10. Supporting statistical data is included in Appendix 9-C.
2. **Approximately two-thirds (3 billion of 5.0 billion) have never heard the Gospel once.** Two point seven of the three billion can only be reached by cross-cultural going. Many of these are in the **over 16,000 unreached people groups.** Many are in the great unevangelized belt of northern Africa, the Middle East, and Aisa. A map showing country by country the location of the unreached people groups is given as Chart 11. The exact number per each country is given in Appendix 9-D.

CHART 3 — WORLD POPULATION GROWTH

Population:

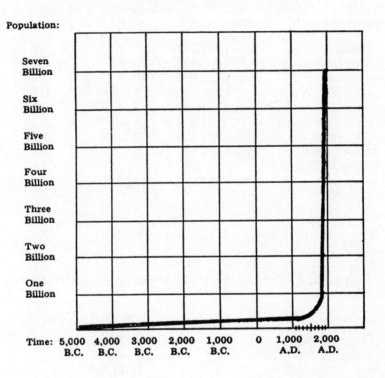

Population:								

Seven Billion

Six Billion

Five Billion

Four Billion

Three Billion

Two Billion

One Billion

Time: 5,000 B.C. 4,000 B.C. 3,000 B.C. 2,000 B.C. 1,000 B.C. 0 1,000 A.D. 2,000 A.D.

TABLE 2 — TEN MOST POPULATED COUNTRIES

	Million			Million
1. China	1,050	6. Brazil		143
2. India	785	7. Japan		122
3. USSR	278	8. Nigeria		105
4. USA	241	9. Bangladesh		104
5. Indonesia	168	10. Pakistan		102

177

TABLE 3 — WORLD POPULATION BY CONTINENTS[3]

Continent	Population	Percent of Total	AGR (%annual growth rate)
Asia	2,909,753,000	58.2	1.8
Africa	589,842,000	11.8	2.8
Europe	498,786,000	10.0	0.3
USSR	283,286,000	5.7	0.5
South America	282,274,000	5.6	2.3
USA & Canada	270,134,000	5.4	0.7
C. Am. & Mexico	109,268,000	2.2	2.7
Caribbean	31,364,000	0.6	1.7
Oceania	25,293,000	0.5	1.3
TOTAL	5,000,000,000	100.0	

TABLE 4 — RELATIVE WORLD AREAS BY CONTINENTS

Area	% of land mass
Africa	20.2%
Asia	18.7
USSR	14.8
USA & Canada	12.9
South America	11.9
Antarctica	10.3
Oceania	6.0
Europe	3.3
Cent. America & Mexico	1.7
Caribbean	0.2
TOTAL	100.0

CHART 4 — RELATIVE WORLD POPULATION
AND AREA BY CONTINENTS

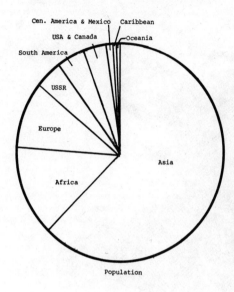

Population

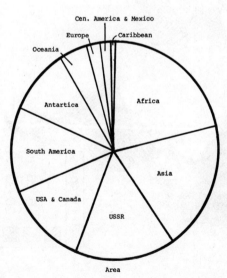

Area

179

CHART 5 — POPULATION

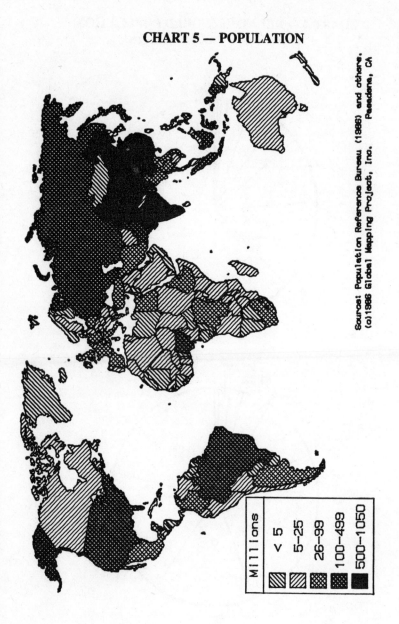

Sources: Population Reference Bureau (1986) and others.
(c)1986 Global Mapping Project, Inc.   Pasadena, CA

Millions
< 5
5–25
26–99
100–499
500–1050

TABLE 5 — WORLD'S LARGEST CITIES (1985)

There are currently ten metropolitan areas with a population of over 10 million:

Name of City	Country	Urban Population
1. Tokyo/Yokohama	Japan	21,300,000
2. Mexico City	Mexico	18,800,000
3. New York	USA	18,200,000
4. Shanghai	China (PRC)	17,000,000
5. Sao Paulo	Brazil	14,500,000
6. Beijing	China (PRC)	14,100,000
7. Cairo	Egypt	10,900,000
8. Los Angeles	USA	10,800,000
9. Buenos Aires	Argentina	10,700,000
10. Rio de Janeiro	Brazil	10,200,000

TABLE 6 — WORLD'S LARGEST CITIES (A.D. 2000)

By A.D. 2000 over half of the world's population will live in large cities. The twenty-five metropolitan areas estimated to have a population of over 10 million by 2000 include:

Name of City	Country	Urban Population
1. Mexico City	Mexico	31,000,000
2. Sao Paulo	Brazil	25,800,000
3. Tokyo/Yokohama	Japan	24,200,000
4. New York	USA	22,800,000
5. Shanghai	China	22,700,000
6. Beijing	China	19,900,000
7. Rio de Janeiro	Brazil	19,000,000
8. Bombay	India	17,100,000
9. Calcutta	India	16,700,000
10. Jakarta	Indonesia	16,600,000
11. Seoul	Korea	14,200,000
12. Los Angeles	USA	14,200,000
13. Cairo	Egypt	13,100,000
14. Madras	India	12,900,000
15. Manila	Philippines	12,300,000
16. Buenos Aires	Argentina	12,100,000
17. Bangkok	Thailand	11,900,000
18. Karachi	Pakistan	11,800,000
19. Delhi	India	11,700,000
20. Bogota	Columbia	11,700,000
21. Paris	France	11,300,000
22. Tehran	Iran	11,300,000
23. Istanbul	Turkey	11,200,000
24. Osaka/Kobe	Japan	11,100,000
25. Baghdad	Iraq	11,100,000

Religious categories of the world's peoples are given in Table 7.

TABLE 7 — WORLD'S RELIGIONS[4]

Religion	Approximate Number
Christian	1,613,000,000
Muslim	925,000,000
Hindu	655,000,000
Anamist	135,000,000
Jews	20,350,000
Buddhists, Chinese, and Japanese folk religions	593,000,000
Non-religious	1,010,000,000
Other (Sikh, spiritists, Bahai, Jain, Parsee, various new religions, etc.)	48,650,000
TOTAL	5,000,000,000
However, just over 6% of the world is truly converted =	320,000,000
94% lost =	4,680,000,000
Total world population =	5,000,000,000

The world's peoples, divided religiously by how close they are to the Gospel, can be seen on Charts 6 though 9. Supporting statistical data is given in Appendix 9-B.

CHART 6 — WORLD-WIDE DISTRIBUTION OF
POPULATION, MISSIONARIES, AND UNREACHED PEOPLES

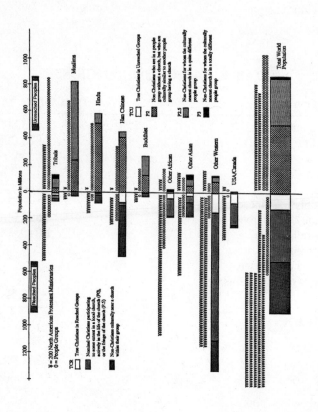

Charts 6-9 are from the U.S. Center for World Mission, 1605 E. Elizabeth, St., Pasadena, Ca 91104.

CHART 7 — THE WORLD IN MISSION PERSPECTIVE

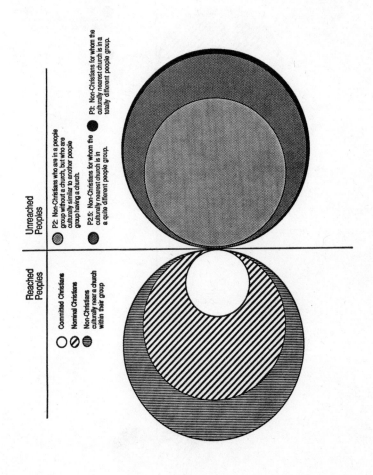

Reached Peoples

◯ Committed Christians
⊘ Nominal Christians
▨ Non-Christians culturally near a church within their group

Unreached Peoples

◉ P2: Non-Christians who are in a people group without a church, but who are culturally similar to another people group having a church.

● P2.5: Non-Christians for whom the culturally nearest church is in a quite different people group.

● P3: Non-Christians for whom the culturally nearest church is in a totally different people group.

CHART 8 — RELATIVELY REACHED BLOCS

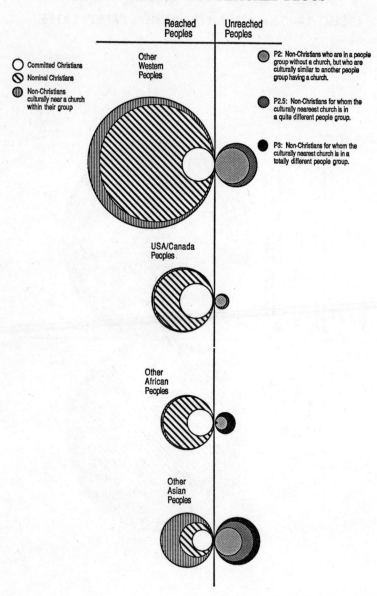

Reached Peoples

Unreached Peoples

○ Committed Christians

⊘ Nominal Christians

▥ Non-Christians culturally near a church within their group

Other Western Peoples

USA/Canada Peoples

Other African Peoples

Other Asian Peoples

P2: Non-Christians who are in a people group without a church, but who are culturally similar to another people group having a church.

P2.5: Non-Christians for whom the culturally nearest church is in a quite different people group.

P3: Non-Christians for whom the culturally nearest church is in a totally different people group.

CHART 9 — RELATIVELY UNREACHED BLOCS

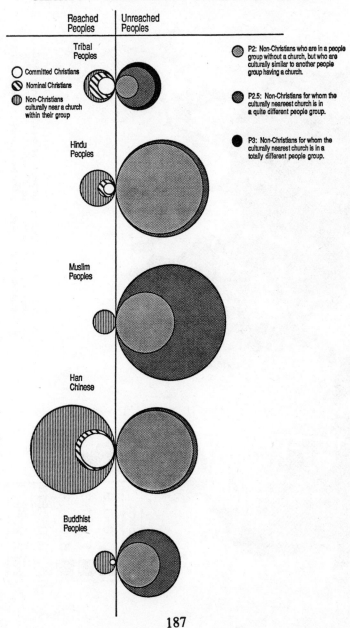

Reached Peoples | Unreached Peoples

Tribal Peoples

Committed Christians

Nominal Christians

Non-Christians culturally near a church within their group

P2: Non-Christians who are in a people group without a church, but who are culturally similar to another people group having a church.

P2.5: Non-Christians for whom the culturally nearest church is in a quite different people group.

P3: Non-Christians for whom the culturally nearest church is in a totally different people group.

Hindu Peoples

Muslim Peoples

Han Chinese

Buddhist Peoples

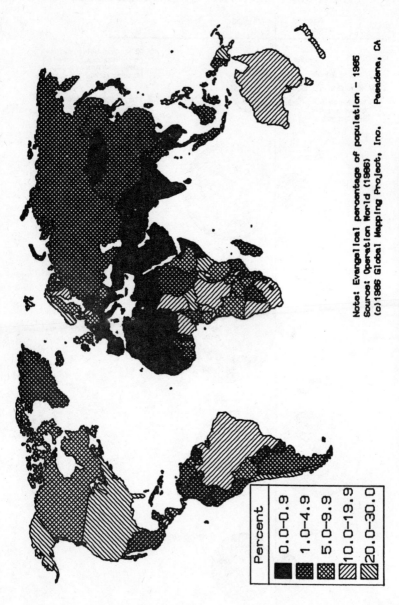

Note: Evangelical percentage of population – 1985
Source: Operation World (1986)
(c)1986 Global Mapping Project, Inc.   Pasadena, CA

Percent
0.0-0.9
1.0-4.9
5.0-9.9
10.0-19.9
20.0-30.0

CHART 10 — DISTRIBUTION OF EVANGELICALS

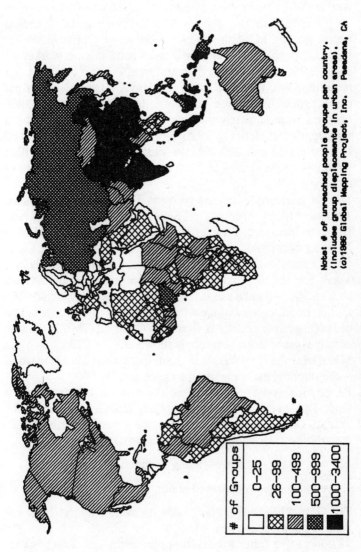

Note: # of unreached people groups per country.
(Includes group displacements in urban areas).
(c)1985 Global Mapping Project, Inc. Pasadena, CA

CHART 11 — UNREACHED PEOPLE GROUPS

# of Groups	
0-25	
26-99	
100-499	
500-999	
1000-3400	

There are approximately 70,000 long-term and 30,000 short-term missionaries in the world. However, most of them are working with the already reached with only about 9,000 long-term missionaries endeavoring to reach the 2.4 billion in the unreached people groups. In North America there is one Christian worker for 1,321 people, while in Asia there is one Christian worker for every 2,760,635 people.[5] In other words, North America has more than two thousand times as many Christian workers per capita as does Asia. There is only one missionary for every million Muslims. Approximately one-fourth (15-20,000) of the long-term missionaries will retire by 1990. (Some of this is seen in Chart 6.) It is estimated that **200,000 new missionaries and $1.5 billion annually are yet needed** to reach the unreached people groups of the world.

3. Some countries have very few converts. They include Afghanistan, Albania, Algeria, Arabian Gulf States, Bhutan, Comoros Islands, Djibouti, Iran, Iraq, Libya, Maldive Islands, Malaysia (Muslim Malays), Mauritania, Mongolia, Morocco, North Korea, Qatar (all Muslim), Saudi Arabia, South Yemen, Turkey, and Zanzibar.

4. There are still approximately **3,600 languages** of the world's about 5,500 **without a single verse of Scripture.** They include 260 million or 5.2 percent of the world's population. The distribution of languages per country is shown on Chart 12. The distribution of languages without Scripture is shown on Chart 13.

5. Ministering the love of Jesus to the desperately needy of the world —the starving, the homeless, the oppressed.

6. Penetrating every segment of society with the will and ways of God. The seven basic areas of society include: the family, the educational institutions, the Church, the government, the media, the arts and entertainment, and business and industry.

Encouraging Trends

We have much to be encouraged about:

1. The Gospel has been initially taken to every country. There are believers in every country.

2. 78,000 people (after substracting for deaths and defections)are turning to Jesus Christ world-wide every week. A map showing

evangelical growth rate, country by country, is given as Chart 14. Supporting statistical information is given in Appendix 9-E.

3. 1,600 new churches are being formed world-wide every week.
4. Muslims are beginning to turn to Christ at an accelerated rate.
5. At present trends, Africa will be the most Christian of all the continents by the year 2000.
6. By 2000, three-fifths of all Christians will be non-white and will live in Asia, Africa, and Latin America. The growth in some of these areas has been tremendous.

In 1900 there were only 50,000 Protestants in all of Latin America; by 1980 it had reached 20 million; and some project 100 million by 2000. Much of this growth has been among Pentecostals, like the Brazil for Christ Church in Sao Paulo, Brazil, that seats 25,000. Another example is the Jotabeche Methodist Pentecostal Church of Santiago, Chile, a church of 90,000 members 12 years of age and older. Their building seats 16,000, so the members only attend once per month. The other Sundays they attend satellite churches. To all of this must be added the many Catholics in Latin America who are coming to really know Jesus in a life-changing way.[6]

The growth in parts of Africa likewise has been phenomenal: 4,000 per day are turning to Christ. One group in east Africa has grown from ten in 1962 to 150,000 in 1984. Another group has grown from thirteen thousand in 1960 to 500,000 by 1980.[7]

In Asia, especially South Korea, there are similar statistics. The world's largest church is there: the Full Gospel Central Church in Seoul with a membership of over 500,000.[8] There are an estimated 50-100 million Christians in China.

7. The number of missionaries going out from Third World, or developing nations, exceeds 18,000.

Current Common Approaches

There are approximately 70,000 long-term Protestant missionaries in the world. 52,000 are from the Western world (40,000 from the USA) and 18,000 from the Third World. They are involved in the following types of ministries:

1. *Church Planting*. God's most basic strategy for the evangelization of the world is the planting of New Testament churches. We see

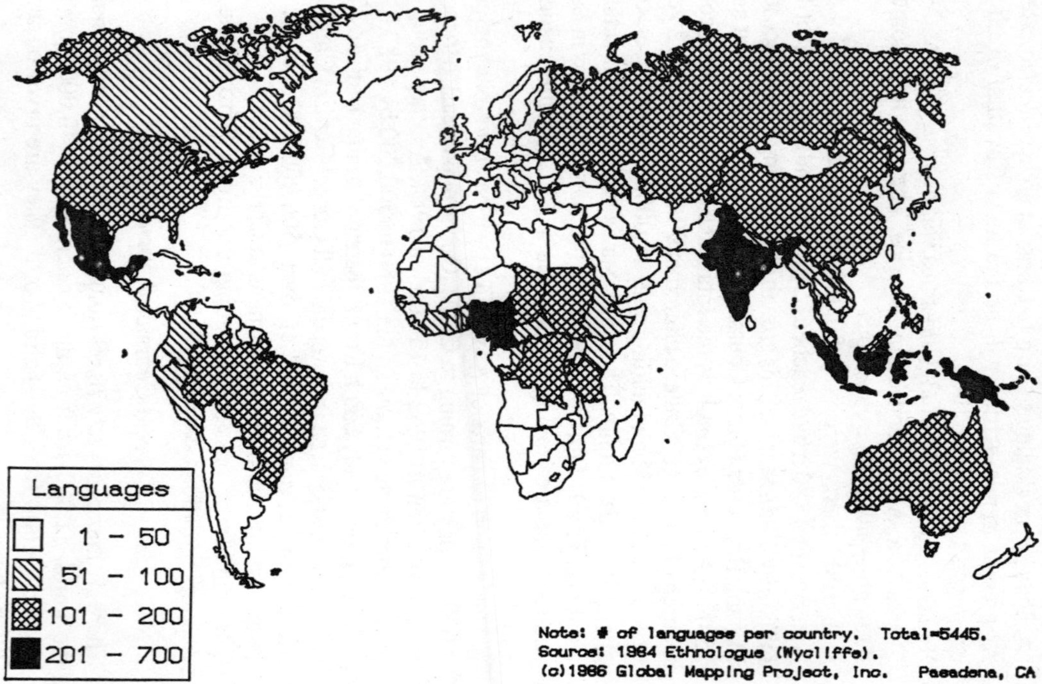

Languages
- 1 – 50
- 51 – 100
- 101 – 200
- 201 – 700

Note: # of languages per country. Total=5445.
Source: 1984 Ethnologue (Wycliffe).
(c)1986 Global Mapping Project, Inc.   Pasadena, CA

CHART 12 — DISTRIBUTION OF LANGUAGES

192

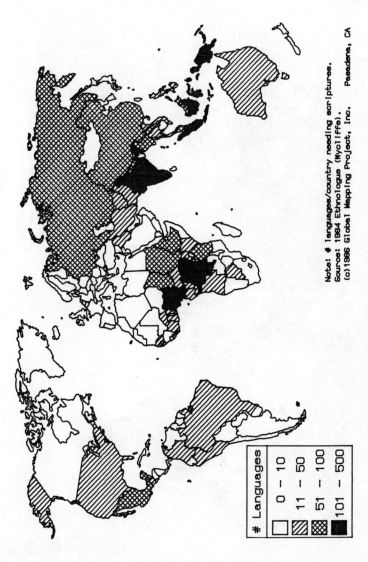

Note: # languages/country needing scriptures.
Source: 1984 Ethnologue (Wycliffe).
(c)1986 Global Mapping Project, Inc.   Pasadena, CA

Languages

☐	0 – 10
▨	11 – 50
▩	51 – 100
■	101 – 500

CHART 13 — LANGUAGES WITHOUT SCRIPTURE

193

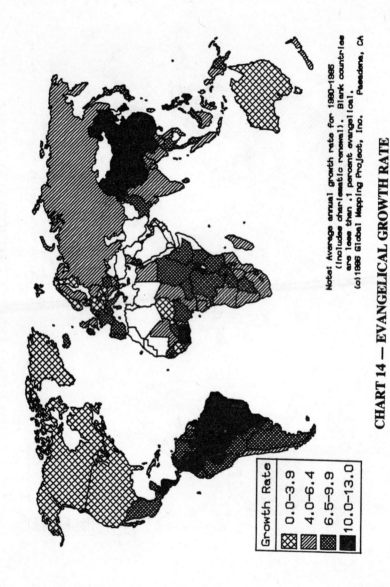

Growth Rate

⊠ 0.0-3.9

▨ 4.0-6.4

▩ 6.5-9.9

■ 10.0-13.0

Note: Average annual growth rate for 1980-1985
(includes charismatic renewal). Blank countries
are less than .1 percent evangelical.
(c)1986 Global Mapping Project, Inc.   Pasadena, CA

CHART 14 — EVANGELICAL GROWTH RATE

this so clearly in the New Testament missionary pattern illustrated in Paul's ministry. These New Testament churches, in turn, went out to evangelize their "world,"their geographic-cultural community (1 Thessalonians 1:8), and they sent others out to evangelize and plant churches in other locations (Acts 13:1-3). One of the most basic strategies must continue to be church planting with the goal of **"a church for every people by the year 2000."**

2. *Bible translation and Bible distribution work.* There are approximately 5,500 known languages in the world. An adequate translation of the entire Bible is now available in 233 languages. There are an additional 501 with an adequate New Testament. Scripture portions in 68 languages need revising. Translation work in over 1,000 languages is in progress, but over 3,600 languages still have no translation work being done in them. There is no portion of God's Word available to 260 million people, or 5.2 percent of the world's population. Revelation 5:9 tells us that Jesus died to purchase those of every tongue. We must believe God for sufficient personnel, technology, and funds so that the Word of God can be in **every language by A.D. 2000.**

Appoximately 500 million Scripture portions and 15 million complete Bibles are distributed around the world annually.[9] Some of the major organizations involved in this work are listed in Appendix 9-F.

One must also mention the work of Dr. Frank Laubach, who, with his "Each One Teach One" program, enabled over 100 million illiterate people in 103 countries and 313 languages to learn to read the Bible in their native language.[10] The adult literacy in the world is shown on Chart 15.

3. *Church Renewal.* There are parts of the world where there is a Christian Church that has lost much of its spiritual life and power. It needs to be renewed, after which it could evangelize the rest of that area as well as be a force for sending more workers to other areas. Examples of churches that need this kind of renewal include the Wesleyan Church in Tonga, the Methodist Church in Fiji, and the Lutheran Church in Denmark. Examples of situations where God is bringing this type of renewal include parts of the Lutheran Church in Iceland, Norway, and Finland; parts of the Catholic

Church in Austria and Belgium; and parts of the Anglican Church in England. Let us continue to pray and work for **renewal of the existing Church world-wide.**

4. *Christian literature and Bible correspondence courses.* The distribution of Christian literature is a major approach to world evangelization. A list of those majoring in literature production and distribution is found in Appendix 9-G.

   The use of Bible correspondence courses, likewise, is a major tool in world evangelization, especially when combined with radio broadcasting into closed Muslim and Communist countries. Many people in these lands hear a Gospel message over the radio, write for a Bible correspondence course, and through this process come to know the Savior.

5. *The media.* The media (Christian radio, television, Gospel recordings, films, the telephone, and audio and video tapes) will play a major note in the evangelization of the world in this generation. There are over one billion radios in the world. Ninety percent of the world's population can hear the Gospel, by radio, tens of thousands of decisions result each month, and many new churches are being formed by listeners. Christian television and satellite networks are likewise now covering much of the earth. The gospel on record is now available in over 4,300 languages and dialects. Audio and video tapes are being used increasingly to communicate the Gospel and to teach the believers. Also, there are those who are using the telephone to evangelize whole areas systematically, and Christian films are reaching many. Ministries specializing in the media are given in Appendix 9-H.

6. *Work Among Students.* There are millions of high school, college, and university students around the world, who, as the leaders of tomorrow, need to be reached with the Gospel of Jesus Christ. Those involved in this ministry are playing a vital role in the evangelization of the world. A list of those primarily involved in this ministry is given in Appendix 9-J.

7. *Medical mission work.* Beginning slowly, by 1925 over 2,000 doctors and nurses from Europe and North America were serving in mission-sponsored hospitals and clinics throughout the world.

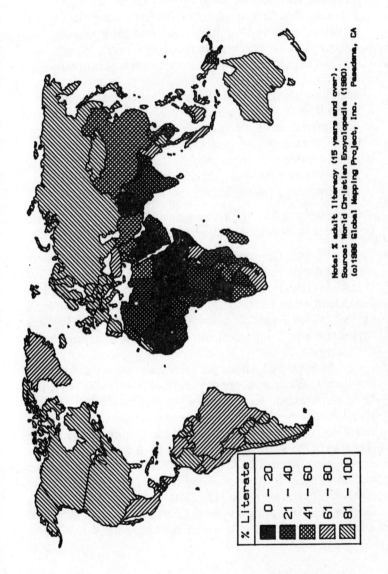

% Literate

▓ (black)	0 – 20
▓	21 – 40
▓	41 – 60
▓	61 – 80
▓	81 – 100

Note: % adult literacy (15 years and over).
Source: World Christian Encyclopedia (1980).
(c)1986 Global Mapping Project, Inc. Pasadena, CA

CHART 15 — ADULT LITERACY

197

"The ministry of missionary medicine during the Twentieth Century has been without a doubt the greatest humanitarian effort the world has ever known, and more than any other force, it has served to disarm the critics of Christian missions. How many times medical specialists forsook lucrative practices and modern facilities in their homelands to work long hours at a feverish pace in utterly primitive conditions. They devoted their lives to raising health standards around the world, often leading the research in diseases in which most Western doctors had little interest, and building hospitals and medical schools from funds they had personally donated or solicited. Among their credits are some of the finest medical schools and hospitals in the world, The Christian Medical College and Hospital in Vellore, India, being a prime example." [11]

There are over 140 North American mission agencies known to be involved in medical, dental, and health mission work today.

8. *Mercy Ministries.* Our world today is filled with tremendous need: refugees, the poor, the hungry, the oppressed. It is estimated that over 40,000 children die each day around the world from lack of food, clean water, sanitation, and adequate medical care. In India alone 3 million a year die before their first birthday.[12] Over one billion people (over one-fifth the world's population) are malnourished.

An additional 500 million are chronically hungry and exist on less than 1,000 calories per day, most of them living in Africa, India, and Bangladesh. Close to a billion people exist on $40-$80 a year, which prevents them from buying adequate seeds, fertilizer, and tools. (A map vividly showing the quality of life of the countries of the world is given as Chart 16. A country-by-country presentation is found in Appendix 9-K.) There are at least ten million refugees in the world, and that number is estimated to climb to fifty million by the year 2000.[13] (A map vividly showing the refugees of the world is given as Chart 17. The actual estimated numbers, per country, is given in Appendix 9-K.) Those organizations specializing in relief and development ministries are listed in Appendix 9-M.)

What a needy world! We must minister to them in Jesus' Name (Matthew 25), and we must get the Gospel to them. Are we doing all that we can? Are we living a sacrificial lifestyle that would be pleasing to the Lord?

9. *International Congresses.* Several international congresses on world evangelization, led by Dr. Billy Graham, Dr. Leighton Ford, and others, have had a major influence on world evangelization strategy since the 1960's. The first congress was the Berlin Congress on World Evangelization held in Berlin, West Germany, in 1966. The next was the International Congress on World Evangelization held in Lausanne, Switzerland, in 1974. Since that time there have been many national and regional conferences; the Consultation on World Evangelization in Pattaya, Thailand, in June 1980; and the Edinburgh 1980 Congress. In 1989 another major congress is scheduled, the International Congress on World Evangelization II. There was also the International Conference for Itinerant Evangelists held in Amsterdam, Netherlands in 1983, and a second conference in 1986 attended by 8,160 evangelists from 174 countries.[14]

There have also been the very effective Urbana, Illinois, missions conventions. In December, 1984, over 18,000 attended the 14th such convention and heard the challenge of world evangelization.

10. *Mission Centers.* The 1974 Lausanne Congress on World Evangelization made a clear distinction between evangelism (sharing the Gospel with people of your own culture) and missions (getting the Gospel to people of another culture). In recent years we have seen a number of mission centers emerge, dedicated to research, mobilization, training, and services in connection with reaching the yet unreached people groups of the world. A list of some of the major mission centers is given in Appendix 9-N.

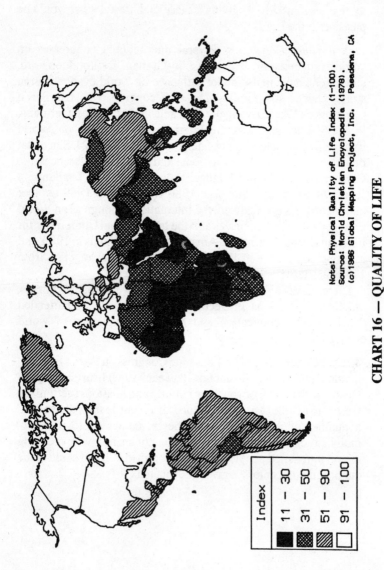

Note: Physical Quality of Life Index (1-100).
Source: World Christian Encyclopedia (1978).
(c)1986 Global Mapping Project, Inc.   Pasadena, CA

Index

■ 11 – 30
▓ 31 – 50
▨ 51 – 90
□ 91 – 100

CHART 16 — QUALITY OF LIFE

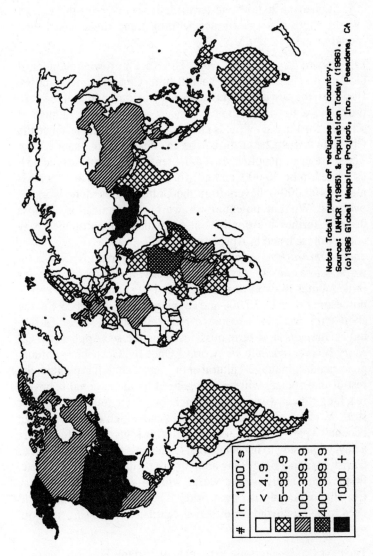

in 1000's

☐	< 4.9
▩	5-99.9
▨	100-399.9
▦	400-999.9
■	1000 +

Note: Total number of refugees per country.
Source: UNHCR (1985) & Population Today (1986).
(c)1986 Global Mapping Project, Inc. Pasadena, CA

CHART 17 — THE REFUGEE STATUS

Part-Time Missionaries

In addition to the 70,000 long-term missionaries serving throughout the world, there is a greatly accelerating trend toward part-time missionary work.

1. *Professional "tent-making" work.* There are a growing number of nations that are not open to full-time Christian missionaries. However, they do allow Christians to be in their nation if they are providing a needed technical service; i.e., teaching English in schools, working in oil fields and construction work, etc. Once the Christian is there, he or she can be an effective witness for Christ. The number of people involved in "tentmaking" ministry is now estimated to be 50,000, and growing rapidly. There are approximately 400,000 believers from the United States alone working overseas. What a potential for world evangelization! (Those desiring further information on tentmaking opportunities may contact those listed in Appendix 9-P.)

2. *Short-term workers.* Another rapidly growing trend is short-term work, where one can serve in an overseas missionary capacity for three months to two years. The number of short-term workers is now estimated to be 30,000 and growing rapidly. About 25% of the short-term workers become career missionaries. (For further information on short-term missionary service, see Appendix 9-Q.)

3. *Every believer reaching his "world."* Once the Gospel has initially penetrated a language-cultural entity, and a church is planted, the rest of that society will be evangelized by the national believers reaching "their world," their neighbors, their fellow factory or store workers, etc. So there is a sense in which every Christian becomes a part-time missionary, living for Jesus twenty-four hours a day, witnessing to his neighbors, leading his fellow employees to Christ, spending time going door-to-door with other believers, etc. In the final analysis, the world will be evangelized as every Christian evangelizes "his world." The Christians of the world need to be mobilized for effective, Spirit-led witnessing and soul winning.

The next two chapters are extremely important. They outline how the Great Commission can be fulfilled in this generation and how you can be involved.

17

HOW THE GREAT COMMISSION CAN BE FULFILLED IN THIS GENERATION

Ninety-four per cent still unsaved; over a **million dying each week, without Jesus;** three billion who have **never heard** the Gospel once; over 16,000 unreached people groups; over three thousand languages without one verse of Scripture: we are left with a staggering task. But **we can fulfill the Great Commission in this generation, by the year 2000, as we implement the following:**

1. The Great Commission will be fulfilled as revival comes to this earth; as God pours out His Spirit upon all mankind (Acts 2:17-21). (See Chapters 1-4.)
2. It will be fulfilled as the Church of the Lord Jesus Christ is fully restored to the purity, spiritual authority and power, purposes, principles and patterns, and fruitfulness of the Early Church. (See Chapters 5-11.)
3. It will be fulfilled as unity comes to the Body of Christ; as Christians learn to lay their lives down for one another (John 13:34-35), and as they begin to function as one body (John 17:20-23). (See Chapters 12 and 13.)
4. It will be fulfilled as all Christians experience the Spirit-filled, Spirit-empowered, Spirit-led life (Acts 1:8, Ephesians 5:18).
5. It will be fulfilled as all Christians become people of the Word: hearing (Luke 11:28), reading (Deuteronomy 17:18-20), studying (Acts 17:11), memorizing (Psalms 119:11), and meditating upon (Psalms 1:1-3), the Word; mastering it, and letting it master them (Matthew 7:13-27, James 1:22-24).

6. It will be fulfilled as all Christians become people of prayer (Luke 18:1, 1 Thessalonians 5:17, etc.).

7. It will be fulfilled as Christians everywhere are conformed to the image of Jesus Christ (Romans 8:28-29, 2 Corinthians 3:18).

8. It will be fulfilled as Christians grow up to maturity (Colossians 1:28, Ephesians 4:13-16).

9. It will be fulfilled as apostles, prophets, evangelists, pastors, and teachers give themselves to equipping and releasing the saints for their various ministries (1 Corinthians 12:4-7, Ephesians 4:11-16).

10. It will be fulfilled as the Church returns to a concept of evangelism that mobilizes every believer (Matthew 4:19, John 15:16), to witness by life and word (Acts 5:42), wherever he goes (Matthew 10:7-8, Acts 8:4), as a natural, normal part of daily life.

11. It will be fulfilled as Christian workers are trained on-the-job (as Jesus and Paul did: Philippians 4:9).

12. It will be fulfilled by the full utilization of both personal evangelism and mass evangelism.

13. It will be fulfilled as God confirms His Word with miracles (Mark 16:20, Acts 5:12).

14. It will be fulfilled as every Christian becomes a soul winner (Proverbs 11:30, Matthew 4:19).

15. It will be fulfilled as new Christians are adequately discipled (Matthew 28:20, 1 Thessalonians 2:7-12).

16. It will be fulfilled as Christians multiply themselves through the lives of others (Acts 15:36, 2 Timothy 2:2).

17. It will be fulfilled as Christians everywhere become more informed about missions.

18. It will be fulfilled as the body of Christ has an accurate, up-to-date picture of the task yet to be accomplished and the available resources.

19. It will be fulfilled as Christians live simpler lifestyles, thereby having more resources to contribute toward world evangelization.

20. It will be fulfilled as all Christians everywhere make the fulfillment of the Great Commission their primary purpose

in life; whether they are missionaries, business people, factory workers, farmers, or home-makers.

21. It will be fulfilled as the local church reaches out and takes the Gospel to its entire community.

22. It will be fulfilled as local churches become training sending bases for world evangelization.

23. It will be fulfilled as we study Church history and learn from the past.

24. It will be fulfilled as Christian leaders jointly plan strategies, thereby eliminating competition and duplication.

25. It will be fulfilled as Church movements (denominations) and para-church movements (interdenominational movements) learn to work together.

26. It will be fulfilled as the resident church and traveling ministries increasingly bless one another.

27. It will be fulfilled as we use the major amount of our resources (people, know-how, technology, finances, and prayer) in reaching the over 16,000 Muslim, Hindu, Buddhist, Chinese, and tribal unreached people groups.

28. It will be fulfilled by a final, massive mobilization of people, knowledge, technology, finances, and prayer for the specific purpose of completing the task.

29. It will be fulfilled as teams increasingly are involved in aggressive, pioneer evangelism and church planting.

30. It will be fulfilled as we reach the great cities of the world.

31. It will be fulfilled as we reach the students of the world.

32. It will be fulfilled by an accelerated ministry of Bible translation and distribution work.

33. It will be fulfilled as renewal comes to areas where there already exists a nominal Christian Church which needs awakening.

34. It will be fulfilled by an accelerated use of the media: telephone, radio, television, films, Gospel recordings, audio and video tapes, and the printed page.

35. It will be fulfilled as a congregation of obedient Christians is formed within every segment of society, i.e., within practical and cultural distance of every person on earth.

36. It will be fulfilled as we demonstrate the love of Christ to the neediest of the world.
37. It will be fulfilled as we penetrate with God's truth the seven basic areas of society: the home, the church, the educational system, the government, the media, the arts and entertainment, and business and industry.
38. It will be fulfilled as we get to know God better, learning of His love and faithfulness (Psalms 145:17, Lamentations 3:21-23, etc.).
39. It will be fulfilled as we do God's work God's way (John 15:5).
40. It will be fulfilled as God enables us to fulfill it, for his glory (John 17:4).

18

HOW CAN YOU GET INVOLVED

The fifth and final wave of world evangelism is gathering momentum. We can see the Great Commission fulfilled by the year 2000. God wants to use each of us in this glorious task. We all need to prepare ourselves. And we all need to become involved (John 9:4)!

You Need be Become Informed

You need to become informed about the great needs that exist and about the opportunities for service. In the Bibliography you will find a list of books about missions recommended for your study. Appendix 9-R gives a list of recommended periodicals for becoming a world Christian. Appendix 9 also gives a number of sources for additional information on the task and how to get involved.

You Need to Pray

Through prayer you can have a world-wide ministry! You can pray for the nations, for unreached people groups, for those who are laboring in various places, and for the Lord to raise up thousands of additional laborers (Matthew 9:38). You are especially encouraged to secure a copy of the book *Operation World*, which gives you details on how to pray for each nation. (Additional sources for prayer information are listed in Appendix 3.)

You Need to Give

It takes money to evangelize the world! Every worker, every piece of literature, every Bible, every Gospel recorder, every radio or television program, every missionary boat or plane costs money. And as the cost of everything escalates in our inflation-ridden world, so does the cost of world evangelization.

Most of the world's wealth is found in the Northern Hemisphere, while most of the poverty is in the Southern Hemisphere. The annual income of the average person in the Northern Hemisphere is over $6,500; in the Southern Hemisphere it is about $600. The United States, with about five per cent of the world's population, consumes over forty percent of the world's resources. Evangelicals in the United States earn $700 billion per year. Of this, they give $21 billion, or 3.0 percent, to the Church. Of that, $2.1 billion, or 0.3 % goes to missions; and, of that, $20 million, or 0.0029 per cent, goes to reach unreached peoples.[1]

The Christians of the world have an annual income of $6.5 trillion. How much more could the Christians of the world give if we really gave sacrificially? How much more would we give if we really believed that a million people were going into eternity each week without Jesus Christ? How much more would God have you to give? For suggestions on how to live more simply in order to have more to give to world evangelism, write The Creative Lifestyle Center, P.O. Box 504, Tacoma, Washington 98401. God will hold us accountable for how we use the resources that He has put at our disposal. May we be faithful, sacrificial stewards — for the sake of the evangelization of the world.

You May Want to Get More Training

As you prepare for short-term or long-term missionary service you may want to get further training. Appendix 9-S gives a list of possible places. But your best teacher is the Holy Spirit and the best textbook, the Bible. Ask God what He would have you to do.

God May Want You to Go

God may want you to become involved full-time in the work of world evangelization. This may involve going to another part of your nation — or another part of the world. Or He may want you to go in a tent-making capacity. Whatever it may be, He knows what is best for you. Your first step is to be willing to go. Isaiah said, "Here am I, send me!" (Isaiah 6:8). Then God can lead you. In Appendix 9 is a partial list of agencies that you may want to consider. What a privilege: to be led by God into the great harvest fields of the world; to be provided for by Him; to be used by Him; for His glory!

Mobilize Others For World Evangelization

As you become informed, begin to pray, give more sacrificially, get better prepared, and get more deeply involved in the evangelization of the world, you also need to mobilize others to do the same (2 Timothy 2:2).

PERSONAL ASSIGNMENT — WORLD EVANGELIZATION

Questions to Answer

1. What are three Scriptures that give the Great Commission?

2. What are the five waves of world evangelization?

3. Who is the "father of modern missions"?

Questions for Meditation and Application

1. Why did the early Church have such success at evangelism and how can that be applied today?

2. Describe the task yet remaining and some present-day encouraging trends.

3. How can the Great Commission be fulfilled in this generation?

Assignment

1. Begin to read several key books on missions. (See Bibliography for a list.)

2. Give yourself to God for the fulfilling of the Great Commission in this generation. Ask God what He would have you do.

PART V — PERSECUTION

"Then they will deliver you to tribulation, and will kill you, and you will be hated by all nations on account of My name."

— Matthew 24:9

"And he causes all, the small and the great, and the rich and the poor, and the free men and the slaves, to be given a mark on their right hand, or on their forehead, and he provides that no one shall be able to buy or to sell, except the one who has the mark, either the name of the beast or the number of his name."

— Revelation 13:16-17

"There is no doubt that global events are preparing the way for the final war of history — the great Armageddon! As the earthly time-clock ticks off each second and the world approaches midnight, this planet, according to the Bible, is going to be plunged into suffering too horrible to imagine or comprehend." [1]

— Billy Graham

"God has everything under control!" [2]

— David Wilkerson

19

END-TIME PERSECUTION

The first four sections of this book are exciting, considering the great things that God has done and will yet do: revival, restoration, unity, and world evangelization. This section will not be exciting to many. In fact, many Christians would like to dispense with the whole idea of end-time persecution; but persecution is clearly taught in the Bible as a part of God's plan.

Persecution in the Old Testament

Persecution is clearly taught in the Old Testament as a part of the life of one who walks with God (Psalm 37:32, 42:3, 94:5, 119:157, 142:6, 143:3, etc.). Also, it is taught in the New Testament as being part of the life of the Old Testament person who walked with God (Hebrews 11:25-27, 33-38). The prophets especially experienced much persecution (Jeremiah 2:30, Matthew 23:34-35, Luke 11:49-51, Acts 7:52, James 5:10, etc.). Consider the persecution that Job, Joseph, and Daniel experienced.

Persecution for the Christian

Persecution is an integral part of being a follower of Jesus (Matthew 5:10-12, 10:16-28, 13:21, 22:22-23; Mark 4:17, 10:30; Luke 6:22-23; John 15:18-20, 16:1-2, 17:14; Acts 7:57-59, 8:1-3, 11:19, 12:2-4, 14:22; Romans 8:17-18, 8:35; Galatians 6:12;

Philippians 1:29, 3:10; 1 Thessalonians 2:14; 2 Thessalonians 1:4; 2 Timothy 2:12, 3:12; Hebrews 13:13; James 1:2-4, 1:12; 1 Peter 2:20-23, 4:12-19; Revelation 1:9, 17:6). Peter's first letter is a manual on how to live under suffering and persecution. Those who are apostles are especially called to a life of persecution (Luke 11:49; Acts 4:3, 5:40-41, 9:16, 13:50, 14:19; 1 Corinthians 4:9-13; 2 Corinthians 4:5-18, 6:4-10, 11:23-27, 12:9-10; Galatians 6:17; Colossians 1:24; 2 Timothy 3:10-11).

End-Times

The Bible talks about a period of time in world history that it calls the "last days." This phrase is mentioned in Genesis 49:1, Isaiah 2:2, Micah 4:1, Acts 2:17, Hebrews 1:2, James 5:3, 2 Timothy 3:1, and 2 Peter 3:3-4. A similar phrase "end (or consummation) of the age" is mentioned in Daniel 8:17, 19, 9:26, 12:4, 9, 13; Matthew 10:22, 13:39, 40, 49, 24:3, 6, 13-14, 28:20; Mark 13:7, 13; Luke 21:9; 1 Corinthians 15:24, and 1 Peter 4:7. Other similar phrases such as "last time," "last day," and "last hour," appear in John 6:39, 40, 44, 54, 11:24, 12:48; James 5:3; 1 Peter 1:5, 20; 1 John 2:18; and Jude 18.[1]

Other passages of Scripture that tell us about "the last days" or "the end time" include Ezekiel 38-39, Daniel 2, 9-12, Matthew 24-25, Mark 13, Luke 17:20-18:8, Luke 21, 1 Corinthians 15:50-58, 1 Thessalonians 4-5, 2 Thessalonians 1-3, 2 Timothy 3, 2 Peter 3, Jude, and Revelation 4-22.

Jesus' Teaching on End-Time Persecution

Jesus' most extensive teaching on the end of the Age is recorded in Matthew 24-25, Mark 13, and Luke 21. (A detailed outline of these chapters is found in Appendix 10.) In His description of events that will take place on earth before the Great Tribulation, Jesus said:

Then they will deliver you to tribulation, and will kill you, and you will be hated by all nations on account of My Name. And at that time many will fall away and will betray one another and hate one another. And many false prophets will arise, and will mislead many. And because lawlessness is increased, most people's love will grow cold. But the one who endures to the end, it is he who shall be saved. And this gospel of the kingdom shall be preached in the whole world for a witness to all the nations, and then the end shall come. (Matthew 24:9-14)

But be on your guard; for they will deliver you to the courts and you will be flogged in the synagogues, and you will stand before governors and kings for My sake, as a testimony to them. And the gospel must first be preached to all the nations. And when they arrest you and deliver you up, do not be anxious beforehand about what you are to say, but say whatever is given you in that hour; for it is not you who speak, but it is the Holy Spirit. And brother will deliver brother to death, and a father his child; and children will rise up against parents and cause them to be put to death. And you will be hated by all on account of My name, but the one who endure to the end will be saved. (Mark 13:9-13)

But before all these things, they will lay their hands on you and will persecute you, delivering you to the synagogues and prisons, bringing you before kings and governors for My name's sake. It will lead to an opportunity for your testimony. So make up your minds not to prepare beforehand to defend yourselves; for I will give you utterance and wisdom which none of your opponents will be able to resist or refute. But you will be betrayed even by parents and brothers and relatives and friends, and they will put some of you to death, and you will be hated by all on account of My name. Yet not a hair of your head will perish. By your perseverence you will win your souls. (Luke 21:12-19)

This sounds like pretty severe persecution of Christians — and it is before the Great Tribulation. So there will be a time of distress, pressure, hardship, suffering, persecution that will lead up to the Great Tribulation.

Jesus goes on to say that there will be even worse persecution during the Great Tribulation as recorded in Matthew 24:15-24, Mark 13:14-23, and Luke 21:20-24. This will be a time of such severe hardship, suffering, and persecution that no one would live through it, except it be shortened "for the sake of the elect."

Some teach that the Church will be raptured, or caught up from the earth to the heavens, to be with Jesus, before the Great Tribulation; some teach that the Church will go part way through the Tribulation;

some teach that the Church will not be caught away until the end of the Great Tribulation; and some don't have an opinion. This book does not take a stand on the question of when the rapture will occur. This author believes that there is severe persecution ahead for Christians world-wide. We need to be ready to be caught up to be with Jesus at any moment. We also need to be ready to face severe persecution.

Persecution Already a Reality in Many Parts of the World

While the Christians of North America, for the most part, are living self-centered lives of ease, materialism, and pleasure, and waiting for the rapture, many of our brothers and sisters in Christ around the world are experiencing hunger, homelessness, and intense persecution. As Corrie ten Boom once stated:

I have been in countries where the saints are already suffering terrible persecution. In China the Christians were told, 'Don't worry, before the tribulation comes, you will be translated — raptured.' Then came a terrible persecution. Millions of Christians were tortured to death. Later I heard a Bishop from China say, sadly, 'We have failed. We should have made the people strong for persecution rather than telling them Jesus would come first.' Turning to me he said, 'You will have time. Tell the people how to be strong in times of persecution, how to stand when the tribulation comes —to stand and not faint.' " [2]

How do we tell the Christians of China, Russia, eastern Europe, many parts of Africa, Afghanistan, southeast Asia, the Middle East, and parts of Central and South America that there will be no end-time persecution? They are already experiencing it; some have for over sixty years!

Trends Leading to World-Wide Anxiety and the Persecution of Christians

The Bible says that the day is coming when there will be "dismay among nations, in perplexity . . . men fainting from fear" (Luke 21:25-26). There are world trends today that are surely leading this planet toward a time of increased dismay and perplexity; a time of unsolvable problems; a time of hardship and difficulty; and a time of

215

world-wide persecution of Christians. Let's take a look at some of these trends.

Population Trends

The population explosion and move toward urbanization was described in Chapter 16. It is the most severe in the already over-populated areas of Asia, Africa, and Latin America. With this population growth and move to the cities, there are growing problems of food supply, water pollution, traffic congestion, shortage of housing, noise pollution, and psychological problems resulting from the sheer numbers of people.

Ecological Trends

Today we see nature and weather increasingly out of control: changing temperature patterns, tornadoes, floods, earthquakes, volcanoes, typhoons, and hurricanes. We are also running out of tillable, fertile land; clean, drinkable water; clean air to breathe; fuel; and a number of natural resources. Much of this will increasingly affect the food supply, which will lead to great turmoil.

Trend toward a Computer-Based Society

The innovations in electronics, computers, and communication satellites are changing forever the way people live; instant communications, electronic banking, work-at-home by computer, robot industries, pilotless vehicles, etc. It also paves the way for the possibility of the total control of information, communications, food, natural resources, money, and all of life, and for a world dictator.

Multi-Choice Trend

Everything is happening so fast! Before A.D. 1500 there were about a thousand new books being written each year. Now there are about two thousand per day! Ninety percent of all scientists who have ever lived are alive today. It is difficult to keep up in one's profession. There are so many choices to choose from, ranging from breakfast cereals to automobiles. The pace of everything is quickening. Nothing is permanent any longer. All of this has tremendous psychological effects.

Decline of Morals Trend

Abortion, homosexuality, adultery, pornography, rape, sodomy, murder, burglary, gambling, lying, cheating, alcohol and drug use, and abuse of children and the elderly: this is a description of today's society. These practices cause a breakdown in interpersonal relations, the family, and all of society, and will certainly bring God's judgment upon us.

Economic Trends

We are living in times of world-wide economic instability and uncertainty characterized by rising taxes, unemployment, declining value of money, runaway debt, inflation, and a growing number of bankruptcies. There is also the trend toward a computerized, cashless economy. All of this will eventually lead to a world-wide financial crisis resulting in the installation of a one-world, electronic monetary system.

Political Trends

International Communism continues to spread its influence, although there are also a few signs of losses. The world's problems are great: wars, terrorism, famine, the arms race, human injustices, inequities and shortages in resources; on the list could go. Mankind increasingly looks to government for answers to its problems with increased government control and a one-world government seen as the ultimate answer.

Religious Trends

There is today the growth of false religions: false Messiahs, Islam, atheistic Communism, humanism, devil worship, witchcraft, ancestral worship, the occult, and the cults. There is also the trend toward a one-world super-church. Praise God, there is also the growing trend toward a revived, restored New Testament Christianity.

Conclusion

What's ahead? Where will the present trends lead us? The world will become increasingly chaotic. In order to try to deal with the world's problems, a one-world political, economic, information, communications, religious system will develop (Revelation 13).

Christians cannot be part of this system (Revelation 14:9-12). In the midst of all this, a revived, restored New Testament Christianity will develop. It will be a very difficult time to be alive (Matthew 24:5-22). But glorious!

217

20

PREPAREDNESS

Jesus said that the day is coming when Christians will be killed and "hated by all nations on account of My name" (Mathew 24:9). He is coming back soon for His Bride. John tells us that a day is coming when "no one should be able to buy or to sell, except the one who has the mark" (Revelation 13:7). There is a growing conviction that all of this could come to pass in the near future. What should Christians do to prepare?

Spiritual Preparedness

God, in His Word, tells us what our attitude and lifestyle should be in view of the soon possibility of Jesus' return, persecution, and hard times.

1. Settle in your heart that you will be persecuted (Matthew 5:10-12, 24:9, Mark 13:9, Luke 6:22-23, Luke 21:12, John 15:18-20, Phillipians 1:29, 2 Timothy 3:12, 1 Peter 2:20-23).
2. Be assured of God's promises to protect and deliver (Deuteronomy 30:7, Psalm 23, 31:15, 63:9-11; 91, 109, 129; Isaiah 51:12-13; Jeremiah 17:17-18, 20:11; John 16:33 2 Thessalonians 3:3, 2 Timothy 2:12)
3. Develop the habit of meditating upon God's Word (Psalm 91; 119:78, 95, 157, 165; John 15:20, 16:1, 2 Timothy 3:13-17).

4. Learn to rejoice at the privilege of being persecuted (Matthew 5:12, Luke 6:23, Acts 5:41, James 1:2, 1 Peter 4:13-16).

5. Learn to not resist your enemy and persecutor (Matthew 5:38-42, Luke 6:29-31).

6. Learn to love, forgive, bless and pray for your enemy and persecutor (Matthew 5:44-48, Luke 6:27-38, Luke 23:34, Acts 7:60, Romans 12:17-21, 1 Peter 3:8-12).

7. Develop a discerning spirit so that you will not be misled or deceived (Matthew 24:4-5, Mark 13:5-6, Luke 21:8, 2 Thessalonians 2:3, 10-12).

8. Do not be fearful or frightened (Matthew 10:19, 24:6, 26-33; Mark 13:7; Luke 21:9; 2 Thessalonians 2:2; 1 Peter 5:7).

9. Be assured that the Holy Spirit will give you the right words when you need them (Matthew 10:19-20, Mark 13:11, Luke 21:14-15).

10. Be busy evangelizing the world (Matthew 24:14, Mark 13:10).

11. Be patient and persevering to the end (Matthew 24:13, Mark 13:13, Luke 21:19, 2 Thessalonians 1:4, 2 Timothy 3:10, James 5:7-11).

12. Be prepared to flee and travel light (Matthew 10:23, 24:16-20; Mark 13:14-18; Luke 21:21-28).

13. Be informed (Matthew 24:25, 33; Mark 13:23, 29; 1 Thessalonians 4:13).

14. Be on the alert (Matthew 24:42, 25:13; Mark 13:9, 23, 33-37; Luke 21:34; 1 Thessalonians 5:1-6; 1 Peter 5:8).

15. Be prayerful (Mark 13:33).

16. Do not be weighed down by giddiness, drunkenness, and worldly concern (Luke 21:34, 1 Thessalonians 5:6-7).

17. Be ready (Matthew 24:44, Mark 13:35-37, Luke 21:36).

18. Be a diligent, faithful soldier of Christ (Matthew 24:45-25:30, Luke 19:13-26).

19. Lift up your head in an attitude of anticipation (Luke 21:28, 2 Peter 3:12-13).

20. Be wise and cautious (Matthew 10:16-17).

21. Be assured that nothing can separate you from God's love (Romans 8:31-39).

22. Be content and assured of God's grace (2 Corinthians 12:8-10).
23. Learn to encourage one another (1 Thessalonians 4:18, 5:11, Hebrews 10:23-25).
24. Be people of faith, love, and hope (1 Thessalonians 5:8, 2 Timothy 3:10, 1 Peter 4:8-10).
25. Be spiritually strong (2 Thessalonians 2:15).
26. Live a disciplined life (2 Thessalonians 3:6-13, 1 Peter 4:1-7).
27. Discipline the unruly (2 Thessalonians 3:6-15).
28. Live holy lives (1 Peter 1:13-19; 2 Peter 3:11; Revelation 22:11).
29. Live submissive lives (1 Peter 2:13-3:7, 5:5-6).
30. Have an undefiled conscience (1 Peter 3:15-22).
31. Keep yourself built up in the love of God (Jude 20-21).

Based on other Biblical teaching, the following additional suggestions are offered:

1. Be an overcomer. Learn to live a life of victory: victory over sin, the devil, circumstances, people, everything!
2. Be filled with the Holy Spirit. Be initially and continually filled with the Holy Spirit. Learn to be led by the Spirit. Live a life of purity and power.
3. Memorize God's Word. Get chapters of God's Word hidden in your heart. If your Bible is taken away, you will still have God's Word with you. Memorize Psalms 3, 4, 23, 46, 91, and other chapters of praise, promise, and assurance.
4. Learn to hear and obey God's voice.
5. Give everything to Jesus. Be a person who, in his heart, has no rights or possessions.
6. Become a person of prayer.
7. Learn to forgive and love everyone.
8. Learn how to do battle with the devil and his demons.
9. Develop a quiet, discerning spirit.
10. Do not fear. Learn to resist every thought of fear and worry.

11. Develop deep, caring relationships with a select group of Christians. Let God show you who they should be.
12. Live supernaturally. Learn to trust God to supply your every need by His great power and abundance.
13. Learn to accept persecution joyfully.
14. Completely die to self — then you will no longer fear death.

Physical Preparedness

A day is coming when one cannot buy or sell without the mark of the beast (Revelation 13:16-18). The elect (Gentile and Jewish Christians going through the Great Tribulation or Gentile and Jewish Christians who are converted during the Great Tribulation, depending on your view) cannot accept this mark (Revelation 14:9-12). They will not be able to live in dependence upon the world system. They will live (1) by providing for themselves, (2) by sharing with other Christians, and (3) by God's supernatural supply.

So, should Christians prepare now for what may lie ahead? Joseph did (Genesis 37-50); and you should, too, as God leads. The important thing is that you be led by the Holy Spirit. Here are some things that you might seek the Lord about:

1. Learn to live more simply.
2. Get out of debt.
3. Get rid of credit cards.
4. Own your own land.
5. Own your own home.
6. Have your own source of heat, light, and electricity.
7. Have your own food and water source and storage.
8. Be able to make your own clothes.
9. Have a means of travel without fuel (horse, bicycle, boat, etc.).
10. Have a supply of basic medicines.
11. Have a way to pay taxes.
12. Be prepared for a nuclear war.

13. Have a supply of gold and silver and extra tools and seeds for bartering.
14. Have a supply of extra Bibles.
15. Begin to move in the direction of the church meeting in homes.
16. Have your own printing press for printing Christian literature.
17. Be ready to minister to those in need (Matthew 25:31-46).

Further information on various facts of physical preparedness can be found in the Bibliography.

God Has Everything Under Control

Do all that you can to be prepared spiritually, and do what God shows you to do to be prepared physically. Most importantly, be assured that God has everything under control. So, rest in Him!

PERSONAL ASSIGNMENT — PERSECUTION

Questions to Answer

1. What are the four chapters in the Gospels that record Jesus' teaching on end times?

2. What are three trends in society today that could lead to end-time persecution?

3. What are three things that should characterize our attitude and approach to life as Christians living in end times?

Questions for Meditation and Application

1. Is persecution a possibility for you during your lifetime?

2. How do you think end-time persecution will come to you?

3. Are you prepared for end-time persecution? If your answer is "no," what should you do to become prepared?

Assignment

1. To get a Biblical perspective of end times, meditate on Matthew 24-25, Mark 13, Luke 21, 1 Thessalonians 4-5, 2 Thessalonians, 2 Timothy 3, 1 Peter, 2 Peter 3, Jude, and Revelation.

2. Prepare yourself spiritually for end-time persecution.

3. Ask God what you should do to prepare physically for the possibility of end-times hardship and persecution.

EPILOGUE

Each of these five characteristics of the Church triumphant at the end of the Age — revival, restoration, unity, world evangelization, and persecution — will affect and enhance the others. The **revival** will further the restoration, further the process of unity, greatly accelerate the evangelization of the world, and help to bring on persecution. The **restoration** will provide new wine skins, which will encourage the revival to continue; it will enhance unity; provide new channels for world evangelization; and will result in a Church better prepared to go through persecution. Great **unity** in the Body of Christ will further the revival, enhance the restoration, greatly accelerate world evangelization; and both bring on, and be preparation for, persecution. **World evangelization** will prolong and increase the revival, enhance the restoration, further unity, and help bring on persecution (the devil hates world evangelization!). **Persecution** will increase revival, help to complete the restoration, enhance unity, and further the evangelization of the world.

I can see it all now. There will soon be a mighty, world-wide, end-time revival, when God will pour out His Spirit on all mankind (every person); bringing new life, purity, and power to His Church; and conviction of sin upon the lost. God's people will be fully restored to all that is part of Bible Christianity: the purity, spiritual authority and power, purposes, principles and patterns, and fruitfulness of the Early Church. Great unity will come to the Body of Christ: God's true followers will function as one, in every location, and world-wide. The Gospel will be taken to every person on earth and multitudes will turn to the Lord Jesus Christ. But all of this will occur in the context of growing persecution. What a glorious time it will be! As Arthur Wallis recently wrote:

> "God will conclude this Age as He commenced it. Great power and glory in the Church, great victories over Satan, but in the context of great persecution and opposition. But the difference will be that what was then confined to one small corner of the globe will in the end be world-wide. I believe that the greatest chapters of the Church's long history have yet to be written, and that it will be said of the generation that brings back the King, 'This was their finest hour.' " [1]

Hallelujah! Make us ready, Lord Jesus, for Your final move. We want to be Your ready army. We know the devil is defeated. We want to see You glorified. All glory, honor, power, and praise belongs to You! Amen.

APPENDIX 1

SCRIPTURES CONTAINING THE WORD "REVIVAL"

Bible Reference	English Trans.	Quotation — New American Standard Bible
Genesis 45:27	chayah	"When they told him all the words of Joseph....the spirit of their father, Jacob, revived."
Judges 15:19	chayah	"When he drank (the water), his strength returned and he revived."
1 Samuel 30:12	shub	"... and he ate; then his spirit revived. For he had not eaten bread or drunk water for three days and three nights."
1 Kings 17:22	chayah	"And the Lord heard the voice of Elijah, and the life of the child returned to him and he revived."
2 Kings 13:21	chayah	"...And when the (dead) man touched the bones of Elisha he revived and stood up on his feet."
Ezra 9:8	michyah	"But now for a brief moment grace has been shown from the Lord our God, to leave us an escaped remnant and to give us a peg in His holy place, that our God may enlighten our eyes and grant us a little reviving in our bondage."
Ezra 9:9	michyah	"For we are slaves; yet in our bondage, our God has not forsaken us, but has extended lovingkindness to us in the

		sight of the kings of Persia, to give us reviving to raise up the house of our God, to restore its ruins, and to give us a wall in Judah and Jerusalem."
Nehemiah 4:2	chayah	"Can they (the Jews) revive the stones from the dusty rubble even the burned ones?"
Psalm 69:32	chayah	"You who seek God, let your heart revive."
Psalm 71:20	chayah	"Thou, who hast shown me many troubles and distresses, wilt revive me again, and wilt bring me up again from the depths of the earth."
Psalm 80:18	chayah	"Revive us, and we will call upon Thy name."
Psalm 85:6	chayah	"Wilt Thou not Thyself revive us again, that Thy people may rejoice in Thee?"
Psalm 119:25	chayah	"Revive me according to Thy word."
Psalm 119:37	chayah	"Turn away my eyes from looking at vanity, and revive me in Thy ways."
Psalm 119:40	chayah	"Revive me through Thy righteousness."
Psalm 119:50	chayah	"This is my comfort in my affliction, that Thy word has revived me."
Psalm 119:88	chayah	"Revive me according to Thy loving-kindness."
Psalm 119:93	chayah	"I will never forget Thy precepts, for by them Thou has revived me."
Psalm 119:107	chayah	"I am exceedingly afflicted; revive me, O Lord, according to Thy word."
Psalm 119:149	chayah	"Hear my voice according to Thy loving-kindness; revive me, O Lord, according to Thine ordinances."

Psalm 119:154	chayah	"Plead my cause and reedem me; revive me according to Thy word."
Psalm 119:156	chayah	"Great are Thy mercies, O Lord; revive me according to Thine ordinances."
Psalm 119:159	chayah	"Consider how I love Thy precepts; revive me, O Lord, according to Thy lovingkindness."
Psalm 138:7	chayah	"Though I walk in the midst of trouble, Thou wilt revive me."
Psalm 143:11	chayah	"For the sake of Thy name, O Lord, revive me. In Thy righteousness bring my soul out of trouble."
Isaiah 57:15	chayah	" . . . I dwell on a high and holy place and also with the contrite and lowly of spirit in order to revive the spirit of the lowly and . . . "
Isaiah 57:15	chayah	"and to revive the heart of the contrite."
Hosea 6:2	chayah	"He will revive us after two days;"
Habakkuk 3:2	chayah	"O Lord, revive Your work in the midst of the years!"
Philippians 4:10	anathallo	"You have revived your concern for me . . .

Quotation — King
James Bible

Romans 7:9	ana zao	"I was alive without the Law once, but when the commandment came, sin revived, and I died."
Romans 14:9	zao	"For to this end Christ both died, and rose, and revived, that He might be Lord both of the dead and living."

229

APPENDIX 2 — TOPICS FOR PRAYER SESSIONS

1. Prayer of confession	Psalm 51:1-19
2. My personal prayer	Psalm 139:23-24
3. God's formula for revival	2 Chronicles 7:14
4. Nehemiah's prayer	Nehemiah 1:1-11
5. Prayer and confession of Ezra	Ezra 9:5-15
6. Jehoshaphat's prayer	2 Chronicles 20:3-25
7. Revival under Hezekiah	2 Chronicles 29:3-36
8. The fire of the Lord fell	1 Kings 18:20-41
9. Prevailing prayer	Genesis 18:23-33
10. Teach us to pray	Luke 11:1-13
11. Praying and not fainting	Luke 18:1-14
12. Instant and earnest prayer	Acts 12:1-19
13. If two of you agree	Matthew 28:19-20
14. Boldly to the throne	Hebrews 4:14-16
15. The prayer of faith	Mark 11:22-26
16. Effective fervent prayer	James 5:16-18
17. Our personal responsibility	Ezekiel 33:1-11
18. The whitened harvest fields	John 4:5-39
19. Sleeping disciples	Matthew 26:36-46
20. Launch out into the deep	Luke 5:1-11
21. Feeding the multitudes	Mark 6:30-44
22. Helping our neighbors	Luke 10:25-37
23. Fruit bearing	John 15:1-19
24. The Holy Spirit	John 16:5-15
25. Our need of power	Acts 2:1-21
26. The Spirit-filled life	Ephesians 5:1-20
27. Our equipment	Ephesians 6:10-18
28. Our dedication to Him	Romans 12:1-21
29. Fellowship with Him	1 John 1:1-10
30. Praise and thanksgiving	Psalm 103:1-22

Taken from Revival Prayer Groups, I.H.C. Heritage House, Salem, OH 44460.

APPENDIX 3 — SOURCES FOR PRAYER INFORMATION

Bibleless Peoples Prayer Project, Wycliffe Bible Translators, Huntington Beach, CA 92647

Block Prayer, Mrs. Wendy Bolton, 32 McKenzie St., Cambridge, Ontario, Canada N1R-4E1

Burning Bush, P.O. Box 31116, Amarillo, Texas 79120

Canadian Prayer Fellowship, c/o Rev. Robert Birch, Burnaby Christian Fellowship, 549 Mac Pherson Avenue, Burnaby, B.C. V5J-4N8

Change the World Ministries, P.O. Box 5838, Mission Hills, CA 91345

Concerned Women for America, P.O. Box 5100, San Diego, CA 92105

Dawson, Joy (Mrs.), YWAM, P.O. Box 591, Tujunga, CA 91042

Global Prayer Digest, Frontier Fellowship, P.O. Box 90970, Pasadena, CA 91109

Great Commission Prayer Crusade, Campus Crusade for Christ, Arrowhead Springs, San Bernardino, CA 92414

Intercessors, The, Lincoln, VA 22078

Intercessors for America, P.O. Box 2639, Reston, VA 22090

International Intercessors, Box O, Pasadena, CA 91109

International Prayer Ministries, P.O. Box 888-850, Atlanta, Ga 30356

Dr. Larry Lea, Church on the Rock, P.O. Box 880, Rockwall, TX 75087

Lydia Fellowship International, P.O. Box 20236, San Jose, CA 95106

National Prayer Committee, P.O. Box 6826, San Bernadino, CA 92412

"Prayer Fuel," Christian Literature Crusade, Fort Washington, PA 19034

"Prayerline" Booklet, Christian Aid, Rt. 1, Box 1, Charlottesville, VA 22901

Satellite Prayer Network, Maranatha Ministries, P.O. Box 1799, Gainesville, FL 32602

"Soviet Prayer Guide," Issachar, P.O. Box 30727, Seattle, WA 98103

The Lord's Handmaidens, 311 Fife Heights Dr. E., Tacoma, WA 98424

Wesley Duewel prayer retreats, OMS International, Greenwood, IN 46142

"World Vision Magazine," 919. W. Huntington Dr., Monrovia, CA 91016.

You will find the following aids helpful as you move into a deeper ministry of intercession:

1. *Global Prayer Digest.* Available from Frontier Fellowship, P.O. Box 90970, Pasadena, CA 91109. Telephone (818) 797-1111. Gives daily prayer items for unreached peoples.
2. *Operation World* by P.J. Johnstone. Available from your local bookstore or from William Carey Library Publishers, P.O. 40129, Pasadena, CA *91104. Telephone (818) 798-0819. Gives prayer information for every country.*
3. *Prayer for Those Who Influence Your Family.* Great Commission Prayer Crusade, CCC, Arrowhead Springs, San Bernardino, CA 92414, 1980.
4. *Prayer Map.* Available from Change the World Ministries, P.O. Box 5838, Mission Hills, CA 91345. Telephone (818)782-1216. Covers the world in prayer in a year.
5. *Principles for Effective Intercession* by Joy Dawson. Available from Youth With A Mission, P.O. Box 296, Sunland, CA 91040-0296. Telephone (818) 896-2755. Tells how to move into a time of effective intercession.
6. *YWAM Prayer Diary.* Available from Youth With A Mission, P.O. Box 1380, Lindale, TX 75711. Telephone (800) 922-2143. Covers the world in prayer in a year.

APPENDIX 4 — ORGANIZATIONS SPECIALIZING IN REVIVAL

Bibles for the World, 1300 Crescent St., Box 805, Wheaton, IL 60187. An excellent leaflet, *Heart Searching for Prayer Preparation and Personal Revival*, available.

Canadian Revival Fellowship, Box 584, Regina, Sask., Canada S4P 3A3

Coalition on Revival, 89 Pioneer Way, Mountain View, CA 94041

Concerts of Prayer, Inter-Varsity Missions, P.O. Box 7895, Madison, WI 53707

David Wilkerson Crusades, P.O. Box 260, Lindale, TX 75771

Fullness Magazine, P.O. Box 79350, Fort Worth, TX 76179

Herald of His Coming, Box 3457, Terminal Annex, Los Angeles, CA 90051

Hour of Revival, 13 Lismore Rd., Eastbourne, Sussex, England

International Intercessors, Box O, Pasadena, CA 91109. Armin Gesswein's articles on prayer and revival available.

International Awakening Ministries, P.O. Box 21, Wheaton, IL 60187

James Robison, P.O. Box 18489, Fort Worth, TX 76118

Last Days Ministries, Box 40, Lindale, TX 75771. Reprints of writings by Charles G. Finney are available.

League of Prayer, P.O. Box 4038, Montgomery, AL 36104

Mario Murrillo Ministries, P.O. Box 9804, Calabasas, CA 91302

Ministers' Prayer Fellowship, Box 5246, Hacienda Heights, CA 91745

Office of Spiritual Awakening, Home Mission Board, Southern Baptist Convention, 1350 Spring Street, N.W., Atlanta, GA 30367

Prayer Summit, P.O. Box 1940, Fallbrook, CA 92028

Rev. Leonard Ravenhill, Rt. 1, Box 102-C, Lindale, TX 78155

Renewal Ministries, YWAM, 133 C St. SE, Washington, DC 20003

Revival Fellowship, 2200 E. Colorado Blvd., Pasadena, CA 91107-3683

Richard Simmons Ministries, P.O. Box 4151, Bellingham, WA 98227

Prepare Ye The Way Ministries, Box 67, Elizabethtown, PA 17022

APPENDIX 5 — WHO GOD IS IN EACH BOOK OF THE BIBLE

References	Who God Is
Genesis 1	He is the Creator of all.
Exodus 3:6-14	I AM WHO I AM
Leviticus 16:2-3, 6	He is the Holy God who requires an atonement for sin.
Deuteronomy 8	He is a covenant-keeping God.
Joshua 6	He is the One who gives victory to His people.
Judges 6:34, 11:29, 13:24-25 14:6, 19, 15:14	He is the One who does exploits through His people by the Holy Spirit (even in the Old Testament!)
Ruth 2:11-12	The One who is mindful of us in every circumstance of life.
1 Samuel 3:8-11, 19-20	The One who speaks to us.
2 Samuel 11:2-4, 26-27, 12:1-14	He's the One who knows our every secret sin.
1 Kings 18:16-24, 33-39	The One who will prove Himself when it is needful.
2 Kings 24:1-4	The One who will judge and destroy a nation that continues to turn its back on Him.
1 Chronicles 29:10-13	He is a great God.
2 Chronicles 7:14	He is a God who hears, forgives, and heals.
Ezra 1:1-4	He is the One who uses even unsaved rulers to accomplish His purposes.
Nehemiah 1:4-11	He is the One who hears and answers prayer.
Esther 2:17, 4:14-16	He is the One who will use a little maiden girl to accomplish His purposes.
Job 42:1-6	He is the One who can not be known intellectually — but must be known by revelation and experience.
Psalm 23	He is our Shepherd.

Proverbs 3:33	He is the One who blesses the righteous.
Ecclesiastes 12:13-14	He is the One who is to be obeyed and respected.
Song of Sol. 2:4, 4:16b	He is our Lover. 6:3, 7:10
Isaiah 53	He is the One who came and died for us to provide wholeness for us.
Jeremiah 32:17, 33:2-3	He is the One who can do all things.
Lamentations 3:21-23	He is a merciful and faithful God.
Ezekiel 34:11-16	He is the One who will shepherd His sheep.
Daniel 3:16-19, 24-30, 6:3-28	He is the One who delivers those who put their trust in Him and are faithful to Him.
Hosea 6:1-3	He is the God of the second chance.
Joel 2:23-32	He is the God who sends revival or Who pours out His Spirit.
Amos 9:9-15	He is the one who watches over Israel.
Obadiah 15	He is the One who judges the nations.
Jonah 3	He is the One who will change His mind when men repent.
Micah 5:2	He is the God who causes things to happen according to His Divine plan.
Nahum 1:1-8	He is a God of wrath.
Habakkuk 3:17-18	He is the One who is to be praised regardless of circumstances.
Zeph. 1:14-15, 3:14-20	He is the God of ultimate victory.
Haggai 2:3-9	He is the God of restoration —greater than before.
Zechariah 12:10, 14:4, 14:16	He is the Jew's Messiah, and the King of the whole earth.
Malachi 3:7-12	The One that won't be out-given.
New Testament	**Who God is**
Matthew 1:21	He is the One who came to save us from our sins.
Mark 16:15	He is the One who has given us a commission.
Luke 8:35-56	He is the miracle worker.
John 3:15-17	He is the One who gives eternal life.

Acts 1:4-8, 2:1-4, 38-39	He is the One who sends the Holy Spirit.
Romans 6:23, 11:22-27, 33-36	He is the One who has a plan of redemption for Jew and Gentile.
1 Corinthians 1:26-31, 12:4-11, 13:4-8a	He is the One who uses the weak to confound the wise.
2 Corinthians 2:14, 4:7, 8:9, 9:8, 12:9-10	He is the God of abundant grace.
Galatians 3:24-29	He is the One who cancels our sins because of our faith in Jesus Christ.
Ephesians 1:10, 18-23	He is the One Who is far above all.
Philippians 2:5-11	He is the One Who chose to humble Himself —but He has been highly exalted.
Colossians 1:15-20	He is the One for whom all things exist.
1 Thessalonians 4:13-18	He is the One Who is coming again.
2 Thessalonians 1:4-9, 2:8-12	He is the One Who is coming to make all things right.
1 Timothy 1:17, 6:15-16	He is the great King.
2 Timothy 2:12-13, 4:7-8	He is the righteous Judge.
Titus 1:3, 2:10, 13 3:4-6	He is God our Saviour.
Philemon 8-9	He is the One who helps us to be forthright with each other — in love.
Hebrews 11:1-6	He is the One we are to put our trust (faith) in.
James 1:17	He is the One who is unchanging.
1 Peter 2:20-24	He is the One who suffered, giving us an example.
2 Peter 2:4-9	He is the righteous Judge.
1 John 4:10	He is the One who loves us.
2 John 2-3	He is the God of all truth.
3 John 3-7	He is the One in whose Name we go.
Jude 24	He is the One who is able to keep you from stumbling
Revelation 1:5, 4:8-11, 5:8-14, 7:10-12, 11:15-17, 15:3-4, 19:1-7, 19:11-16	He is the reigning King Who is to be worshipped.

236

APPENDIX 6 — CHRISTIAN LEGAL ORGANIZATIONS

Christian Conciliation Service
1700 Alhambra Blvd.,
Suite 108
Sacramento, CA 95816

Utilizes Biblical peacemaking
procedures as an alternative
to legal
disputes among Christians.

Christian Legal Fellowship
60 Bowden St.
Toronto, Ont. M4K 2X4 Canada

Christian Legal Society
P.O. Box 1492
Maryfield, VA 22116

Concerned Women for American
Education & Legal Defense
Foundation
122 "C" St., NW, Suite 800
Washington, D.C. 20001

Dave Haigler, Attorney
Lexacomp., Inc.
P.O. Box 61782
Dallas, TX 75261-0782

Mr. Haigler contributes a
regular column, "Casenotes,"
to Counsel of Chalcedon,
3032 Hacienda Court, Marietta,
GA 30066

International Movement of Roman
Catholic Lawyers
315 E. 47th St.
New York, NY 10017

Law School
CBN University
Virginia Beach, VA 23463

National Christian Center
133 "C" Street SE
Washington, D.C. 20003

Legal liaison concerning
religious freedom.

Creation Science Legal Defense
Fund
P.O. Box 1238
Little Rock, AR 72203

Established to seek legislation and
court rulings mandating that public
schools give unbiased treatment to the
creation and evolution theories of
origins.

Christian Civil Liberties Union c/o Simon Greenleaf School of Law, 3855 E. La Palma Anaheim, CA 92807	To represent Christians in civil liberties cases.
The Christian Law Association P.O. Box 30290 Cleveland, OH 44130	Publishes information on cases handled by the law firm of David C. Gibbs and Charles Craze. Also, the association sponsors annual Biblical Legal Seminars.
The Rutherford Institute P.O. Box 510 Manassas, VA 22110-9990	The foundation's purpose is to establish a network of lawyers who can handle First Amendment (freedom of religion) cases when they arise.
Simon Greenleaf School of Law 3855 La Palma Avenue Anaheim, CA 92807	A law school from a Christian perspective. Graduate program in human rights.
William A. Owen, Director The Christian Legal Defense and Education Foundation P.O. Box 41209 Jacksonville, FL 32203-1209	Publishes monthly newsletter.

APPENDIX 7 — TRANSLATION AND USE OF THE GREEK WORD "EKKLESIA" IN THE ENGLISH BIBLE

Summary

How Translated	No. of Times	How Used	Denoted in Study
Assembly	3	An assembly of people other than Christians	—
Congregation	2	An assembly of the children of Israel	—
Church(es)	13	Church universal	1
109 times total	30	All the believers in a given city, seen as a unit	2
	17	A group of believers who met together	3
	37	Groups of believers across a wide area	4
	9	Believers in general	5
	3	None of the above	6
	114		

Ref.	Trans.	Immediate Context	How Used	Denoted
Matthew				
16:18	Church	I will rebuild My Church	Talking about all believers during Church Age	1
18:17	Church	Tell it to the Church	A group of believers	3
18:17	Church	Refuses to listen even to the Church	The same group of believers	3
Acts				
5:11	Church	Great fear came upon the whole Church	All of the believers in Jerusalem who were gathered together	2,3
7:38	Cong.	In the congregation-the children of Israel gathered at Mt. Sinai		
8:1	Church	A great persecution rose against the Church in Jerusalem	All the believers in Jerusalem in general	2
8:3	Church	Saul began ravaging the Church, entering house after house	Some of the believers in Jerusalem in their homes	6
9:31	Church	So the church throughout all Judea and Galilee and Samaria	All the believers in three provinces	4
11:22	Church	The church at Jerusalem, and they sent Barnabas	All the believers in Jerusalem functioning as one body	2
11:26	Church	They met with the Church, and taught considerable multitudes	All the believers in Antioch, considered as a unit	2
12:1	Church	Herod..laid hands on some who belonged to the Church	Some believers who were part of the believers in general	6

Ref.	Trans.	Immediate Context	How Used	Denoted
12:5	Church	Prayer...was being made fervently by the Church of God	All, or a group of, believers in Jerusalem	3
13:1	Church	At Antioch, in the Church that was there	All the believers at Antioch, functioning as a unit	2
14:23	Church	Appointed elders for them in every Church	The believers in Lystra, Iconium, and Antioch	2
14:27	Church	Gathered the Church together	All the believers of Antioch gathered together	2,3
15:3	Church	Being sent on their way by the Church	The believers of Antioch functioning as a body	2
15:4	Church	They were received by the Church and apostles and elders	Refers to the believers of Jerusalem in general	2
15:22	Church	It seemed good to the apostles and the elders, with the whole Church	All the believers in Jerusalem functioning as one body	2
15:41	Churches	Traveling through Syria and Cilicia	The various groups of believers in two provinces	4
16:5 (w/16:4)	Churches	The churches were being strengthened in the faith	Groups of believers in various cities	4
18:22	Church	He went and greeted the church	The believers at Caesarea	2
19:32	Assembly	The assembly was in confusion	An assembly of people other than Christians	2
19:39	Assembly	The lawful assembly	A governmental body, not Christians	2

Ref.	Trans.	Immediate Context	How Used	Denoted
19:41	Assembly	He dismissed the assembly	An assembly of people other than Christians	
20:17	Church	He . . . called to him the elders of the Church	The believers of Ephesus functioning as one body	2
20:28	Church	Overseers, to shepherd the Church of God	The believers of Ephesus functioning as one body	2
Romans				
16:1	Church	The Church which is at Cenchrea	All the believers of Cenchrea seen as one body	2
16:4	Churches	All the churches of the Gentiles	Various groups of believers in the Gentile world	4
16:5	Church	The church that is in their house	A functioning group of believers living or meeting in a house	3
16:16	Churches	All the Churches of Christ greet you	All the groups of believers to which Paul was related	4
16:23	Church	Gaius, host . . . to the whole Church	All the believers in Corinth, who met in Gaius' home	3
1 Cor.				
1:2	Church	To the Church of God which is at Corinth	All the believers at Corinth	2
4:17	Church	I teach everywhere in every church	Functioning groups of believers	4

Ref.	Trans.	Immediate Context	How Used	Denoted
6:4	Church	In the church	The believers of Corinth seen as a unit	
7:17	Churches	In all the churches	All the groups of believers to which Paul is related	4
10:32	Church	The Church of God	All believers in general	5
11:16	Churches	The Churches of God	The various groups of believers to which Paul is related	4
11:18	Church	When you come together as a church	All the believers in Corinth gathered together as one unit	4
11:22	Church	Do you despise the Church of God	Referring to the believers of Corinth	6
12:28	Church	God has appointed some in the Church	Probably referring to the Church universal	2
14:4	Church	Edifies the Church	A group of believers gathered together	1
14:5	Church	The Church may receive edifying	A group of believers gathered together	3
14:12	Church	The edification of the Church	A group of believers gathered together	3
14:19	Church	In the Church	A group of believers gathered together	3
14:23	Church	The whole Church should assemble together	All the believers in Corinth, gathered together	2,3

243

Ref.	Trans.	Immediate Context	How Used	Denoted
14:28	Church	Keep silent in the Church	A group of believers gathered together	3
14:33	Churches	All the churches of the saints	All the groups of believers to which Paul was related	4
14:34	Churches	Keep silent in the churches	All the groups of believers in Corinth, or everywhere to which Paul is related	4
14:35	Church	Improper for a woman to speak in church	Any group of believers	5
15:9	Church	Persecuted the Church of God	The believers in general that Paul persecuted	5
16:1	Churches	The Churches of Galatia	The groups of believers in the province of Galatia	5
16:19	Church	The church that is in their house	A functioning group of believers living or meeting in a house, probably in Ephesus	4
2 Cor. 1:1	Church	To the Church of God which is at Corinth	The believers at Corinth, seen as a unit	3
8:1	Churches	The churches of Macedonia	The groups of believers in the province of Macedonia	2
8:18	Churches	Through all the churches	The groups of believers where Titus was known	4

244

Ref.	Trans.	Immediate Context	How Used	Denoted
8:19	Churches	Appointed by the churches	Groups of believers that appointed Titus to travel with Paul	4
8:23	Churches	Messengers of the churches	Groups sending apostles	4
8:24	Churches	Openly before the churches	Groups of churches in Corinth(?)	3
11:8	Churches	I robbed other churches	Groups of believers Paul served and that blessed him financially	4
11:28	Churches	Concern for all the churches	All the groups of believers for whom Paul had apostolic oversight	4
12:13	Churches	The rest of the churches	The groups of believers that Paul had oversight of except Corinth	4
Galatians				
1:2	Churches	To the churches of Galatia	Paul writing to groups of believers in the province of Galatia	4
1:13	Church	Persecute the Church of God	The believers in general	5
1:22	Churches	The churches of Judea	The groups of believers in Judea	4
Ephesians				
1:22	Church	Head over all things to the Church	The Universal Church	1
3:10	Church	Wisdom...known through the Church	The Universal Church	1
3:21	Church	To Him the glory in the Church	The Universal Church	1
5:23	Church	Christ...the Head of the Church	The Universal Church	1

245

Ref.	Trans.	Immediate Context	How Used	Denoted
5:24	Church	The Church is subject to Christ	The Universal Church	1
5:25	Church	Christ also loved the Church	The Universal Church	1
5:27	Church	Present to Himself the Church	The Universal Church	1
5:29	Church	Christ also does the Church	The Universal Church	1
5:32	Church	Christ and the Church	The Universal Church	1
Philp.				
3:6	Church	A persecutor of the Church	The believers in general	5
4:15	Church	No Church shared with me	The groups of believers related to Paul	4
Col.				
1:18	Church	Head of the Body, the Church	The Universal Church	1
1:24	Church	His Body (which is the Church)	The Universal Church	1
4:15	Church	The Church that is in her house	A group of believers that lived or met in a home	3
4:16	Church	The Church of the Laodiceans	The believers of Laodicea	2
1 Thess.				
1:1	Church	To the Church of the Thessalonians	All the believers in Thessalonica	2
2:14	Churches	The churches...in Judea	The groups of believers in Judea	4
2 Thess.				
1:1	Church	The Church of the Thessalonians	All the believers in Thessalonica	2
1:4	Churches	Among the churches	The groups to which Paul is related	4

Ref.	Trans.	Immediate Context	How Used	Denoted
1 Tim.				
3:5	Church	Take care of the Church	Believers in general	5
3:15	Church	The Church of the living God	Believers in general	5
5:16	Church	Let not the Church be burdened	Believers in general	5
Philm.				
1:2	Church	The Church in your house	A group of believers that lived or met in a house	3
Hebrews				
2:12	Cong.	In the midst of the congregation	Assembly of the children of Israel	6
12:23	Church	The Church of the first-born we are enrolled in heaven	Those in heaven	6
James				
5:14	Church	Call for the elders of the Church	Believers in general	5
3 John				
6	Church	Your love before the Church	A group of believers that are told of Gaius' ministry	3
9	Church	I wrote something to the Church	Believers of whom Gaius is part	3
10	Church	Puts them out of the Church	The believers of whom Gaius is a part	3
Rev.				
1:4	Churches	The 7 churches	The believers in 7 cities	4
1:11	Churches	The 7 churches	The believers in 7 cities	4

247

Ref.	Trans.	Immediate Context	How Used	Denoted
1:20	Churches	The angels of the 7 churches	The believers in 7 cities	4
1:20	Churches	The 7 churches	The believers in 7 cities	4
2:1	Church	The Church in Ephesus	Believers in the City of Ephesus	2
2:7	Churches	What the Spirit says to the Churches	The 7 groups of believers, or all groups of believers	4
2:8	Church	The Church in Smyrna	The believers in the city of Smyrna	2
2:11	Churches	What the Spirit says to Churches	Same as 2:7	
2:12	Church	The Church in Pergamum	The believers in the City of Pergamum	2
2:17	Churches	What the Spirit says to Churches	Same as 2:7	2
2:18	Church	The Church in Thyatira	Believers in the City of Thyatira	2
2:23	Churches	All the Churches will know	The believers in the city	4
2:29	Churches	What the Spirit says to Churches	Same as 2:7	2
3:1	Church	The Church in Sardis	The believers in the City of Sardis	2
3:6	Churches	What the Spirit says to Churches	Same as 2:7	4
3:7	Church	The Church in Philadelphia	The believers in the City of Philadelphia	
3:13	Churches	What the Spirit says to Churches	Same as 2:7	2
3:14	Church	The Church in Laodicea	The believers in the City of Laodicea	4
3:22	Churches	What the Spirit says to Churches	Same as 2:7	2
22:16	Churches	The Churches	All the groups of believers all over the earth	4

248

APPENDIX 8 — TRAVELING MINISTRIES
IN THE NEW TESTAMENT

Ref.	Person	Goes Where	Sent By	Does What
Acts				
18:1-3	Philip	City of Samaria	Scattered by persecution	Preaches, heals, casts out demons, baptizing, much rejoicing
8:14-17	Peter & John	City of Samaria	Sent by apostles in Jerusalem	Prayed for Samarian believers to receive the Holy Spirit
8:26-39	Philip	Gaza	Goes in obedience to an angel	Preaches to Ethiopian eunuch, baptizes him
8:40	Philip	Azotus to Caesarea	Transported by Holy Spirit	Preached the Gospel to all the cities
9:1-9, 20-25	Saul	Damascus	Went to arrest the believers, interrupted by the ascended Christ, ministered to by Ananias	Preached Jesus, has converts
9:10-19	Ananias	A house in Damascus	By the Lord through a vision, and instruction	Prayed for Saul: healing and infilling of the Holy Spirit baptizes Saul (?)

249

Ref.	Person	Goes Where	Sent By	Does What
9:29-30	Saul	Tarsus	Sent by "the brethren"	
9:32-35	Peter	Traveling throughout region—stopped in Lydda		Heals Aeneas, many turn to the Lord
9:36-43	Peter	Joppa	Invited by disciples in Joppa	Raises Tabitha from the dead, many believed, stays many days
10:01-11:18	Peter	Caesarea	Spoken to in vision, the voice of the Lord, and the Holy Spirit; and invited by 3 men, sent by Cor-nelius, spoken to by an angel.	Preaches to people assembled by Cornelius, Holy Spirit falls, baptized
11:19-21	Men of Cyprus	Antioch		Preached the Lord Jesus, large number turned to the Lord
11:22-26	Barnabas	Antioch	Church at Jerusalem	Encourages the new believers, more be-lieved, gets Saul, both met with the church and taught many for a year

250

Ref.	Person	Goes Where	Sent By	Does What
11:27-29	Prophets, incl Agabus	Antioch		Told, by the Spirit, of a coming famine, contribution sent
11:29-30	Barnabus & Saul	Judea	Church at Antioch	Take contribution to elders at Jerusalem
12:17	Peter	"another place"	Just goes	?
12:25	Barnabas, Saul & John Mark	Antioch	Return to where they were sent from	
13:1-14:26	Barnabas, Saul (John Mark as helper)	Many cities	"Set apart" and sent out by the Holy Spirit and the church with laying on of hands	Proclaimed Gospel, healed, converts, planted churches, appointed elders in each new church.
14:26-28	Note: They returned to Antioch and again related to the church there.			
15:1-21	Paul and Barnabas & "certain others"	Jerusalem	The church	Consider the matter of circumcision with the apostles and elders in Jerusalem
15:22-32	Judas & Silas to to go with Paul & Barnabas	Antioch	Apostles, elders, and whole church	Share personally the decision reached at Jerusalem

Ref.	Person	Goes Where	Sent By	Does What
15:33	Judas & Silas	Jerusalem	Sent back to Jerusalem	Returning home
15:36-39	Barnabas & Mark	Cyprus	?	?
15:36-41	Paul & Silas	Syria & Cilicea	"Committed by the brethren to the grace of the Lord"	Strengthening the churches
16:1-3	Timothy	With Paul	"Well spoken of by the brethren"	To travel with Paul (& Silas)
16:6-10	Paul (& Silas & Timothy)	Macedonia	Forbidden by the Spirit to go to Asia; called through a vision to go to Macedonia	To evangelize
17:14	Paul	Athens	"the brethren"	Leaves Berea for safety
17:15	Silas & Paul	Athens	Commanded by Paul	to join him
18:1-3	Paul	Corinth	?	
18:5	Silas & Timothy	Corinth to be with Paul	?	
18:18-19	Paul, Priscilla & Aquila	Ephesus	He "took leave of the brethren"	to be with Paul Leaves Priscilla & Aquila there

Ref.	Person	Goes Where	Sent By	Does What
	and Trophimus of Asia			
21:1-4	Paul & others	Tyre	?	Stayed with disciples seven days ("we") Goes anyway!
21:4-7	Paul & others ("we")	Ptolemais, Caesarea	Warned not to go	
21:10-14	Agabus	Caesarea	?	Had a word for Paul
21:8-16	Paul, "we," and some disciples	Cyprus		
21:17-23:10	Paul and "we"	Jerusalem		Shares what God has done, arrested
23:11-26:29	Paul	Caesarea	Sent by commander	Gave defense and witnessed before Felix, Festus, and King Agrippa
26:30	Paul and "we"	En route to Rome	Agrippa, because he had appealed to Caesar	Ministered along the way
28:15		Rome		
28:16-31	Paul		Under house arrest	Preaches and teaches to all who came to him

Ref.	Person	Goes Where	Sent By	Does What
18:22	Paul	Antioch	?	Greets the church, spends some time there
18:23	Paul	Province of Phrygia	?	Strengthening the disciples
19:1-20:1	Paul	Ephesus	?	Minister for two years
19:22	Timothy & Erastus	Macedonia	Paul	?
20:1-3	Paul	Macedonia & Greece	?	Exhorts them
20:3-38	Paul, with Sopater of Berea, Aristacchus and Secundus of Thessa lonica, Gauis of Derbe, Timothy and Tychicus	Troas, Azsos Miletus	Ministering to churches & elders	

Additional Notes Regarding the Church
of the New Testament

The church at Jerusalem was quite large (large numbers of converts are mentioned in Acts 2:41, 4:4, 5:14, 6:1, 6:7, etc.). It is doubtful that they all met together, at least on a regular basis. We do know that they were gathering in their homes (Acts 5:11, 11:22, 15:14, 15:22).

The church at Antioch all seemed to come together at times (Acts 13:1, 14:27). But other times it's not clear whether they were all in one place or not (Acts 11:26). However, all of the believers in Antioch were seen as one church (Acts 11:26, 13:1, 14:27, 15:3).

At Corinth, there were times when, it seems that all of the believers met at Gaius' home (Romans 16:23), probably a very large one, since there were many believers in Corinth (Acts 18:8). However many there were, and whenever they met, they were seen as one church (Romans 16:23, 1 Corinthians 1:2, 11:22, 2 Corinthians 1:1), and sometimes all came together (1 Corinthians 11:18, 14:23).

Other cities where the believers were all seen as one church, the "called out ones" of that city, include Lystra (Acts 14:23), Iconium (Acts 14:23), Antioch of Pisidia (Acts 14:23), Caesarea (Acts 18:22), Ephesus (Acts 20:17, Revelation 2:1), Cenchrea (Romans 16:1), Laodicea (Colossians 4:16, Revelation 3:14), Thessalonica (1 Thessalonians 1:1, 2 Thessalonians 1:1), Smyrna (Revelation 2:8), Pergamum (Revelation 2:12), Thyatira (Revelation 2:18), Sardis (Revelation 3:1), and Philadelphia (Revelation 3:7).

Seventeen times the word "church" refers to a group of people who regularly met together (Matthew 18:17; Romans 16:23; 1 Corinthians 14:4-5, 14:12, 14:19, 14:28; 3 John 6, 9, 10, etc.), usually in someone's home (Romans 16:5, 1 Corinthians 16:19, Colossians 4:15, Philemon 2).

Thirty-seven times these words "church" and "churches" refer to groups of believers in more than one location over a large area, i.e., "the churches throughout all Judea and Galilee and Samaria" (Acts 9:31). Nine times they refer to believers in general, i.e., "if a man does not know how to manage his own household, how will he take care of the church of God?" (1 Timothy 3:5).

APPENDIX 9 — HELPFUL INFORMATION ON WORLD EVANGELIZATION

9-A — The 223 Countries of the World

1 Afghanistan
2 Albania
3 Algeria
4 American Samoa
5 Andorra
6 Angola
7 Anguilla
8 Antigua
9 Argentina
10 Australia
11 Austria
12 Bahamas
13 Bahrain
14 Bangladesh
15 Barbados
16 Belgium
17 Belize
18 Benin
19 Bermuda
20 Bhutan
21 Bolivia
22 Botswana
23 Brazil
24 British Antarctic Territory
25 British Indian Ocean Territory
26 British Virgin Islands
27 Brunei
28 Bulgaria
29 Burkina Faso (former Upper Volta)
30 Burma
31 Burundi
32 Cameroon
33 Canada
34 Canton & Enderbury Islands
35 Cape Verde
36 Cayman Islands
37 Central African Republic
38 Chad
39 Channel Islands
40 Chile
41 China
42 China (Taiwan)
43 Christmas Islands
44 Cocos Islands
45 Colombia
46 Comoros
47 Congo
48 Cook Islands
49 Costa Rica
50 Cuba
51 Cyprus
52 Czechoslavakia
53 Denmark
54 Djibouti
55 Dominica
56 Dominican Republic
57 Ecuador
58 Egypt
59 El Salvador
60 Equatorial Guinea
61 Ethiopia
62 Faeroe Islands
63 Falkland Islands
64 Fiji
65 Finland
66 France
68 French Polynesia

256

67 French Guiana	107 Korea (North)
69 French Southern & Antarctic Territory	108 Korea (South)
	109 Kuwait
70 Gabon	110 Laos
71 Gambia	111 Lebanon
72 German Democratic Republic (East)	112 Lesotho
	113 Liberia
73 Germany (West)	114 Libya
74 Ghana	115 Liechtenstein
75 Gibraltar	116 Luxembourg
76 Greece	117 Macao
77 Greenland	118 Madagascar
78 Grenada	119 Malawai
79 Guadeloupe	120 Malaysia
80 Guam	121 Maldives
81 Guatemala	122 Mali
82 Guinea	123 Malta
83 Guinea-Bissau	124 Martinique
84 Guyana	125 Mauritania
85 Haiti	126 Mauritius
86 Holy See	127 Mayotte
87 Honduras	128 Mexico
88 Hong Kong	129 Midway Islands
89 Hungary	130 Monaco
90 Iceland	131 Mongolia
91 India	132 Montserrat
92 Indonesia	133 Morocco
93 Iran	134 Mozambique
94 Iraq	135 Namibia
95 Ireland	136 Nauru
96 Isle of Man	137 Nepal
97 Israel	138 Netherlands
98 Italy	139 Netherlands Antilles
99 Ivory Coast	140 New Caledonia
100 Jamaica	141 New Zealand
101 Japan	142 Nicaragua
102 Johnston Island	143 Niger
103 Jordan	144 Nigeria
104 Kampuchea	145 Niue Island
105 Kenya	146 Norfolk Island
106 Kiribati	147 Northern Solomons

148	Norway	188	Sudan
149	Oman	189	Surinam
150	Pacific Islands Trust Territory	190	Svalbard and Jan Mayen Islands
151	Pakistan	191	Swaziland
152	Palestine	192	Sweden
153	Panama	193	Switzerland
154	Panama Canal Zone	194	Syria
155	Papua New Guinea	195	Tanzania
156	Paraguay	196	Thailand
157	Peru	197	Timor
158	Philippines	198	Togo
159	Pitcairn Islands	199	Tokelau Islands
160	Poland	200	Tonga
161	Portugal	201	Trinidad and Tobago
162	Puerto Rico	202	Tunisia
163	Qatar	203	Turkey
164	Reunion	204	Turks and Caicos Islands
165	Romania	205	Tuvalu
166	Rwanda	206	Uganda
167	Sahara	207	Union of Soviet Socialist Republics
168	St. Helena	208	United Arab Emirates
169	St. Kitts-Nevis	209	United Kingdom of Great Britain & Northern Ireland
170	St. Lucia	210	United States of America
171	St. Pierre and Miquelon	211	United States Virgin Islands
172	St. Vincent and Grenadines	212	Uruguay
173	Samoa	213	Vanuatu
174	San Marino	214	Venezuela
175	Sao Tome and Principe	215	Viet Nam (North and South)
176	Saudi Arabia	216	Wake Island
177	Senegal	217	Wallis and Futuna Islands
178	Seychelles	218	Yemen (North)
179	Sierra Leone	219	Yemen (South)
180	Sikkim	220	Yugoslavia
181	Singapore	221	Zaire
182	Solomon Islands	222	Zambia
183	Somalia	223	Zimbabwe
184	South Africa		
185	Spain		
186	Spanish North Africa		
187	Sri Lanka		

Appendix 9-B — Information basis for Charts 6-9

	A. Reached People Groups						B. Unreached People Groups													
Tribal	1,000	20	25	20	65	6,000	5,000	0.001	35	70	30	135	4,000	3,000	6,000	200	10,000	2,000	2,000
Muslim	30	0.2	0	34	34	600	4,000	0.01	235	587	0	822	250	580	4,030	856	850	500	2,000
Hindu	300	8	12	60	80	1,800	3,000	0.52	514	73	0	588	100	500	3,300	668	1,900	2,000	4,000
Han Chinese	1,200	80	22	379	481	2,400	2,000	0.02	407	44	0	451	200	200	3,200	932	2,600	1,500	200
Buddhists	20	2	1	27	30	800	1,000	0.01	129	146	0	275	200	100	1,020	305	1,000	2,000	1,200
Subtotal	2,550	110	60	520	690	11,600	15,000	0.561	1,320	920	30	2,271	4,750	4,380	17,550	2,961	16,350	8,000	9,400
Other African	2,450	45	124	11	180	12,500	1,000	0.21	11	5	10	26	950	300	3,450	206	13,450	6,000	5,000
Other Asian	1,000	28	47	106	181	7,000	600	0.21	50	51	33	134	1,650	700	1,600	315	8,650	5,000	4,000
Other Western	1,000	147	955	229	1,331	28,000	400	0.01	82	36	11	129	1,850	130	1,400	1,460	29,850	3,000	1,600
(USA,Canada)	500	76	161	18	255	4,000	100	0.001	9	3	1	13	500	30	600	268	4,500	300	600
Subtotal	4,450	220	1,126	346	1,692	47,500	2,000	0.43	143	92	54	289	4,450	1,130	6,450	1,981	51,950	14,000	10,600
Grand Total	7,000	330	1,186	866	2,382	59,100	17,000	0.991	1,463	1,012	84	2,560	9,200	5,510	24,000	4,942	68,300	22,000	20,000

Evangelism and "Domestic" Missions — Among Reached Peoples

Frontier Missions — Among Unreached Peoples

259

Appendix 9-C — Distribution of Evangelicals
Sorted Alphabetically

Country	%	Country	%	Country	%
AFGHANISTA	0.0	GREECE	0.1	P.N.G.	21.0
ALBANIA	0.0	GREENLAND	3.8	PAKISTAN	0.2
ALGERIA	0.0	GUAM	7.6	PANAMA	9.8
ANGOLA	7.7	GUATEMALA	19.0	PARAGUAY	2.5
ARGENTINA	4.7	GUINEA	0.4	PERU	3.0
AUSTRALIA	17.0	GUINEA-BIS	0.7	PHILIPPINE	6.4
AUSTRIA	0.6	GUYANA	8.7	POLAND	0.2
BAHAMAS	30.0	HAITI	12.3	PORTUGAL	0.6
BAHRAIN	1.0	HONDURAS	8.8	PUERTO RIC	20.8
BANGLADESH	0.1	HUNGARY	3.7	QATAR	1.4
BELGIUM	0.4	ICELAND	3.0	ROMANIA	7.8
BELIZE	12.0	INDIA	0.7	RWANDA	16.0
BENIN	1.2	INDONESIA	4.3	S. AFRICA	15.0
BHUTAN	0.0	IRAN	0.0	S. KOREA	18.0
BOLIVIA	6.5	IRAQ	0.0	SAO TOME &	2.5
BOTSWANA	4.0	IRELAND	0.6	SAUDI ARAB	0.0
BRAZIL	16.0	ISRAEL	0.2	SENEGAL	0.1
BRUNEI	0.4	ITALY	0.6	SEYCHELLES	0.5
BULGARIA	0.5	IVORY COAS	3.7	SIERRA LEO	1.5
BURKINA FA	1.4	JAMAICA	14.0	SOMALIA	0.0
BURMA	3.1	JAPAN	0.2	SPAIN	0.3
BURUNDI	9.5	JORDAN	0.3	SRI LANKA	0.2
CAMEROON	4.0	KAMPUCHEA	0.0	SUDAN	1.6
CANADA	6.5	KENYA	26.5	SURINAM	3.0
CAPE VERDE	3.0	KUWAIT	0.2	SWAZILAND	19.0
CEN AF REP	28.0	LAOS	1.2	SWEDEN	5.6
CHAD	11.0	LEBANON	0.6	SWITZERLAN	4.0
CHILE	21.6	LESOTHO	2.7	SYRIA	0.1
CHINA	4.6	LIBERIA	7.1	TAIWAN	2.5
COLOMBIA	2.4	LIBYA	0.0	TANZANIA	9.0
COMOROS	0.0	LUXEMBOURG	0.1	THAILAND	0.2
CONGO	15.0	MADAGASCAR	1.8	TOGO	1.2
COSTA RICA	6.5	MALAWI	14.8	TRINIDAD &	11.0
CUBA	2.1	MALAYSIA	1.2	TUNISIA	0.0
CYPRUS	0.4	MALI	0.6	TURKEY	0.0
CZECHOSLOV	2.1	MAURITANIA	0.0	U.A.E.	0.2
DENMARK	5.0	MAURITIUS	3.5	U.K.	7.0
DJIBOUTI	0.0	MEXICO	3.1	UGANDA	24.9
DOM. REP.	4.7	MONGOLIA	0.0	URUGUAY	1.9
E. GERMANY	11.0	MOROCCO	0.0	USA	23.0
ECUADOR	3.2	MOZAMBIQUE	4.5	USSR	2.5
EGYPT	0.7	N. KOREA	0.0	VENEZUELA	2.1
EL SALVADO	12.8	NAMIBIA	17.0	VIETNAM	0.5
EQ. GUINEA	2.7	NEPAL	0.3	W. GERMANY	7.0
ETHIOPIA	9.6	NETH. ANT.	2.7	W. SAHARA	0.0
FALKLANDS	7.0	NETHERLAND	8.0	YEMEN-ADEN	0.0
FINLAND	16.0	NEW ZEALAN	16.7	YEMEN-SANA	0.0
FR. GUIANA	4.3	NICARAGUA	6.3	YUGOSLAVIA	0.2
FRANCE	0.6	NIGER	0.1	ZAIRE	17.6
GABON	5.7	NIGERIA	14.0	ZAMBIA	7.3
GAMBIA	0.1	NORWAY	20.0	ZIMBABWE	7.0
GHANA	9.0	OMAN	0.1		

NOTE: Evangelical percentage of population - 1985

Distribution of Evangelicals
Sorted by Data

BAHAMAS	30.0	GABON	5.7	LEBANON	0.6
CEN AF REP	28.0	SWEDEN	5.6	MALI	0.6
KENYA	26.5	DENMARK	5.0	PORTUGAL	0.6
UGANDA	24.9	ARGENTINA	4.7	BULGARIA	0.5
USA	23.0	DOM. REP.	4.7	SEYCHELLES	0.5
CHILE	21.6	CHINA	4.6	VIETNAM	0.5
P.N.G.	21.0	MOZAMBIQUE	4.5	BELGIUM	0.4
PUERTO RIC	20.8	FR. GUIANA	4.3	BRUNEI	0.4
NORWAY	20.0	INDONESIA	4.3	CYPRUS	0.4
GUATEMALA	19.0	BOTSWANA	4.0	GUINEA	0.4
SWAZILAND	19.0	CAMEROON	4.0	JORDAN	0.3
S. KOREA	18.0	SWITZERLAN	4.0	NEPAL	0.3
ZAIRE	17.6	GREENLAND	3.8	SPAIN	0.3
AUSTRALIA	17.0	HUNGARY	3.7	ISRAEL	0.2
NAMIBIA	17.0	IVORY COAS	3.7	JAPAN	0.2
NEW ZEALAN	16.7	MAURITIUS	3.5	KUWAIT	0.2
BRAZIL	16.0	ECUADOR	3.2	PAKISTAN	0.2
FINLAND	16.0	BURMA	3.1	POLAND	0.2
RWANDA	16.0	MEXICO	3.1	SRI LANKA	0.2
CONGO	15.0	CAPE VERDE	3.0	THAILAND	0.2
S. AFRICA	15.0	ICELAND	3.0	U.A.E.	0.2
MALAWI	14.8	PERU	3.0	YUGOSLAVIA	0.2
JAMAICA	14.0	SURINAM	3.0	BANGLADESH	0.1
NIGERIA	14.0	EQ. GUINEA	2.7	GAMBIA	0.1
EL SALVADO	12.8	LESOTHO	2.7	GREECE	0.1
HAITI	12.3	NETH. ANT.	2.7	LUXEMBOURG	0.1
BELIZE	12.0	PARAGUAY	2.5	NIGER	0.1
CHAD	11.0	SAO TOME &	2.5	OMAN	0.1
E. GERMANY	11.0	TAIWAN	2.5	SENEGAL	0.1
TRINIDAD &	11.0	USSR	2.5	SYRIA	0.1
PANAMA	9.8	COLOMBIA	2.4	AFGHANISTA	0.0
ETHIOPIA	9.6	CUBA	2.1	ALBANIA	0.0
BURUNDI	9.5	CZECHOSLOV	2.1	ALGERIA	0.0
GHANA	9.0	VENEZUELA	2.1	BHUTAN	0.0
TANZANIA	9.0	URUGUAY	1.9	COMOROS	0.0
HONDURAS	8.8	MADAGASCAR	1.8	DJIBOUTI	0.0
GUYANA	8.7	SUDAN	1.6	IRAN	0.0
NETHERLAND	8.0	SIERRA LEO	1.5	IRAQ	0.0
ROMANIA	7.8	BURKINA FA	1.4	KAMPUCHEA	0.0
ANGOLA	7.7	QATAR	1.4	LIBYA	0.0
GUAM	7.6	BENIN	1.2	MAURITANIA	0.0
ZAMBIA	7.3	LAOS	1.2	MONGOLIA	0.0
LIBERIA	7.1	MALAYSIA	1.2	MOROCCO	0.0
FALKLANDS	7.0	TOGO	1.2	N. KOREA	0.0
U.K.	7.0	BAHRAIN	1.0	SAUDI ARAB	0.0
W. GERMANY	7.0	EGYPT	0.7	SOMALIA	0.0
ZIMBABWE	7.0	GUINEA-BIS	0.7	TUNISIA	0.0
BOLIVIA	6.5	INDIA	0.7	TURKEY	0.0
CANADA	6.5	AUSTRIA	0.6	W. SAHARA	0.0
COSTA RICA	6.5	FRANCE	0.6	YEMEN-ADEN	0.0
PHILIPPINE	6.4	IRELAND	0.6	YEMEN-SANA	0.0
NICARAGUA	6.3	ITALY	0.6		

REFERENCES: Operation World (1986)
GLOBAL MAPPING PROJECT. INC. Pasadena. CA 08/05/87

Appendix 9-D — The Unreached
Sorted Alphabetically

Country	#	Country	#	Country	#
AFGHANISTA	110	GREECE	5	P.N.G.	675
ALBANIA	10	GREENLAND	1	PAKISTAN	150
ALGERIA	30	GUAM	0	PANAMA	10
ANGOLA	50	GUATEMALA	21	PARAGUAY	15
ARGENTINA	40	GUINEA	37	PERU	95
AUSTRALIA	170	GUINEA-BIS	47	PHILIPPINE	190
AUSTRIA	9	GUYANA	10	POLAND	15
BAHAMAS	0	HAITI	5	PORTUGAL	0
BAHRAIN	3	HONDURAS	4	PUERTO RIC	1
BANGLADESH	60	HUNGARY	5	QATAR	12
BELGIUM	10	ICELAND	3	ROMANIA	15
BELIZE	10	INDIA	3400	RWANDA	3
BENIN	45	INDONESIA	1640	S. AFRICA	57
BHUTAN	10	IRAN	116	S. KOREA	30
BOLIVIA	39	IRAQ	27	SAO TOME &	0
BOTSWANA	40	IRELAND	5	SAUDI ARAB	40
BRAZIL	150	ISRAEL	27	SENEGAL	55
BRUNEI	11	ITALY	55	SEYCHELLES	1
BULGARIA	10	IVORY COAS	200	SIERRA LEO	76
BURKINA FA	82	JAMAICA	7	SOMALIA	20
BURMA	200	JAPAN	100	SPAIN	15
BURUNDI	2	JORDAN	9	SRI LANKA	10
CAMEROON	215	KAMPUCHEA	40	SUDAN	340
CANADA	114	KENYA	66	SURINAM	10
CAPE VERDE	0	KUWAIT	10	SWAZILAND	0
CEN AF REP	47	LAOS	80	SWEDEN	13
CHAD	200	LEBANON	4	SWITZERLAN	8
CHILE	13	LESOTHO	8	SYRIA	15
CHINA	1625	LIBERIA	74	TAIWAN	60
COLOMBIA	110	LIBYA	15	TANZANIA	131
COMOROS	10	LUXEMBOURG	1	THAILAND	55
CONGO	42	MADAGASCAR	20	TOGO	60
COSTA RICA	2	MALAWI	16	TRINIDAD &	3
CUBA	8	MALAYSIA	240	TUNISIA	9
CYPRUS	8	MALI	48	TURKEY	40
CZECHOSLOV	5	MAURITANIA	5	U.A.E.	15
DENMARK	8	MAURITIUS	4	U.K.	45
DJIBOUTI	11	MEXICO	150	UGANDA	90
DOM. REP.	8	MONGOLIA	100	URUGUAY	5
E. GERMANY	0	MOROCCO	60	USA	360
ECUADOR	10	MOZAMBIQUE	35	USSR	560
EGYPT	10	N. KOREA	0	VENEZUELA	61
EL SALVADO	6	NAMIBIA	20	VIETNAM	160
EQ. GUINEA	16	NEPAL	85	W. GERMANY	14
ETHIOPIA	155	NETH. ANT.	0	W. SAHARA	60
FALKLANDS	0	NETHERLAND	10	YEMEN-ADEN	21
FINLAND	6	NEW ZEALAN	0	YEMEN-SANA	12
FR. GUIANA	7	NICARAGUA	10	YUGOSLAVIA	20
FRANCE	55	NIGER	37	ZAIRE	300
GABON	34	NIGERIA	781	ZAMBIA	72
GAMBIA	24	NORWAY	5	ZIMBABWE	47
GHANA	100	OMAN	25		

NOTE: # of unreached people groups per country
includes group displacements in urban areas

The Unreached
Sorted by Data

INDIA	3400	GUINEA-BIS	47	KUWAIT	10
INDONESIA	1640	ZIMBABWE	47	NETHERLAND	10
CHINA	1625	BENIN	45	NICARAGUA	10
NIGERIA	781	U.K.	45	PANAMA	10
P.N.G.	675	CONGO	42	SRI LANKA	10
USSR	560	ARGENTINA	40	SURINAM	10
USA	360	BOTSWANA	40	AUSTRIA	9
SUDAN	340	KAMPUCHEA	40	JORDAN	9
ZAIRE	300	SAUDI ARAB	40	TUNISIA	9
MALAYSIA	240	TURKEY	40	CUBA	8
CAMEROON	215	BOLIVIA	39	CYPRUS	8
BURMA	200	GUINEA	37	DENMARK	8
CHAD	200	NIGER	37	DOM. REP.	8
IVORY COAS	200	MOZAMBIQUE	35	LESOTHO	8
PHILIPPINE	190	GABON	34	SWITZERLAN	8
AUSTRALIA	170	ALGERIA	30	FR. GUIANA	7
VIETNAM	160	S. KOREA	30	JAMAICA	7
ETHIOPIA	155	IRAQ	27	EL SALVADO	6
BRAZIL	150	ISRAEL	27	FINLAND	6
MEXICO	150	OMAN	25	CZECHOSLOV	5
PAKISTAN	150	GAMBIA	24	GREECE	5
TANZANIA	131	GUATEMALA	21	HAITI	5
IRAN	116	YEMEN-ADEN	21	HUNGARY	5
CANADA	114	MADAGASCAR	20	IRELAND	5
AFGHANISTA	110	NAMIBIA	20	MAURITANIA	5
COLOMBIA	110	SOMALIA	20	NORWAY	5
GHANA	100	YUGOSLAVIA	20	URUGUAY	5
JAPAN	100	EQ. GUINEA	16	HONDURAS	4
MONGOLIA	100	MALAWI	16	LEBANON	4
PERU	95	LIBYA	15	MAURITIUS	4
UGANDA	90	PARAGUAY	15	BAHRAIN	3
NEPAL	85	POLAND	15	ICELAND	3
BURKINA FA	82	ROMANIA	15	RWANDA	3
LAOS	80	SPAIN	15	TRINIDAD &	3
SIERRA LEO	76	SYRIA	15	BURUNDI	2
LIBERIA	74	U.A.E.	15	COSTA RICA	2
ZAMBIA	72	W. GERMANY	14	GREENLAND	1
KENYA	66	CHILE	13	LUXEMBOURG	1
VENEZUELA	61	SWEDEN	13	PUERTO RIC	1
BANGLADESH	60	QATAR	12	SEYCHELLES	1
MOROCCO	60	YEMEN-SANA	12	BAHAMAS	0
TAIWAN	60	BRUNEI	11	CAPE VERDE	0
TOGO	60	DJIBOUTI	11	E. GERMANY	0
W. SAHARA	60	ALBANIA	10	FALKLANDS	0
S. AFRICA	57	BELGIUM	10	GUAM	0
FRANCE	55	BELIZE	10	N. KOREA	0
ITALY	55	BHUTAN	10	NETH. ANT.	0
SENEGAL	55	BULGARIA	10	NEW ZEALAN	0
THAILAND	55	COMOROS	10	PORTUGAL	0
ANGOLA	50	ECUADOR	10	SAO TOME &	0
MALI	48	EGYPT	10	SWAZILAND	0
CEN AF REP	47	GUYANA	10		

GLOBAL MAPPING PROJECT, INC. Pasadena, CA 08/05/87

Appendix 9-E — Evangelical Growth Rate
Sorted Alphabetically

AFGHANISTA	4.0	GREECE	2.0	P.N.G.	7.2
ALBANIA	3.0	GREENLAND	3.5	PAKISTAN	7.2
ALGERIA	6.0	GUAM	3.5	PANAMA	8.0
ANGOLA	5.0	GUATEMALA	13.0	PARAGUAY	9.0
ARGENTINA	9.5	GUINEA	2.5	PERU	8.0
AUSTRALIA	3.0	GUINEA-BIS	4.0	PHILIPPINE	12.5
AUSTRIA	3.5	GUYANA	7.0	POLAND	6.0
BAHAMAS	2.0	HAITI	4.0	PORTUGAL	6.5
BAHRAIN	3.3	HONDURAS	12.0	PUERTO RIC	6.0
BANGLADESH	4.0	HUNGARY	1.5	QATAR	4.0
BELGIUM	2.5	ICELAND	8.0	ROMANIA	7.5
BELIZE	8.5	INDIA	6.0	RWANDA	9.0
BENIN	6.0	INDONESIA	5.0	S. AFRICA	5.0
BHUTAN	3.0	IRAN	4.5	S. KOREA	12.5
BOLIVIA	6.5	IRAQ	3.0	SAO TOME &	2.5
BOTSWANA	6.5	IRELAND	6.5	SAUDI ARAB	8.0
BRAZIL	11.5	ISRAEL	7.0	SENEGAL	9.0
BRUNEI	4.0	ITALY	8.0	SEYCHELLES	5.7
BULGARIA	4.0	IVORY COAS	13.0	SIERRA LEO	4.0
BURKINA FA	8.0	JAMAICA	5.0	SOMALIA	7.0
BURMA	5.0	JAPAN	7.2	SPAIN	7.0
BURUNDI	6.0	JORDAN	7.0	SRI LANKA	7.0
CAMEROON	6.0	KAMPUCHEA	7.0	SUDAN	6.5
CANADA	3.0	KENYA	6.5	SURINAM	7.0
CAPE VERDE	4.5	KUWAIT	7.0	SWAZILAND	6.5
CEN AF REP	7.0	LAOS	4.0	SWEDEN	4.0
CHAD	5.5	LEBANON	7.0	SWITZERLAN	3.5
CHILE	5.0	LESOTHO	4.0	SYRIA	4.0
CHINA	11.0	LIBERIA	5.0	TAIWAN	4.5
COLOMBIA	10.2	LIBYA	7.0	TANZANIA	8.0
COMOROS	1.5	LUXEMBOURG	3.5	THAILAND	7.0
CONGO	6.0	MADAGASCAR	5.0	TOGO	8.5
COSTA RICA	11.5	MALAWI	9.0	TRINIDAD &	5.0
CUBA	5.0	MALAYSIA	7.2	TUNISIA	4.0
CYPRUS	4.0	MALI	4.0	TURKEY	6.0
CZECHOSLOV	1.5	MAURITANIA	7.2	U.A.E.	5.5
DENMARK	3.5	MAURITIUS	2.3	U.K.	5.5
DJIBOUTI	6.0	MEXICO	7.2	UGANDA	10.0
DOM. REP.	9.4	MONGOLIA	6.5	URUGUAY	6.5
E. GERMANY	3.5	MOROCCO	3.5	USA	3.5
ECUADOR	9.5	MOZAMBIQUE	6.0	USSR	4.5
EGYPT	5.0	N. KOREA	4.0	VENEZUELA	7.5
EL SALVADO	12.0	NAMIBIA	5.0	VIETNAM	4.0
EQ. GUINEA	6.0	NEPAL	10.0	W. GERMANY	3.5
ETHIOPIA	8.0	NETH. ANT.	6.0	W. SAHARA	5.0
FALKLANDS	4.5	NETHERLAND	4.5	YEMEN-ADEN	4.0
FINLAND	3.0	NEW ZEALAN	4.0	YEMEN-SANA	7.0
FR. GUIANA	6.0	NICARAGUA	12.0	YUGOSLAVIA	5.0
FRANCE	7.5	NIGER	3.0	ZAIRE	7.0
GABON	4.5	NIGERIA	7.5	ZAMBIA	7.0
GAMBIA	9.0	NORWAY	3.5	ZIMBABWE	6.0
GHANA	10.0	OMAN	1.5		

NOTE: average annual growth rate 1980-1985
       (includes Charismatic renewal)

GUATEMALA	13.0	SRI LANKA	7.0	IRAN	4.5
IVORY COAS	13.0	SURINAM	7.0	NETHERLAND	4.5
PHILIPPINE	12.5	THAILAND	7.0	TAIWAN	4.5
S. KOREA	12.5	YEMEN-SANA	7.0	USSR	4.5
EL SALVADO	12.0	ZAIRE	7.0	AFGHANISTA	4.0
HONDURAS	12.0	ZAMBIA	7.0	BANGLADESH	4.0
NICARAGUA	12.0	BOLIVIA	6.5	BRUNEI	4.0
BRAZIL	11.5	BOTSWANA	6.5	BULGARIA	4.0
COSTA RICA	11.5	IRELAND	6.5	CYPRUS	4.0
CHINA	11.0	KENYA	6.5	GUINEA-BIS	4.0
COLOMBIA	10.2	MONGOLIA	6.5	HAITI	4.0
GHANA	10.0	PORTUGAL	6.5	LAOS	4.0
NEPAL	10.0	SUDAN	6.5	LESOTHO	4.0
UGANDA	10.0	SWAZILAND	6.5	MALI	4.0
ARGENTINA	9.5	URUGUAY	6.5	N. KOREA	4.0
ECUADOR	9.5	ALGERIA	6.0	NEW ZEALAN	4.0
DOM. REP.	9.4	BENIN	6.0	QATAR	4.0
GAMBIA	9.0	BURUNDI	6.0	SIERRA LEO	4.0
MALAWI	9.0	CAMEROON	6.0	SWEDEN	4.0
PARAGUAY	9.0	CONGO	6.0	SYRIA	4.0
RWANDA	9.0	DJIBOUTI	6.0	TUNISIA	4.0
SENEGAL	9.0	EQ. GUINEA	6.0	VIETNAM	4.0
BELIZE	8.5	FR. GUIANA	6.0	YEMEN-ADEN	4.0
TOGO	8.5	INDIA	6.0	AUSTRIA	3.5
BURKINA FA	8.0	MOZAMBIQUE	6.0	DENMARK	3.5
ETHIOPIA	8.0	NETH. ANT.	6.0	E. GERMANY	3.5
ICELAND	8.0	POLAND	6.0	GREENLAND	3.5
ITALY	8.0	PUERTO RIC	6.0	GUAM	3.5
PANAMA	8.0	TURKEY	6.0	LUXEMBOURG	3.5
PERU	8.0	ZIMBABWE	6.0	NORWAY	3.5
SAUDI ARAB	8.0	SEYCHELLES	5.7	SWITZERLAN	3.5
TANZANIA	8.0	CHAD	5.5	USA	3.5
FRANCE	7.5	U.A.E.	5.5	W. GERMANY	3.5
NIGERIA	7.5	U.K.	5.5	BAHRAIN	3.3
ROMANIA	7.5	ANGOLA	5.0	ALBANIA	3.0
VENEZUELA	7.5	BURMA	5.0	AUSTRALIA	3.0
JAPAN	7.2	CHILE	5.0	BHUTAN	3.0
MALAYSIA	7.2	CUBA	5.0	CANADA	3.0
MAURITANIA	7.2	EGYPT	5.0	FINLAND	3.0
MEXICO	7.2	INDONESIA	5.0	IRAQ	3.0
P.N.G.	7.2	JAMAICA	5.0	NIGER	3.0
PAKISTAN	7.2	LIBERIA	5.0	BELGIUM	2.5
CEN AF REP	7.0	MADAGASCAR	5.0	GUINEA	2.5
GUYANA	7.0	MOROCCO	5.0	SAO TOME &	2.5
ISRAEL	7.0	NAMIBIA	5.0	MAURITIUS	2.3
JORDAN	7.0	S. AFRICA	5.0	BAHAMAS	2.0
KAMPUCHEA	7.0	TRINIDAD &	5.0	GREECE	2.0
KUWAIT	7.0	W. SAHARA	5.0	COMOROS	1.5
LEBANON	7.0	YUGOSLAVIA	5.0	CZECHOSLOV	1.5
LIBYA	7.0	CAPE VERDE	4.5	HUNGARY	1.5
SOMALIA	7.0	FALKLANDS	4.5	OMAN	1.5
SPAIN	7.0	GABON	4.5		

GLOBAL MAPPING PROJECT, INC.   Pasadena, CA   08/05/87

9-F — Organizations Primarily Involved in Bible Distribution

American Bible Society, 1865 Broadway, New York, NY 10023

Bibles for the Nations, YWAM, P.O. Box 7, Elm Springs, AR 72728

Bibles for the World, P.O. Box 805, Wheaton, IL 60189

Gideons International, 2900 Lebanon Road, Nashville, TN 37214

International Bible Society, East Brunswick, NJ 08816

Living Bibles International, 11809 C. Mill St., Naperville, IL 60540

Open Doors, P.O. Box 2020, Orange, CA 92669

Pocket Testament League, P.O. Box 368, Lincoln Park, NJ 07035

United Bible Societies, Bible House, P.O. Box 810340, 7000 Stuttgart 80, West Germany

World Home Bible League, South Holland, IL 60473

9-G — Organizations Majoring in Christian Literature Production and Distribution

Christian Literature Crusade, Box C, Fort Washington, PA 19034. Christian Bookstore and literature distribution.

Evangelical Literature Overseas, Box 725, Wheaton, IL 60187

Life Messengers, P.O. Box 1967, Seattle, WA 98111. Produce literature for others to distribute.

Operation Mobilization, P.O. Box 148, Midland Park, NJ 07432. Distribute thousands of books and millions of pieces of literature each year through their ships and door-to-door.

World Literature Crusade, 20232 Sunburst St., Chatsworth, CA 91311. Have as their goal to take a piece of literature to every home in the world by the year 1996.

World Missionary Press, P.O. Box 120, New Paris, IN 46553. Produce 2,500,000 Scripture booklets per month for free distribution.

9-H — Organizations Specializing in Christian Media

Radio Ministries

Far East Broadcasting Company, P.O. Box 1, La Mirada, CA 90637

HCJB, World Radio Missionary Fellowship, P.O. Box 553000, Opa Locka, FL 33055

Trans World Radio, P.O. Box 98, Chatham, NJ 09728

Gospel Recordings

Gospel Recordings, 122 Glendale Blvd., Los Angeles, CA 90026

Telephone

Televisitation, P.O. Box 71654, Los Angeles, CA 90071

Christian Television and Satellite Networks

Baptist Radio and TV Commission, Southern Baptist Convention, 6350 West Freeway, Fort Worth, TX 76105

Christian Broadcasting Network, CBN Center, Virginia Beach, VA 23463

Church Satellite Network, P.O. Box 15000, Phoenix, AZ 85060

Crossroads Christian Communications, 100 Huntley St., Toronto, Ontario, Canada M4Y 2L1

Dominion Network, P.O. Box 9060, Farmington Hills, MI 48018

Gibraltar Satellite Network, P.O. Box 707, Buffalo, NY 14217

Kenneth Copeland Evangelistic Assoc., P.O. Box 8720, Ft. Worth, TX 76112

Power Satellite Network, P.O. Box 9009, Tyler, TX 75711

PTL Broadcasting Network, P.O. Box 15000, Charlotte, NC 28210

Robert Tilton Ministries, P.O. Box 81900, Dallas, TX 75381

Teaching and Evangelistic Network, P.O. Box 15086, Austin, TX 78761

Trinity Broadcasting Network, P.O. Box A, Santa Ana, CA 92711

World Satellite Network, P.O. Box 23000, Houston, TX 77228

9-J —Organizations Specializing in Working With Students

Campus Crusade for Christ, Arrowhead Springs, San Bernardino, CA 92414

International Students, Inc., Star Ranch, P.O. Box C, Colorado Springs, CO 80901.

Inter-Varsity, PO Box 7895, Madison, WI 53707

Maranatha Ministries, P.O. Box 1799, Gainesville, FL 32602

The Navigators, P.O. Box 6000, Colorado Springs, CO 80934

Overseas Students Mission, 5028 Wisconsin Ave., Washington, DC 20016

Young Life, 720 W. Monument, Colorado Springs, CO 80901

Youth For Christ, P.O. Box 419, Wheaton, IL 60187

Youth With A Mission, P.O. Box 4600, Tyler, TX 75712

Appendix 9-K — Quality of Life
Sorted Alphabetically

Country	PQLI	Country	PQLI	Country	PQLI
AFGHANISTA	18	GREECE	88	P.N.G.	35
ALBANIA	72	GREENLAND	90	PAKISTAN	38
ALGERIA	41	GUAM	80	PANAMA	80
ANGOLA	15	GUATEMALA	51	PARAGUAY	73
ARGENTINA	85	GUINEA	20	PERU	59
AUSTRALIA	93	GUINEA-BIS	11	PHILIPPINE	71
AUSTRIA	93	GUYANA	82	POLAND	91
BAHAMAS	88	HAITI	32	PORTUGAL	78
BAHRAIN	61	HONDURAS	51	PUERTO RIC	90
BANGLADESH	35	HUNGARY	91	QATAR	31
BELGIUM	93	ICELAND	96	ROMANIA	90
BELIZE	70	INDIA	43	RWANDA	25
BENIN	23	INDONESIA	48	S. AFRICA	48
BHUTAN	20	IRAN	44	S. KOREA	82
BOLIVIA	43	IRAQ	39	SAO TOME &	20
BOTSWANA	45	IRELAND	93	SAUDI ARAB	28
BRAZIL	67	ISRAEL	89	SENEGAL	24
BRUNEI	65	ITALY	92	SEYCHELLES	72
BULGARIA	91	IVORY COAS	28	SIERRA LEO	27
BURKINA FA	16	JAMAICA	84	SOMALIA	19
BURMA	51	JAPAN	96	SPAIN	91
BURUNDI	22	JORDAN	47	SRI LANKA	82
CAMEROON	25	KAMPUCHEA	40	SUDAN	35
CANADA	95	KENYA	39	SURINAM	83
CAPE VERDE	53	KUWAIT	74	SWAZILAND	35
CEN AF REP	18	LAOS	29	SWEDEN	97
CHAD	18	LEBANON	79	SWITZERLAN	95
CHILE	77	LESOTHO	48	SYRIA	54
CHINA	57	LIBERIA	26	TAIWAN	86
COLOMBIA	68	LIBYA	44	TANZANIA	27
COMOROS	30	LUXEMBOURG	95	THAILAND	68
CONGO	26	MADAGASCAR	41	TOGO	25
COSTA RICA	85	MALAWI	30	TRINIDAD &	80
CUBA	84	MALAYSIA	62	TUNISIA	47
CYPRUS	60	MALI	14	TURKEY	55
CZECHOSLOV	93	MAURITANIA	14	U.A.E.	33
DENMARK	96	MAURITIUS	77	U.K.	94
DJIBOUTI	30	MEXICO	73	UGANDA	34
DOM. REP.	64	MONGOLIA	45	URUGUAY	87
E. GERMANY	93	MOROCCO	40	USA	94
ECUADOR	67	MOZAMBIQUE	24	USSR	91
EGYPT	42	N. KOREA	45	VENEZUELA	79
EL SALVADO	64	NAMIBIA	48	VIETNAM	45
EQ. GUINEA	28	NEPAL	25	W. GERMANY	93
ETHIOPIA	19	NETH. ANT.	85	W. SAHARA	80
FALKLANDS	90	NETHERLAND	96	YEMEN-ADEN	27
FINLAND	94	NEW ZEALAN	94	YEMEN-SANA	27
FR. GUIANA	70	NICARAGUA	53	YUGOSLAVIA	84
FRANCE	94	NIGER	13	ZAIRE	28
GABON	21	NIGERIA	25	ZAMBIA	30
GAMBIA	25	NORWAY	96	ZIMBABWE	43
GHANA	34	OMAN	30		

NOTE: Physical Quality of Life Index (1-100)

Quality of Life
Sorted by Data

SWEDEN	97	PORTUGAL	78	PAKISTAN	38
DENMARK	96	CHILE	77	BANGLADESH	35
ICELAND	96	MAURITIUS	77	P.N.G.	35
JAPAN	96	KUWAIT	74	SUDAN	35
NETHERLAND	96	MEXICO	73	SWAZILAND	35
NORWAY	96	PARAGUAY	73	GHANA	34
CANADA	95	ALBANIA	72	UGANDA	34
LUXEMBOURG	95	SEYCHELLES	72	U.A.E.	33
SWITZERLAN	95	PHILIPPINE	71	HAITI	32
FINLAND	94	BELIZE	70	QATAR	31
FRANCE	94	FR. GUIANA	70	COMOROS	30
NEW ZEALAN	94	COLOMBIA	68	DJIBOUTI	30
U.K.	94	THAILAND	68	MALAWI	30
USA	94	BRAZIL	67	OMAN	30
AUSTRALIA	93	ECUADOR	67	ZAMBIA	30
AUSTRIA	93	BRUNEI	65	LAOS	29
BELGIUM	93	DOM. REP.	64	EQ. GUINEA	28
CZECHOSLOV	93	EL SALVADO	64	IVORY COAS	28
E. GERMANY	93	MALAYSIA	62	SAUDI ARAB	28
IRELAND	93	BAHRAIN	61	ZAIRE	28
W. GERMANY	93	CYPRUS	60	SIERRA LEO	27
ITALY	92	PERU	59	TANZANIA	27
BULGARIA	91	CHINA	57	YEMEN-ADEN	27
HUNGARY	91	TURKEY	55	YEMEN-SANA	27
POLAND	91	SYRIA	54	CONGO	26
SPAIN	91	CAPE VERDE	53	LIBERIA	26
USSR	91	NICARAGUA	53	CAMEROON	25
FALKLANDS	90	BURMA	51	GAMBIA	25
GREENLAND	90	GUATEMALA	51	NEPAL	25
PUERTO RIC	90	HONDURAS	51	NIGERIA	25
ROMANIA	90	INDONESIA	48	RWANDA	25
ISRAEL	89	LESOTHO	48	TOGO	25
BAHAMAS	88	NAMIBIA	48	MOZAMBIQUE	24
GREECE	88	S. AFRICA	48	SENEGAL	24
URUGUAY	87	JORDAN	47	BENIN	23
TAIWAN	86	TUNISIA	47	BURUNDI	22
ARGENTINA	85	BOTSWANA	45	GABON	21
COSTA RICA	85	MONGOLIA	45	BHUTAN	20
NETH. ANT.	85	N. KOREA	45	GUINEA	20
CUBA	84	VIETNAM	45	SAO TOME &	20
JAMAICA	84	IRAN	44	ETHIOPIA	19
YUGOSLAVIA	84	LIBYA	44	SOMALIA	19
SURINAM	83	BOLIVIA	43	AFGHANISTA	18
GUYANA	82	INDIA	43	CEN AF REP	18
S. KOREA	82	ZIMBABWE	43	CHAD	18
SRI LANKA	82	EGYPT	42	BURKINA FA	16
GUAM	80	ALGERIA	41	ANGOLA	15
PANAMA	80	MADAGASCAR	41	MALI	14
TRINIDAD &	80	KAMPUCHEA	40	MAURITANIA	14
W. SAHARA	80	MOROCCO	40	NIGER	13
LEBANON	79	IRAQ	39	GUINEA-BIS	11
VENEZUELA	79	KENYA	39		

REFERENCES: World Christian Encyclopedia (1978)
GLOBAL MAPPING PROJECT, INC. Pasadena, CA   08/05/87

Appendix 9-L — The Refugee Status
Sorted Alphabetically

AFGHANISTA	0	GREECE	4100	P.N.G.	10900
ALBANIA	0	GREENLAND	0	PAKISTAN	2500000
ALGERIA	167000	GUAM	0	PANAMA	1100
ANGOLA	92000	GUATEMALA	70000	PARAGUAY	0
ARGENTINA	11500	GUINEA	0	PERU	600
AUSTRALIA	89000	GUINEA-BIS	0	PHILIPPINE	15100
AUSTRIA	20500	GUYANA	0	POLAND	0
BAHAMAS	0	HAITI	0	PORTUGAL	600
BAHRAIN	0	HONDURAS	38000	PUERTO RIC	0
BANGLADESH	0	HUNGARY	0	QATAR	0
BELGIUM	36400	ICELAND	0	ROMANIA	1000
BELIZE	3000	INDIA	7200	RWANDA	49000
BENIN	3600	INDONESIA	7890	S. AFRICA	0
BHUTAN	0	IRAN	1000000	S. KOREA	0
BOLIVIA	0	IRAQ	0	SAO TOME &	0
BOTSWANA	3600	IRELAND	500	SAUDI ARAB	0
BRAZIL	5300	ISRAEL	0	SENEGAL	5000
BRUNEI	0	ITALY	15100	SEYCHELLES	0
BULGARIA	0	IVORY COAS	600	SIERRA LEO	0
BURKINA FA	0	JAMAICA	0	SOMALIA	700000
BURMA	0	JAPAN	1500	SPAIN	9900
BURUNDI	256300	JORDAN	800000	SRI LANKA	0
CAMEROON	13700	KAMPUCHEA	0	SUDAN	690000
CANADA	353000	KENYA	8000	SURINAM	0
CAPE VERDE	0	KUWAIT	0	SWAZILAND	6600
CEN AF REP	42000	LAOS	1200	SWEDEN	90600
CHAD	0	LEBANON	300000	SWITZERLAN	31200
CHILE	2500	LESOTHO	11500	SYRIA	280000
CHINA	179800	LIBERIA	0	TAIWAN	0
COLOMBIA	0	LIBYA	0	TANZANIA	178000
COMOROS	0	LUXEMBOURG	0	THAILAND	127476
CONGO	1000	MADAGASCAR	0	TOGO	1800
COSTA RICA	16000	MALAWI	0	TRINIDAD &	0
CUBA	2000	MALAYSIA	9155	TUNISIA	0
CYPRUS	0	MALI	0	TURKEY	2600
CZECHOSLOV	0	MAURITANIA	0	U.A.E.	0
DENMARK	8500	MAURITIUS	0	U.K.	135000
DJIBOUTI	16700	MEXICO	170000	UGANDA	151000
DOM. REP.	6000	MONGOLIA	0	URUGUAY	0
E. GERMANY	0	MOROCCO	800	USA	1000000
ECUADOR	900	MOZAMBIQUE	800	USSR	0
EGYPT	5500	N. KOREA	0	VENEZUELA	1400
EL SALVADO	0	NAMIBIA	0	VIETNAM	21000
EQ. GUINEA	0	NEPAL	0	W. GERMANY	126600
ETHIOPIA	72000	NETH. ANT.	0	W. SAHARA	0
FALKLANDS	0	NETHERLAND	15000	YEMEN-ADEN	0
FINLAND	500	NEW ZEALAN	4500	YEMEN-SANA	0
FR. GUIANA	0	NICARAGUA	18500	YUGOSLAVIA	1600
FRANCE	167300	NIGER	0	ZAIRE	329000
GABON	0	NIGERIA	4000	ZAMBIA	94000
GAMBIA	0	NORWAY	10000	ZIMBABWE	50000
GHANA	0	OMAN	0		

NOTE: Total number of refugees per country

The Refugee Status
Sorted by Data

Country	Value	Country	Value	Country	Value
PAKISTAN	2500000	DOM. REP.	6000	GAMBIA	0
IRAN	1000000	EGYPT	5500	GHANA	0
USA	1000000	BRAZIL	5300	GREENLAND	0
JORDAN	800000	SENEGAL	5000	GUAM	0
SOMALIA	700000	NEW ZEALAN	4500	GUINEA	0
SUDAN	690000	GREECE	4100	GUINEA-BIS	0
CANADA	353000	NIGERIA	4000	GUYANA	0
ZAIRE	329000	BENIN	3600	HAITI	0
LEBANON	300000	BOTSWANA	3600	HUNGARY	0
SYRIA	280000	BELIZE	3000	ICELAND	0
BURUNDI	256300	TURKEY	2600	IRAQ	0
CHINA	179800	CHILE	2500	ISRAEL	0
TANZANIA	178000	CUBA	2000	JAMAICA	0
MEXICO	170000	TOGO	1800	KAMPUCHEA	0
FRANCE	167300	YUGOSLAVIA	1600	KUWAIT	0
ALGERIA	167000	JAPAN	1500	LIBERIA	0
UGANDA	151000	VENEZUELA	1400	LIBYA	0
U.K.	135000	LAOS	1200	LUXEMBOURG	0
THAILAND	127476	PANAMA	1100	MADAGASCAR	0
W. GERMANY	126600	CONGO	1000	MALAWI	0
ZAMBIA	94000	ROMANIA	1000	MALI	0
ANGOLA	92000	ECUADOR	900	MAURITANIA	0
SWEDEN	90600	MOROCCO	800	MAURITIUS	0
AUSTRALIA	89000	MOZAMBIQUE	800	MONGOLIA	0
ETHIOPIA	72000	IVORY COAS	600	N. KOREA	0
GUATEMALA	70000	PERU	600	NAMIBIA	0
ZIMBABWE	50000	PORTUGAL	600	NEPAL	0
RWANDA	49000	FINLAND	500	NETH. ANT.	0
CEN AF REP	42000	IRELAND	500	NIGER	0
HONDURAS	38000	AFGHANISTA	0	OMAN	0
BELGIUM	36400	ALBANIA	0	PARAGUAY	0
SWITZERLAN	31200	BAHAMAS	0	POLAND	0
VIETNAM	21000	BAHRAIN	0	PUERTO RIC	0
AUSTRIA	20500	BANGLADESH	0	QATAR	0
NICARAGUA	18500	BHUTAN	0	S. AFRICA	0
DJIBOUTI	16700	BOLIVIA	0	S. KOREA	0
COSTA RICA	16000	BRUNEI	0	SAO TOME &	0
ITALY	15100	BULGARIA	0	SAUDI ARAB	0
PHILIPPINE	15100	BURKINA FA	0	SEYCHELLES	0
NETHERLAND	15000	BURMA	0	SIERRA LEO	0
CAMEROON	13700	CAPE VERDE	0	SRI LANKA	0
ARGENTINA	11500	CHAD	0	SURINAM	0
LESOTHO	11500	COLOMBIA	0	TAIWAN	0
P.N.G.	10900	COMOROS	0	TRINIDAD &	0
NORWAY	10000	CYPRUS	0	TUNISIA	0
SPAIN	9900	CZECHOSLOV	0	U.A.E.	0
MALAYSIA	9155	E. GERMANY	0	URUGUAY	0
DENMARK	8500	EL SALVADO	0	USSR	0
KENYA	8000	EQ. GUINEA	0	W. SAHARA	0
INDONESIA	7890	FALKLANDS	0	YEMEN-ADEN	0
INDIA	7200	FR. GUIANA	0	YEMEN-SANA	0
SWAZILAND	6600	GABON	0		

REFERENCES: UNHCR (1985) & Population Today (1986)
GLOBAL MAPPING PROJECT, INC. Pasadena, CA 08/05/87

9-M — Christian Organizations Specializing in Relief and Development

Bread for the World, 802 Rhode Island Ave. N.E., Washington, DC 20018

Catholic Relief Services, 1011 First Avenue, New York, NY 10022

Christian Blind Mission International, P.O. Box 715, Wheaton, IL 60187

Christian Medical Foundation, 7522 N. Himes Ave., Tampa, FL 33614

Christian Medical Society, P.O. Box 830689, Richardson, TX 75083-0689

Compassion International, P.O. Box 7000, Colorado Springs, CO 80933

ECHO (Educational Concerns for Hunger Organization), RR #2 Box 852, North Fort Meyers, FL 33903

Food For the Hungry, P.O. Box "E," Scottsdale, AZ 85252

Gooddeeds, P.O. Box 66400, Seattle, WA 98166

Harvest, 3080 North Civic Center Plaza, Suite 10, Scottsdale, AZ 85251

Hope International, P.O. Box 4116, Pasadena, CA 91106-0116

Hospital Christian Fellowship, P.O. Box 353, Kempton Park, 1620, South Africa.

IMPACT (International Missions Program for Assembling Consulting and Technical Teams), Pacific & Asia Christian University, 75-5851 Kuakini Highway, Kailua-Kona, Hawaii 96740-2199

Lifewater, P.O. Box 1126, Arcadia, CA 91006

Lutheran World Relief, 360 Park Avenue S., New York, NY 10010

MAP International (Medical Assistance Program), P.O. Box 50-M, Wheaton, IL 60189-0050

Mennonite Central Committee, 21 South 12th St., Akron, PA 17501

Mercy Corps International, 115 N. 8th, Suite 102, Seattle, WA 98103

Salvation Army World Service Office, 1025 Vermont Ave., NW., Washington, DC 20005

The Evangelical Alliance Relief Fund (TEAR Fund), 11 Station Road, Tedding, Middlesex, England TW11-9AA

TEAM, P.O. Box 969, Wheaton, IL 60189

Youth With A Mission, P.O. Box 4600, Tyler, TX 75712

World Concern, P.O. Box 33000, Seattle, WA 98133

World Medical Mission, Inc., P.O. Box 3000, Boone, NC 28607

World Opportunity International, 1415 N. Canuenga Blvd., Hollywood, CA 90028

World Relief, P.O. Box WRC, Wheaton, IL 60189-9936

World Vision International, 919 W. Huntington Dr., Monrovia, CA 91016

9-N — Directory of Mission Centers

Africa

Africa Centre for World Mission, Private Bag, Walkerville 1876, South Africa

Daystar Research Unit, P.O. Box 44400, Nairobi, Kenya

Asia

Brisbane Centre for World Mission, P.O. Box 175, Annerby, QLD 4103, Australia

Chinese Church Research Centre, P.O. Box 312, Sha Tin Center P.O., Sha Tin, N.T., Hong Kong

Chinese Coordination Centre of World Evangelism, P.O. Box 98435 Tsimshatsul, Kowloon, Hong Kong

Church Growth Research Centre, Post Bag 768, Kilpauk, Madras 600010, India

East-Western Center for Missions, Research & Development, CPO Box 2732, Seoul, Korea

Hong Kong Center for Frontier Missions, P.O. Box 71728, Kowloon CPO, Hong Kong

Indian Evangelical Mission Center, 38 Langford Road, Bangalore 5600025, India

Kansal Mission Research Center, 3-52-Chome, Nakajima-dori, Chuo-ku, Kobe 651, Japan

Navajeevodayam Centre for World Mission, P.O. Box 16 Tiruvalla, Kerala 689101, India

Singapore Center for Evangelism and Mission, 209 Bible House, 7 Armenian Street, Singapore 0617

World Missionary Training Institute, 1370 Soongin-Dong, Jongro-KLu, Seoul 110, Korea

Europe

German Center for World Mission, Breite Strasse 16, 5300 Bonn 1, Germany

Missions Center, Moholms Herrgard, 54050 Moholm, Sweden

Norwegian Center for World Mission, Nordregate 20, 0551 Oslo 5, Norway

Oxford Centre for Mission Studies, P.O. Box 70, St. Phillip & St. James Ch., Woodstock Road, Oxford, England

Scottish Centre for World Mission, 10 Prince Albert Road, Glasgow G129NW, United Kingdom

Latin America

Brazilian Center for Mission Information, Caixa Postal 72, 24400 Sao Goncalo, R.J., Brazil

Missionary Information Bureau, C.P. 1498, Sao Paulo, S.P. 01000, Brazil

PROLADES, Apartado 1307, San Jose, Costa Rica

PUENTE, Casilla 8559, Qito, Ecuador

North America

Billy Graham Center, Wheaton College, Wheaton, IL 60187

Canadian Centre for World Mission, 52 Carondale Crescent, Agincourt, Ont. M1W 2B1 Canada

Midwest Center for World Mission, 156 N. Oak Park Ave., Oak Park, IL 60301

Missions Advanced Research and Communication Center, 919 Huntington Dr., Monrovia, CA 91016;

Northwest Centre for World Mission, P.O. Box 1076, Station A, Surrey, B.C. V3S 4P5, Canada

U.S. Center for World Mission, 1605 Elizabeth Street, Pasadena, CA 91104

(Prepared by Darrell R. Dorr, U.S. Center for World Mission, 1605 Elizabeth Street, Pasadena, CA 91104.)

9-P — Tentmaking Information

Friends of the Tentmakers, 2606 Dwight Way, Berkeley, CA 94704

Global Opportunities, 1594 N. Allen #7, Pasadena, CA 91104

Issachar, P.O. Box 30727, Seattle, WA 98103

Tentmakers International, P.O. Box 33836, Seattle, WA 98133

9-Q — Short Term Service

Campus Crusade for Christ, Arrowhead Springs, San Bernardino, CA 92414

Christian Service Corps, 8501 Houston St., Silver Springs, MD 20910

Gospel Recordings, 122 Glendale Blvd., Los Angeles, CA 90026

International Crusades, P.O. Box 203, Prospect Heights, IL 60070

Inter-Varsity Missions, 233 Langdon, Madison, WI 53703

Operation Mobilization, P.O. Box 148, Midland Park, NJ 07432

Teen Missions, P.O. Box 1056, Merritt Island, FL 32952-1056

Vacation Samaritans, 57610 Crestline Dr., Yucca Valley, CA 92284

Wycliffe Bible Translators, Huntington Beach, CA 92647

Youth With A Mission, P.O. Box 4600, Tyler, TX 75712

9-R —Recommended Periodicals for Becoming a World Christian

Asian Report, P.O. Box 9000 Mission Viejo, CA 92690.

Chinese Around the World, P. O. Box 98435, TST, Hong Kong. Free upon request.

Christianity Today, 465 Gunderson Dr., Carol Stream, IL 60187. A good overview of North American evangelical thought and activity.

Comscam, P.O. Box 30727, Seattle, WA 98103. Developments in Communist dominated areas.

Evangelical Missions Quarterly, P.O. Box 794, Wheaton, IL 60189. A missionary journal giving practical contemporary information. Read in over 120 countries by thousands of missionaries.

Foreign Quarters, Issachar, P.O. Box 30727, Seattle, WA 98103. Gives background of information on frontier mission areas.

Global Church Growth, Corunna, IN 46730.

Global Prayer Digest, Frontier Fellowship, Inc., P.O. Box 90970, Pasadena, CA 91109. Gives daily prayer information related to fulfilling the Great Commission.

Global Report, World Evangelical Fellowship, P.O. Box WEF, Wheaton, IL 60189. Free upon request. Brief, every other month report of world-wide mission and church activities.

IFMA News, (Interdenominational Foreign Mission Association, P.O. Box 395, Wheaton, IL 60189-0395. Free upon request. Gives current information of mission activities of all IFMA member organizations. (About eighty mission agencies.)

International Bulletin of Missionary Research, Circulation Dept., P.O. Box 1308-E, Fort Lee, NJ 07024. Scholarly missions information.

International Journal of Frontier Missions, P.O. Box 40638, Pasadena, CA 91104-7638.

MARC Newsletter, World Vision International, 919 West Huntington Dr., Monrovia, CA 91016. Magazine subscription.

Missionary News Service, Evangelical Missions Information Service, P.O. Box 794, Wheaton, IL 60187. Twice a month missions news digest.

Personal Prayer Diary, P.O. Box 1380, Lindale, TX 75771.

Pulse, Evangelical Missions Information Service, P.O. Box 794, Wheaton, IL 60187. Twice a month missions reports and analysis.

Sharing God's Love with Muslims, Box 365, Altadena, CA 91001

The Church Around the World, Tyndale House Publishers, 336 Gunderson Dr., Wheaton, IL 60189. Brief digest of world-wide mission and church happenings.

World Christian, P.O. Box 40010, Pasadena, CA 91104. A "must."

World Evangelization, 8008 Corporate Center Dr., Suite 401, Charlotte, NC 28211. Free.

Periodicals that tell primarily of one organization's activities

Many denominational periodicals.

American Bible Society Record, American Bible Society, 1865 Broadway, New York, NY 10023. Tells of world-wide activities of the American Bible Society.

Bibles for the World, P.O. Box 805, Wheaton, IL 60189.

Christian Mission, Christian Aid Mission, Rt. 10, Box 1, Charlottesville, VA 22901. Free upon request. Tells of activities of Third World missionaries associated with Christian Aid Mission.

Disciple, The Navigators, P.O. Box 6000, Colorado Springs, CO 80901.

Frontlines, Youth With A Mission, P.O. Box 4600, Tyler, TX 75712. Free upon request. Tells of world-wide activities of Youth With A Mission.

In Other Words, Wycliffe Bible Translators, Huntington Beach, CA 92648. Free upon request. Tells of activities of Wycliffe Bible Translators.

Mission Frontiers, U.S. Center for World Mission, 1605 E. Elizabeth St., Pasadena, CA 91104. Missions information from the U.S. Center for World Mission.

Open Doors, Brother Andrew, P.O. Box 2020, Orange, CA 92669. Tells of world-wide activities of Brother Andrew's Bible distribution work.

The Broadcaster Magazine, Far East Broadcasting Co., P.O. Box 1, La Mirada, CA 90637.

The Flame, CBN (Christian Broadcasting Network), Virginia Beach, VA 23463.

World Vision Magazine, 919 W. Huntington Dr., Monrovia, CA 91016. Free upon request. Tells of activities of World Vision; also reports on other mission activities.

Worldwide Challenge, Campus Crusade for Christ, Arrowhead Springs, San Bernardino, CA 92414. Helpful information, CCC activities.

9-S — For Further Training

Short-term training available through those listed in 9-P and the following:

English Language Institute/China, P.O. Box 265, San Dimas, CA 91773

Institute of International Studies, 1605 E. Elizabeth St., Pasadena, CA 91104

LIFE (Language Institute for Evangelism), P.O. Box 200, Alhambra, CA 91802

Missionary Internship, 36200 Freedom Road, Farmington, MI 48024

Overseas Ministries Study Center, 6315 Ocean Ave., Ventnor, NJ 08406

U.S. Center for World Mission, 1605 Elizabeth St., Pasadena, CA 91104

For Bible school and Christian college directors write

American Association of Bible Colleges, P.O. Box 1523, Fayetteville, AK 72702. Request: Directory of American Association of Bible Colleges.

Christian College Coalition, 1776 Massachusetts Ave., NW., Washington, DC 20036

Youth For Christ International, P.O. Box 419, Wheaton, IL 60187. Request: Guide to Christian Colleges

Seminaries and universities with a major in missions

Asbury Theological Seminary, 204 N. Lexington Ave., Wilmore, KY 40390

Azusa Pacific University Graduate Program, Citrus and Alosta, Azusa, CA 91702

Bethel Theological Seminary, 3949 Bethel Dr., St. Paul, MN 55112

Biola University, La Mirada, CA

California Theological Seminary, 2515 West Shaw, Fresno, CA 93711

CBN University, CBN Center, Virginia Beach, VA 23463

Columbia Graduate School of Bible and Missions, P.O. Box 3122, Columbia, SC 29230

Concordia Theological Seminary, Fort Wayne, IN

Dallas Theological Seminary, 3909 Swiss Ave., Dallas, TX 75204

Denver Conservative Baptist Seminary, P.O. Box 10,000, Denver, CO 80210

Eastern Baptist Theological Seminary, Lancaster & City Avenues, Philadelphia, PA 19151

Fuller Theological Seminary, 135 N. Oakland Ave., Pasadena, CA 91101

Gordon-Conwell Theological Seminary, 130 Essex St., S. Hamilton, MA 01982

Grace Theological Seminary, 200 Seminary Dr., Winona Lake, IN 46590

North American Baptist Seminary, 1321 West 22nd St., Sioux Falls, SD 57105

Ontario Theological Seminary, 25 Ballyconnor Court, Willowdale, Ont. Canada M2M 4B3

Oral Roberts University, 7777 S. Lewis, Tulsa, OK 74171

Pacific & Asia Christian University, 75-5851 Kuakini Hwy., Kailua-Kona, HI 96740

Regent College, 2130 Westbrook Mall, Vancouver, B.C. Canada V6T 1W6

Rhema Bible Training School, P.O. Box 50126, Tulsa, OK 74150

Southwestern Baptist Theological Seminary, Fort Worth, TX

Talbot Theological Seminary, 13800 Biola Ave., La Mirada, CA 90639

Trinity Evangelical Divinity School, 2065 Half Day Road, Deerfield, IL 60015

Westminster Theological Seminary in Pennsylvania, P.O. Box 27009, Philadelphia, PA 19118

Wheaton College, Wheaton, IL 60187

William Carey International University, 1605 Elizabeth St., Pasadena, CA 91104

Additional information in Directory: North American Protestant Schools and Professors of Missions, available from MARC

9-T — Places of Service

Get information from:

Your denominational missions department.

Association of International Mission Services, P.O. Box 64534, Virginia Beach, VA 23464

Evangelical Foreign Missions Association, 1430 "K" St., N.W., Suite 900, Washington, DC 20005, (202) 628-7911

Intercristo, 19303 Fremont Ave., N., P.O. Box 33487, Seattle, WA 98133, (800) 426-1342 or (206) 546-7330.

Interdenominational Foreign Mission Association, P.O. Box 395, Wheaton, Il 60187, (312) 682-9270.

Other agencies listed throughout this Appendix 9.

9-U — For Detailed Strategy Information

Global Mapping Project, 1605 E. Elizabeth St., Pasadena, CA 91104

Issachar, P.O. Box 30727, Seattle, WA 98103

Lausanne Committee for World Evangelization, 8008 Corporate Center Dr., Suite 401, Charlotte, NC 28211

MARC, World Vision International, 919 West Huntington Dr., Monrovia, CA 91016

U.S. Center for World Mission, 1605 E. Elizabeth St., Pasadena, CA 91104

APPENDIX 10 — SUMMARY OF JESUS' TEACHING ON END-TIMES

As Found in Matthew 24-25, Mark 13, Luke 21

Matt 24	Mark 13	Lk 21	Summary of Events (Outline form)	Similar Scriptures
			I. Introduction	
1-2	1-2	5-6	1. Jesus talking about destruction of temple	
3	3-4	7	2. Disciples ask Jesus about end-times	
			II. Before the Great Tribulation	
			A. The beginning of birth pangs	
4	5-6	8	1. Take heed that you are not misled by false Christs	
6-7a	7-8a	9-10	2. Wars and rumors of wars, do not be troubled, must take place, end not yet, nation against nation, kingdom against kingdom	
7b	8b	11	3. Upheaval of nature—earthquakes, famines, plagues, terrors, great signs from heaven	
8	8c	—	4. The beginning of birth pangs (#1-3)	
			B. Just before the Tribulation	
9-12	9,11-13a	12-17	1. Pre-tribulation persecution—beaten in synagogues, before rulers, hated, killed,	Matt. 10:17-22 Luke 12:10-12

Matt 24	Mark 13	Lk 21	Summary of Events (Outline form)	Similar Scriptures
			many fall away, betrayed by relatives and friends, false prophets, lawlessness, love cold. God will protect and give words to speak.	
13	13b	19	2. Must endure	
14	10	—	3. Gospel to all peoples	
			III. The Great Tribulation	Luke 17:22-37
15-20	14-18	20-21, 23a	1. Abomination of desolation, Jerusalem surrounded by armies, flee to mountains	
21-22	19-20	22, 23b	2. Great tribulation—shortened for the sake of the elect	
—	—	24	3. Fall by the sword, led captive into all nations, Jerusalem trodden down by Gentiles until time of Gentiles fulfilled	
—	—	24	4. Do not be misled by false Christs and false prophets	
29a	24a	—	IV. After the Great Tribulation	
29b	24b-25	25-26	1. In sky—sun darkened, moon not give light, stars fall, powers of the heavens shaken. On earth—anxiety, perplexity, and fainting	
30-31	26-27	27	2. Jesus comes in clouds with great power and	I Cor. 15:50-58

Matt 24	Mark 13	Lk 21	Summary of Events (Outline form)	Similar Scriptures
			glory, angels, and trumpets to gather His elect	I Thes. 4:13-18
			V. Concluding Exhortations	
—	—	28	1. Be encouraged	
32-41	28-32	29-33	2. You will know approximately when Jesus is to return, but not the exact day	
42-51 Also Ch.25	33-37	34-36	3. Lifestyle of watchfulness (take heed, be alert, pray) and faithful service	Luke 18:1-8

FOOTNOTES

Preface

[1]All Scripture quotations are from The New American Standard Bible unless otherwise noted.

PART I — REVIVAL

[1]Ralph Mahoney, *Is A New Wave of Revival Coming?*, World Missionary Assistance Plan, Burbank, CA, 1982, p. viii.
[2]Statement made at the International Prayer Assembly in Seoul, Korea, June 5-11, 1984.

Chapter 1 — Definition and Biblical Basis

[1]Ron Boehme, *Revive Thy Work*, Youth With A Mission, 133 "C" Street S.E., Washington, D.C. 20003, 1979, p. 1.
[2]*The American College Dictionary*, Random House, N.Y., N.Y., 1951, S.V. "revival."
[3]Arthur Wallis, *Rain From Heaven*, Hodder and Stoughton, Kent, England, 1979, p. 13.
[4]Wallis, p. 15.
[5]Wallis, p. 15.
[6]Boehme, p. 1.
[7]Boehme, p. 1.
[8]Boehme, p. 1.
[9]"News Service of the Southern Baptist Convention," Nashville, TN, February 19, 1982, p. 1.
[10]Owen Murphy, "This is Revival," *Herald of His Coming*, Box 3457, Terminal Annex, Los Angeles, CA 90051, December, 1982, p. 1.
[11]Bill Bright, "Revival," *Worldwide Challenge*, San Bernardino, CA 92414, March, 1983, p. 6.
[12]Charles Finney, *Finney on Revival*, Bethany House Publishers, Minneapolis, MN 55438, p. 9.

[13]Dr. A. Skevington Wood, "Characteristics of Holy Spirit Revival," *Convention Herald,* Salem, OH, April, 1981, p. 4.

[14]Charles Spurgeon, "Genuine Revival," *Herald of His Coming,* May, 1983.

[15]Taken from Ron Boehme, *Revive Thy Work,* Youth With A Mission, 133 "C" Street S.E., Washington, D.C. 20003, 1971.

Chapter 2 — Revivals Throughout Church History (A.D. 100-1900)

[1]William E. Allen, *The History of Revivals of Religion,* Revival Publishing Company, Belfast, North Ireland, 1951, p. 7.

[2]Allen, p. 8.

[3]Allen, p. 9.

[4]Allen, p. 9-10.

[5]Allen, p. 10-11.

[6]Allen, p. 13-14.

[7]Allen, p. 15-16.

Kenneth S. Latourette, *A History of Christianity,* Harper & Row, New York, NY, 1975, p. 893, 897.

Ruth A. Tucker, *From Jerusalem to Irian Jaya,* Zondervan, Grand Rapids, MI 49506, 1983 p. 69-74.

[8]*America's Great Revivals,* compiled by Bethany Fellowship, Minneapolis, MN 55438, p. 5-25.

Boehme, *Revive Thy Work,* p. 4.

Keith J. Hardman, *The Spiritual Awakeners,* Moody Press, Chicago, IL 1983, p. 31-36.

Richard F. Lovelace, *Dynamics of Spiritual Life,* Inter-Varsity Press, Downers Grove, IL 60151, 1980, p. 35-46.

J. Edwin Orr, *The Re-Study of Revival and Revivalism,* Fuller Theological Seminary, 135 N. Oakland Ave., Pasadena, CA 91101, 1981, p. 5-8.

[9]Orr, *The Re-Study,* p. 7.

[10]Orr, *The Re-Study,* p. 7.

[11]Allen, p. 25-26.

Christian History Magazine, Volume 11, No. 1, "Special Commemorative Issue devoted to John Wesley," Worcester, PA 19490, 1984, p. 7-8.

Hardman, p. 75-97.

Latourette, p. 1023-1035.

Lovelace, p. 35-46.

Orr, *The Re-Study,* p. 3.

[12]Allen, p. 30-34.

America's Great Revivals, p. 26-51.

Hardman, p. 109-146.

Latourette, p. 1037-1055.

Lovelace, p. 46-48.

J. Edwin Orr, *Evangelical Awakenings in Africa,* Bethany Fellowship, Minneapolis, MN, 55438, 1975, p. 1-6, 26-46.

Orr, *The Re-Study,* p. 9-24.

J. Edwin Orr, "The Role of Prayer in Spiritual Awakening," Oxford Association for Research in Revival, Los Angeles, CA, p. 1-3.

[13]*America's Great Revivals,* p. 52-72.

Ron Boehme, "Revival Born in a Prayer Meeting," *Revive Thy Work,* Youth With A Mission, 133 "C" Street S.E., Washington, D.C. 20003, p. 1.

J. Edwin Orr, *America's Great Revival,* McBeth Press, Elizabethtown, PA, 1957, p. 5-29.

Orr, *Evangelical Awakenings in Africa,* p. 47- 52.

Orr, *The Re-Study,* p. 25-40.

Orr, "The Role of Prayer . . .," p.4-5.

Orr, *The Second Evangelical Awakening in America,* Marshall, Morgan and Scott, London, 1952, p. 21-22.

[14]J. Edwin Orr, *The Re-Study,* p. v.

Chapter 3 — Revivals in Modern Times (1900-Present)

[1]Latourette, p. 1167.

[2]Timothy L. Smith, *Revivalism and Social Reform,* Abingdon Press, New York, N.Y., p. 135-142.

[3]Frank Bartleman, *Azusa Street,* Logos International, Plainfield, NJ 07060, 1980, p. xi.

Manual, Church of the Nazarene, Nazarene Publishing House, Kansas City, MO, 1980, p. 15-22.

[4]Bartleman, p. 8-42.

[5]George T. B. Davis, "A Spiritual Awakening," *Herald of His Coming,* Box 3457, Terminal Annex, Los Angeles, CA 90051, May, 1983, p. 3.

[6]J. Edwin Orr, *Evangelical Awakenings in the South Seas,* Bethany Fellowship, Inc., Minneapolis, MN 55438, 1976, p. 106.

Orr, *Evangelical Awakenings, 1900-,* Moody Press, Chicago, IL, 1973, p. 152.

[7]Jonathan Goforth, "Pentecost Was Merely a Specimen Day," *Herald of His Coming,* February, 1981, p. 1.

[8]Allen, p. 52-53.

Phil Bartell, "American History: The Rest of the Story," from *Worldwide Challenge,* Arrowhead Springs, San Bernardino, CA, March, 1983, Volume 10, #3, p. 17-18.

Charles Clarke, *Pioneers of Revival,* Logos, Plainfield, NJ 07060, p. 25-30.

Herald of His Coming, December, 1980, p. 5.

Herald of His Coming, December, 1982, p. 1.

Orr, *South Seas,* p. 99-100.

Orr, "The Role of Prayer," p. 5-7.

[9]Orr, *Evangelical Awakenings, 1900 -,* p. 20.

[10]Orr, *Evangelical Awakenings in the South Seas,* p. 100.

Orr, *The Role of Prayer,* p. 7, 8.

[11]Orr, *The Flaming Tongue,* entire book.

Orr, *The Re-Study,* p. 44-45.

[12]Orr, *Evangelical Awakenings, 1900 -,* p. 191.

Orr, *South Seas,* p. 100-103.

[13]Bartelman, *Azusa Street,* entire book.

Logos, Logos International Fellowship, Inc., Plainfield, NJ 07060, Volume II, No. 2, March/April, 1981, p. 4,10-13.

Aimee Semple McPherson, *The Story of My Life,* Word Books, Waco, TX 76796, 1973, entire book.

Vinson Synan, *In the Latter Days,* Servant Books, Ann Arbor, MI 48107, 1984, p. 32-34.

[14]Stanley H. Frodsham, *With Signs Following,* Gospel Publishing House, Springfield, MO 65802, 1946, p. 7-17.

[15]Interview with Frank and Kay Baynes of Cranbrook, B.C., Canada.

Logos, March/April, 1981, p. 15.

[16]Orr, *The Re-Study,* p. 57-58.

[17]A tape of a message given by Duncan Campbell in a church in Wisconsin in the 1960's.

Herald of His Coming, December, 1982, p. 1.

[18]Author's correspondence with some of these colleges.

Orr, *Campus Aflame,* Regal Books, Ventura, CA 93003, p. 165-179.

[19]"Nagaland Revival Continues," from YWAM *Advance,* Holmstead Manor, Staplefield Road, Cuckfield, West Sussex RH17-5FJ, England, Issue 13.

Interview with Ken Wright of New Zealand in July, 1986.

[20]*Logos,* March/April, 1981, p. 14-16.

"Spiritual Sparks Ignite Some Mainstream Churches," from *Christianity Today,* 465 Gunderson Drive, Carol Stream, IL 60188, August 8, 1981, p. 29-31.

Vinson Synan, *In The Latter Days,* most of the book.

"What Does the Future Holy for Charismatic Renewal?," *Christianity Today,* May 16, 1986, p. 38-44.

[21]Mel Tari, *Like A Mighty Wind,* Creation House, Carol Stream, IL, 1971, entire book.

[22]Kurt E. Koch, *God Among the Zulus,* Kregel Publishers, Grand Rapids, MI, 1981, excerpts in *Herald of His Coming,* January 1982, p. 1, 4-5.

[23]Robert E. Coleman, *One Divine Moment,* Fleming H. Revell Company, Old Tappan, NJ 07675, 1970, entire book.

Orr, *Campus Aflame,* p. 209.

[24]Orr, *Campus Aflame,* p. 210-212.

[25]Erwin W. Lutzer, *Flames of Freedom,* Moody Press, Chicago, IL, 1978, entire book.

[26]*Herald of His Coming,* March, 1981, p. 11.

Chapter 4 — A Soon-Coming, Mighty, World-Wide, End-Time Revival

[1]Sources for statistical information are given in Chapter 16.

[2]Revival Prayer Fellowship, News Sheet #147, W. B. Grant, 349 Latymer Court, London W6 7LH, England.

[3]W.H. Offiler, *The Harmonies of Divine Revelation,* Bethel Temple, Seattle, WA, 1946, p. 116-124.

[4]Graham Truscott, *The Power of His Presence,* World Map Press, Burbank, CA 91502, 1969, p. 6, 325-326.

[5]Harold Lindsell, *The Holy Spirit in the Latter Days,* Thomas Nelson, Nashville, TN, 1983, p. 180.

[6]*Charisma,* 190 N. Westmonte Dr., Altamonte Springs, Fl 32714, August 1984, p. 65.

The Church Around The World, Volume 14, #1, Tyndale House Publishers, Wheaton, IL, December, 1983.

World Evangelical Fellowship Global Report, Volume 13, #2, April, 1983.

World-Wide Challenge, May/June, 1984, p. 58.

[7]"President Reagan and the Bible," *Christianity Today,* 465 Gundersen Drive, Carol Stream, IL, March 4, 1983, p. 46.

[8]*U.S. News & World Report,* "Special Report: Religion's New Turn, A Search for the Sacred," April 4, 1983, p. 35-36.

[9]*U.S. News & World Report,* "Special Report: Protestants Shift from Issues to Prayer," April 4, 1983, p. 36-38.

[10]*U.S. News & World Report,* "Special Report: For Catholics, It's No Longer 'Pray, Pay and Obey,'" April 4, 1983, p. 42.

[11]Ron Boehme, *Network,* Youth With A Mission, Washington, D.C., 20003. Further information may be obtained from Coalition on Revival, 89 Pioneer Way, Mountain View, CA 94041.

[12]*Church Around the World,* "International Prayer Assembly—1984," Volume 14, #1, Tyndale House Publishers, Carol Stream, IL, December, 1983.

[13]James Robison, "Receive or Resist?" *Charisma,* December, 1983, p. 49, 50.

[14]E. M. Bounds, *Power Through Prayer,* Zondervan Publishing House, Grand Rapids, MI 49506, p. 9.

[15]*Herald of His Coming,* "A Call For Prayer," September, 1982, p. 6.

[16]*Herald,* September, 1982, p. 7.

[17]*Breaking up the Fallow Ground,* Last Days Ministries, Pretty Good Printing, Box 40, Lindale, TX 75771-0040, 1979.

PART II — RESTORATION

[1]Frank Bartleman, *Another Wave of Revival,* Whitaker House, Pittsburgh and Colfax Streets, Springdale, PA 15144, 1982, p. 135.

[2]Arthur Wallis, "Revival and Recovery," Frank Bartleman, *Another Wave of Revival,* p. 168.

Chapter 5 — The Principle of Restoration

[1]*The American College Dictionary,* 1951, S.V. "restoration."

[2]The Lockman Foundation, *New American Standard Bible Concordance,* Holman Bible Publishers, Nashville, TN, 1975, p. 1011, 1602.

[3]NASB Concordance, p. 1011, 1634.

[4]This writer first heard of a restoration interpretation of Church history from a Church of God pastor in Oklahoma in about 1962. He then saw it in some of Claxton Monro's writings (an evangelical Episcopal priest in Houston, Texas). Then he discovered it as an Epilogue to the book, *Another Wave Rolls In,* (currently under the title *Another Wave of Revival*), by Frank Bartleman (edited by John Walker), Voice Christian Publications, Northridge, CA, 1962. Then, he saw it in some of Bob Mumford's teachings. More recently he has discovered it in the writings of Dick Iverson, pastor of Bible Temple in Portland, Oregon: *Present Day Truths,* Bible Press, 7545 N.E. Glisan Street, Portland, OR 97213, 1975. Finally, in 1981 this writer discovered it in the preaching of Aimee Semple McPherson, founder of the International Church of the Foursquare Gospel: *The Foursquare Gospel,* comp. by Raymond L. Cox, Foursquare Publishing, Los Angeles, CA 90026, 1969, p. 20-38.

[5]Bartleman, p. 139-140.

[6]Dick Iverson, *Present Day Truths,* Bible Press, 7545 N.E. Glisan Street, Portland, OR 97213, 1975, p. 52.

[7]McPherson, *The Foursquare Gospel,* p. 37.

[8]Bartleman, p. 135.

[9]Wallis, p. 155.

[10]Wallis, p. 168.

[11]Donald F. Durnbaugh, *The Believers' Church,* Herald Press, Scottsdale, PA, p. 216-17.

[12]Durnbaugh, p. 218.

[13]Durnbaugh, p. 219.

[14]E. H. Broadbent, *The Pilgrim Church,* Pickering & Inglis Ltd., London, England, 1963, p. 2.

[15]"Search For the New Testament Church," by Maxwell Whyte, *Christian Life Magazine,* January, 1984, p. 39, Wheaton, IL 60188.

Chapter 6 — The Early Church

[1]Arthur Wallis, "Revival and Recovery," (Frank Bartleman, *Another Wave of Revival*), p. 155-156.

Chapter 7 — The Decline From New Testament Christianity

[1]Elgin S. Moyer, Th. D., *Great Leaders of the Christian Church,* Moody Press, Chicago, IL 60645, 1951, p. 77.

[2]Iverson, p. 23.
[3]Iverson, p. 23.
Bruce L. Shelley, *Church History in Plain Language,* Word Books
Publishers, Waco, TX 76703, 1982, p. 85.
[4]Iverson, p. 23.
Latourette, p. 115-119, 129-133, 182-185.
Moyer, p. 96-101.
[5]Broadbent, p. 9.
Iverson, p. 23.
[6]Latourette, p. 79, 91-93, 204.
[7]Latourette, p. 81-91.
Moyer, p. 51.
[8]Latourette, p. 91-94.
Moyer, p. 105-108.
Shelley, p. 108-109.
[9]Broadbent, p. 36-37.
[10]Broadbent, p. 24-26.
Latourette, p. 173-179.
[11]Latourette, p. 185.
Moyer, p. 155-156.
[12]Latourette, p. 339.
Moyer, p. 154-165.
[13]Latourette, p. 365-367.
Moyer, p. 198-210, 229, 234, 235.
[14]Latourette, p. 482-486.
Moyer, p. 272-275.
[15]Broadbent, p. 58-59, 85, 89.
Moyer, p. 275-279.
World Book, Childcraft Int'l., Inc., Chicago, IL, 1964, Volume 5, p.
248.
[16]Moyer, p. 378.
[17]Latourette, p. 455-458.
 Moyer, p. 370-378.
[18]Latourette, p. 456.
[19]Broadbent, p. 102.
Latourette, p. 487.
[20]Latourette, p. 1088, 1092-1095.
[21]Latourette, p. 1363.

Chapter 8 — The Process of Restoration
Throughout Church History

[1]Broadbent, p. 12-13.
Latourette, p. 128-129.
Moyer, p. 78-91.
Shelley, p. 80-81.
Synan, p. 27.
Some Historians see the Montanists as heretical, while others, including the author, see them as a restoration movement, although they may have had some excesses.
[2]Broadbent, p. 31-33.
Latourette, p.221-235.
Shelley, p. 131-139.
[3]Latourette, p. 342-349.
J. Herbert Kane, *A Global View of Christian Missions,* Baker Book House, Grand Rapids, MI 49506, 1977, p. 37-42.
Moyer, p. 170-179.
[4]Broadbent, p. 74-84.
Latourette, p. 166-170, 322-325, 590-591.
Moyer, p. 183-189.
Shelley, p. 126-128.
Tucker, p. 45.
[5]Broadbent, p. 42-55.
[6]Broadbent, p. 36-60.
[7]Some writers indicate that the Cathari, or Albigenses, may have had some questionable beliefs. This was not true of the Waldenses, who adhered strictly to the Scriptures.
[8]Broadbent, p. 87-89.
Latourette, p. 453-455.
Moyer, p. 277-278.
[9]Latourette, p. 453.
[10]Durnbaugh, p. 47.
[11]Latourette, p. 452.
[12]Broadbent, p. 89-94.
Latourette, p. 451-453.
Moyer, p. 278-279.
Shelley, p. 225-227.
World Book, Volume 20, p. 7.

[13]Latourette, p. 424-425.
 Moyer, p. 251-252.
[14]Latourette, p. 425-426, 539.
[15]Latourette, p. 539-540.
[16]Latourette, p. 643-644.
[17]Latourette, p. 541-543, 646-654, 850-854.
[18]Latourette, p. 429-433.
 Moyer, p. 241-251.
[19]Latourette, p. 437-439.
 Moyer, p. 248-249.
[20]Latourette, p. 439.
[21]Latourette, p. 662-666.
 Moyer, p. 292-295.
 Shelley, p. 343-348.
[22]Latourette, p. 666-669.
 Moyer, p. 295-297.
 Shelley, p. 248-251.
[23]Durnbaugh, p. 51-63.
[24]*World Book,* Volume 2, p. 219.
 World Book, Volume 8, p. 428-429.
[25]Latourette, p. 671-675.
 Moyer, p. 297-298.
[26]Latourette, p. 670-671.
[27]Latourette, p. 661-662, 747.
 Moyer, p. 288, 298, 303-304, 313, 318, 336.
 Shelley, p. 286.
 World Book, Volume 6, p. 269.
[28]Latourette, p. 703-742.
 Moyer, p. 305-314.
 Shelley, p. 255-264.
 World Book, Volume 12, p. 458-459.
[29]Moyer, p. 317-350.
 Shelley, p. 274-288, 309-318.

Chapter 9 — The Process of Restoration Throughout Church History (Continued)

[1]Latourette, p. 778-786.
 Moyer, p. 353-365.

Shelley, p. 265-273.

[2]Moyer, p. 312-313.

[3]Latourette, p. 821.

Moyer, p. 319, 326-332.

[4]Moyer, p. 342.

[5]Latourette, p. 765.

Moyer, p. 425-432.

World Book, Volume 1, p. 681.

[6]E. H. Broadbent, p. 85-101.

[7]Latourette, p. 779, 818, 1037-1038, 1178-1182.

[8]Latourette, p. 813-816.

[9]Broadbent, p. 249-253.

Latourette, p. 822-823.

[10]Broadbent, p. 255-270.

[11]Latourette, p. 895-896.

[12]Broadbent, p. 347-400.

Latourette, p. 1185-1290.

Moyer, p. 394-396.

[13]Latourette, p. 1040-1042.

World Book, Volume 3, p. 405, 423-424.

[14]James Burns, *Revival, Their Laws and Leaders,* Baker Book House, Grand Rapids, MI 49506, 1960, p. 15, 36-41.

Latourette, p. 1023-1030.

Moyer, p. 417-428, 455-464.

Shelley, p. 350-360.

[15]Kane, p. 3-47, 57-71.

[16]Kane, p. 73-77.

[17]Kane, p. 77-78.

[18]Kane, p. 78-80.

Latourette, p. 897.

Shelley, p. 407-410.

World Book, Volume 13, p. 656-657.

[19]Kane, p. 83-86.

Latourette, p. 1033.

Moyer, p. 435-439.

Shelley, p. 394-396.

Tucker, p. 114-121.

Ralph D. Winter, *Protestant Mission Societies: The American Experience,*

William Carey Library, Pasadena, CA 91104, 1979, p. 145-146.

[20]Tucker, p. 114-121.

[21]Latourette, p. 128.

[22]Latourette, p. 227-228, 645-646.

[23]Smith, *Revivalism & Social Reform*, Abingdon Press, Nashville, TN, 1957, entire book.

[24]Latourette, p. 1185-1186.

[25]McPherson, entire book.

[26]Adolf Harnack, *The Mission and Expansion of Christianity in the First Three Centuries*, 2 Volumes, Putnam, New York, 1908, p. 153.

[27]Latourette, p. 1185- 1186.

Moyer, p. 430.

Shelley, p. 432-433.

[28]Latourette, p. 1173-1177.

Shelley, p. 433.

[29]Latourette, p. 1066, 1103-1104, 1162.

[30]Smith, p. 148-177.

[31]Smith, p. 178-224.

[32]Latourette, p. 1263-1624.

Shelley, p. 434-436.

[33]Latourette, p. 1199-1200, 1336.

World Book, Volume 14, p. 463.

World Book, Volume 16, p. 180.

[34]Iverson, p. 23.

[35]Moyer, p. 427.

[36]Latourette, p. 1167.

[37]Tucker, p. 292.

[38]An excellent book, *All Things are Possible*, by David E. Harrel, Jr., Indiana University Press, Bloomington, IL 47405,1975. Tells of the 1947-1960 healing revival.

Winkie Pratney, *Revival*, Whitaker House, Springdale, PA 15144, 1983, p. 189-207.

"The Latter Rain and Healing Revivals," *New Wine*, Ft. Lauderdale, FL, October, 1980, p. 30-32.

[39]Latourette, p. 1184-1185.

[40]Editors of *Christian Life Magazine* with C. Peter Wagner, "Signs and Wonders Today," Christian Life Missions, Wheaton, IL 60187, 1982, p. 23-24.

[41]*Christian Life Magazine,* "Signs and Wonders Today," p. 35.

[42]For further information contact The Navigators, P.O. Box 6000, Colorado Springs, CO 80901, and Mr. Jerry Lucas, Memory Ministries, P.O. Box 58600, Manhattan Beach, CA 90266.

Chapter 10 — Today-The Completion of the Restoration

[1]Dr. J. Edwin Orr, "Playing the Good News Melody Off-key," *Christianity Today,* Carol Stream, IL 60188, January 1, 1982, p. 24-25.

[2]Alan Langstaff, "A New Day is Dawning for the Church," *Charisma,* 190 N. Westmonte Dr., Altmonte Springs, FL 32714, March, 1983, p. 37.

[3]Dick Mills, *The New Wave of the Holy Spirit,* Harrison House, P.O. Box 35035, Tulsa, OK 74153, 1983, p. 7, 15-16.

[4]*U.S. News & World Report,* March 28, 1983, p. 14.

U.S. News & World Report, February 13, 1984, p. 10.

[5]Literature from Association of Christian Schools, P.O. Box 4097, Whittier, CA 90607.

U.S. News & World Report, March 5, 1984, p. 46.

[6]*Intercessors For America,* P.O. Box 2639, Reston, VA 22040, February 1, 1984, p. 2.

[7]Information from Bill Gothard at lecture in Portland, Oregon, March, 1984.

[8]Dr. Carl F. H. Henry, "The Road to Eternity," *Christianity Today,* Carol Stream, IL 60188, July 17, 1981, p. 33.

[9]*Salt Shakers,* Inc., P.O. Box 30114, Portland, OR, Volume III, No. 5-6, May-June, 1983.

Chapter 11 — The Completion of the Restoration (Continued)

[1]The author has gleaned much of this from an excellent series on authority by Ralph Mahoney in *World Map Digest,* 900 N. Glenoaks, Burbank, CA 90502, November/December, 1983 and January/ February, 1984.

PART III — UNITY

[1]Paul E. Billheimer, *Love Covers,* Christian Literature Crusade, Fort Washington, PA 19034, 1981, p. 31.

[2]Francis A. Schaeffer, *The Church at the End of the Twentieth Century*, Inter-Varisity Press, Downers Grove, IL 60515, 1970, p. 153.

Chapter 12 — Basic Definitions and Concepts

[1]*The American College Dictionary*, 1951, S.V. "unity."
[2]David B. Barrett, *World Christian Encyclopedia*, Oxford University Press, New York, NY, 1982, p. 17.
[3]Moyer, p. 222-223.

Chapter 13 — Practical Application Today   NONE

PART IV — WORLD EVANGELIZATION

[1]C. Peter Wagner, *On the Crest of the Wave*, Regal Books, A Div. of G/L Publication, Ventura, CA 93006, 1983, back cover.
[2]Robert E. Coleman, *The Master Plan of Evangelism*, Fleming H. Revell Co., Old Tappan, NJ 07675, 1963, p. 21, 31, 37.

Chapter 14 — Definitions and Biblical Basis   NONE

Chapter 15 — World Evangelization Throughout Church History

[1]Kane, p. 3-35.
Latourette, p. 3-266.
William Steuart McBirnie, *The Search for the Twelve Apostles*, Tyndale House Publishers, Wheaton, IL 60189, 1973, entire book.
Shelley, p. 9-158.
[2]Latourette, p. 269-415.
Kane, p. 14, 37-47.
[3]Dr. Donald A. McGavran, Conference on Revival, Missions, and Church Growth at Fuller Theological Seminary, Pasadena, CA 91101, on June 6, 1986.
[4]*World Book*, Volume 15, p. 174.
[5]Moyer, p. 169-170.
Latourette, p. 101-102.
[6]Kane, p. 49-55.
Latourette, p. 269-415.
[7]Latourette, p. 924-951.
Kane, p. 57-71.
World Book, Volume 20, p. 450.

[8]Len Bartlotti, "A Call For a Mission Renewal Movement," *International Journal of Frontier Missions*, Pasadena, CA 91104, 1980, all of the publication.

Church History Magazine, Box 540, Worcester, PA 19490, Volume 1, #1.

Durnbaugh, *The Believers' Church*, p. 233.

International Bulletin of Missionary Research, P.O. Box 1308-E, Fort Lee, NJ 07024-9958 April, 1983, p. 56.

Kane, p. 73-89.

Tucker, p. 67-417.

Ralph Winter, *Perspectives on the World Christian Movement*, William Carey Library, Pasadena, CA 91104, 1981, p. 167-174, 202, 206-252, 599.

Chapter 16 — World Evangelization Today

[1]We are talking about waves of evangelism activity during the present Church Age. There may be further evangelism activity during the Millenium which is not covered in this book.

[2]Statistical information throughout this chapter is based on information available in 1986 and has been verified by U.S. Center for World Mission, Pasadena, CA; MARC, Monrovia, CA; and Issachar, Seattle, WA; but final responsibility rests with the author.

[3]Data Source: World Population Data sheet (interpolation).

[4]Data Source: *Operation World*, by Patrick Johnstone, Fourth edition, 1986, WEC Publications, Bulstrode, Gerrards Cross, Bucks, SL9-85Z, England. Verified by Global Mapping Project, 1605 E. Elizabeth St., Pasadena, CA 91104.

[5]*World Evangelization*, LCFWE, Box 2308, Charlotte, NC 28211, June 1985, p. 15.

[6]C. Peter Wagner, *On the Crest of the Wave*, Regal Books, a Division of G/L Publications, Ventura, CA 93006, 1983, p. 21-25.

[7]Wagner, p. 25-28.

[8]Wagner, p. 28-31.

[9]"The Bible: The Year in Review," *Christianity Today*, Carol Stream, IL 60188, October 4, 1985, p. 23-29.

[10]"The Legacy of Frank Charles Laubach," *International Bulletin of Missionary Research*, P.O. Box 1308-E, Fort Lee, NJ 07024-9958 April, 1983, p. 58-62.

[11]Tucker, p. 327.

[12]Information supplied by Food for the Hungry International Coordination Center, Switzerland, taken from *Hope Magazine,* December 1982, March/April, 1983.

[13]*World Vision,* 919 W. Huntington Dr., Monrovia, CA 91016 September 1982, and March 1983.

[14]Billy Graham Evangelistic Association, Minneapolis, MN 55440.

Chapter 17 — How the Great Commission Can Be Fulfilled In This Generation   NONE

Chapter 18 — How You Can Get Involved

[1]*Mission Frontiers,* 1605 Elizabeth St., Pasadena, CA 91104, March 1984, p. 5.

World Concern, 19303 Fremont Ave. N., Seattle, WA 98133, March 1982, p. 21.

World Concern, April 1982, p. 2.

PART V — PERSECUTION

[1]Billy Graham, *Till Armageddon,* World Wide, 1303 Hennepin Ave., Minneapolis, MN 55403, 1981, p. 15.

[2]David Wilkerson, *The Vision,* Fleming H. Revell Co., Old Tappan, NJ 07675, 1974, p. 116.

Chapter 19 — End-Time Persecution

[1]Nate Krupp, *The Omega Generation?,* New Leaf Press, Inc., Harrison, AR 72601, 1977, p. 120.

[2]Jim McKeever, *Christians Will Go Through the Tribulation,* Omega Publications, P.O. Box 4130, Medford, OR 97501, 1978, p. 5.

Chapter 20 — Preparedness   NONE

Epilogue

[1]Arthur Wallis, *Rain From Heaven,* Hodder and Stoughton, London, England, 1974, p. 124.

BIBLIOGRAPHY

Listed here are all books and articles that are quoted or mentioned in this book. Also listed is additional recommended reading and sources for further information. The starred (*) ones are especially recommended.

PART I — REVIVAL

Allen, William E., *The History of the Revivals of Religion,* Revival Publishing Company, Belfast, North Ireland, 1951.

American College Dictionary, Random House, New York, NY 10022, 1951.

Bartell, Phil, "American History: The Rest of the Story," *Worldwide Challenge,* San Bernardino, CA 92414, March 1983, Volume 10, #3.

Bartleman, Frank, *Azusa Street,* Logos International, Plainfield, NJ 07060, 1980. About the 1906 Pentecostal revival.

Bethany Fellowship, Inc., *America's Great Revivals,* 6820 Auto Club Rd., Minneapolis, MN 55438, 1970.

Boehme, Ron, *Revive Thy Work,* Youth With A Mission, 133 C St., S.E., Washington, DC 20003.

Bohlen, John Roy, *How to Rule the World* or *"Seek 1st the Kingdom of God",* John Roy Bohlen, P.O. Box 7123, Minneapolis, MN 55407

Bounds, E.M., *A Treasury of Prayer,* Bethany House Publishers, 6820 Auto Club Rd., Minneapolis, MN 55435, 1981.

*Bounds, E.M., *Power Through Prayer,* Zondervan Publishing Company, Grand Rapids, MI 49506, 1972.

Bright, Bill, "Revival," *Worldwide Challenge,* San Bernardino, CA 92414, March, 1983.

Bryant, Al, *The John Wesley Reader,* Minister's Personal Library, Waco, TX, 76796, 1984.

*Cairns, Earle E., *An Endless Line of Splendor,* Tyndale House, Wheaton, IL 1986. Revivals and their leaders from Great Awakening to the present.

Cho, Paul Y., *Prayer: Key to Revival,* Word Books, Waco, TX 76796, 1984.

Christian History Magazine, "Special Commerative Issue devoted to John Wesley," Worcester, PA 19400, Volume II, No. 1, 1984.

Christianity Today, "Christianity Comes of Age in the NFL," Carol Stream, IL 60188, January 13, 1984.

Christianity Today, "President Reagan and the Bible," Carol Stream, IL 60188, March 4, 1983.

Church Around the World, Tyndale House Publishers, Wheaton, IL 60189, Volume 14, December, 1983.

Church Around The World, "Religion on Campus," Tyndale House Publishers, Wheaton, IL 60189, April, 1984.

Clarke, Charles, *Pioneers of Revival,* Logos, Plainfield, NJ, 07060.

Coleman, Robert E., *One Divine Moment,* Fleming H. Revell Company, Old Tappan, NJ 07675, 1970. About the 1970 revival at Asbury College.

Coleman, Robert E., *Dry Bones Can Live Again,* Fleming H. Revell Company, Old Tappan, NJ, 07675.

Dawson, Joy, *Intimate Friendship With God,* Chosen Books, Fleming H. Revell Company, Old Tappan, New Jersey. A study of the fear of God.

Drummond, Lewis A., *The Awakening That Must Come,* Broadman, Nashville, TN 37234, 1979.

Finney, Charles, "Breaking Up The Fallow Ground," Last Days Ministries, Pretty Good Printing, Box 40, Lindale, TX 75771-0040.

Goforth, Jonathan, *When The Spirit's Fire Swept Korea,* Bethel Publishing, 1819 S. Main, Elkhart, IN 46516.

Goforth, Jonathan, *By My Spirit,* Bethel Publishing, 1819 S. Main, Elkhart, IN 46516, 1983.

Graham, Dr. John, *The Coming Wave of God's Spirit,* King's Publishing Co., 3000 Fairfield Ave., Shreveport, LA 71104, 1984.

*Grubb, Norman, *Rees Howells, Intercessor,* Christian Literature Crusade, Fort Washington, 701 Penn. Ave., PA 19034. An intercessor who changed the world.

Hardman, Keith J., *The Spirit Awakeners,* Moody Press, Chicago, IL 60610, 1983.

Harper, Michael, *The Twentieth Century Pentecostal Revival,* Logos International, Plainfield, NJ 07060, 1965.

Hawkins, O.S., *After Revival Comes,* Broadman, Nashville, TN 37234.

Herald of His Coming, Gospel Revivals, Box 3457 Terminal Annex, Los Angeles, CA 90051. Free upon request. Excellent on revival and other deeper-life subjects.

*Hessin, Roy, *The Calvary Road,* Christian Literature Crusade, Fort Washington, 701 Penn. Ave., PA 19034, 1976. The pathway to revival.

Howard, Linda, "Milton Green: Missionary to the Southern Baptists," *Charisma,* 190 N. Westmonte Dr., Altamonte Springs, FL 32714, December, 1983.

Intercessors For America, P.O. Box 1289, Elyria, OH 44036, Volume 10, 11, Nov. 1, 1983.

James, Keith, *Lord, Bend the Church,* Harvest Intercession Ministries, P.O. Box 15122, Wellington, New Zealand. An urgent appeal to prepare for God's sovereign revival through obedience, holiness, and prayer.

Kaiser, Walter C., Jr., *Quest for Revival,* Moody Press, Chicago, IL 60610, 1986. Personal revival in the Old Testament.

Koch, Kurt E., *God Among the Zulus,* Kregal Publishers, Grand Rapids, MI 49501, 1981.

Lindsay, Gordon, *They Saw It Happen,* Christ For The Nations, Dallas, TX, 75224. About pentecostal revival in the 20th century.

Lindsell, Harold, *The Holy Spirit in the Latter Days,* Thomas Nelson Publishers, Box 141000, Nashville, TN 37214.

Lockman Foundation (The), *New American Standard Bible Concordance,* Holman Bible Publishers, Nashville, TN 37234, 1975.

Lockyer, Herbert, *All The Prayers of the Bible,* Zondervan Publishing House, Grand Rapids, MI 49506, 1959.

Logos, entire issue, Plainfield, NJ 07060, March-April, 1981.

Lovelace, Richard F., *Dynamics of Spiritual Life,* Inter-Varsity Press, Downers Grove, IL 60151, 1980. The theology of revival.

Lloyd-Jones, Martyn, *Revival,* Crossway Books, Good News Publishers, Westchester, IL 60153

Lutser, Erwin W., *Flames of Freedom,* Moody Press, Chicago, IL 60610, 1976. About the 1971-72 revival in western Canada.

McPherson, Aimee Semple, *The Story of My Life,* Word Books, Waco, TX 76796, 1973.

*Mahoney, Ralph, *Is a New Wave of Revival Coming?,* World Missionary Assistance Plan, Burbank, CA 91502, 1982. Coming revival to United States and the world. Interesting thought on timing.

*Marshall, Peter, *The Light and the Glory,* Fleming H. Revell Co., Old Tappan, NJ 07675, 1977. America's spiritual foundation.

Marshall, Peter and Manuel, David, *From Sea to Shining Sea,* Revell, Old Tappan, NJ 07675, 1986. America's spiritual history from 1787 to 1837.

Mallone, George, CanadianRevival: *It's Our Turn,* Welch Publishing Co. Burlington, Ontario, Canada, 1985.

McGraw, Francis, *Praying Hyde,* Dimension Books, Bethany Fellowship, Inc., Minneapolis, MN 55438, 1970.

Murillo, Mario, *Critical Mass,* Anthony Douglas Publishing Co., Chatsworth, CA 91311, 1985. A strategy for revival in North America.

Murphy, Owen, "This Is Revival," *Herald of His Coming,* Los Angeles, CA 90051, December, 1982.

Murray, Andrew, *The Ministry of Intercession,* Bethany House Publishers, 6820 Auto Club Rd., Minneapolis, MN 55435.

Murray, Andrew, *Humility,* Whitaker House, Springdale, PA 15144, 1982.

"News Service of the Southern Baptist Convention," 460 James Robertson Parkway, Nashville, TN 37219, February 19, 1982.

Offiler, W.H., *The Harmonies of Divine Revelation,* Bethel Temple, Seattle, WA, 1946.

*National Prayer Leaders Newsletter, The National Prayer Committee, P.O. Box 6826, San Bernardino, CA 92412. Networks all prayer ministries in North America.

*Olford, Stephen F., *Heart- Cry for Revival,* Fleming H. Revell Co., Old Tappan, NJ 07675, 1962. Challenging messages about revival.

Orr, J. Edwin, *America's Great Revival,* McBeth Press, Elizabethtown, PA, 1957. About the 1857-59 revival.

Orr, J. Edwin, *Campus Aflame,* Regal Books, 2300 Knoll Dr., Ventura, CA 93003.

Orr, J. Edwin, *Evangelical Awakenings in Africa,* Bethany Fellowship, Inc., Minneapolis, MN 55438, 1975.

Orr, J. Edwin, *Evangelical Awakenings in Eastern Asia,* Bethany Fellowship, Inc., Minneapolis, MN 55438, 1975.

Orr, J. Edwin, *Evangelical Awakenings in Latin America,* Bethany Fellowship, Inc., Minneapolis, MN 55438, 1978.

Orr, J. Edwin, *Evangelical Awakenings in Southern Asia,* Bethany Fellowship, Inc., Minneapolis, MN 55438, 1975.

Orr, J. Edwin, *Evangelical Awakenings in the South Seas,* Bethany Fellowship, Minneapolis, MN 55438, 1975.

*Orr, J. Edwin, *The Flaming Tongue,* Moody Press, Chicago, IL 60610, 1973. About the 1905 revival.

Orr, J. Edwin, *The Re-Study of Revival and Revivalism,* Fuller Theological Seminary, 135 N. Oakland Ave., Pasadena, CA 91101, 1981.

Orr, J. Edwin, *The Outpouring of the Spirit in Revival and Awakening and Its Issue in Church Growth,* 135 N. Oakland Ave., Pasadena, Ca 91101, 1984.

*Dr. Orr's extensive teaching on the great awakenings is also available on video and film from Campus Crusade for Christ.

*Pratney, Winkie, *Revival,* Whitaker House, Springdale, PA 15144, 1983. History and principles of revival.

**Proposal for City-wide Prayer Rallies,* Intervarsity Mission, P.O. Box 7895, Madison, WI 53707-7895. Excellent.

Quebedeaux, Richard, *The New Charismatics II,* Harper & Row, New York, NY 10022, 1983.

Renewal, edited by Richard Lovelace, 4 issues, published papers, Box 162, S. Hamilton, MA 01936.

*Ravenhill, Leonard, *America Is Too Young To Die,* Bethany House, Minneapolis, MN 55438, 1983.

Ravenhill, Leonard, *A Treasury of Prayer,* Fires of Revival, Zachery, LA 70791, 1961.

Ravenhill, Leonard, *Revival God's Way,* Bethany Publishing, Minneapolis, MN 55438, 1983.

Ravenhill, Leonard, *Sodom Had No Bible,* Bethany House, Minneapolis, MN, 55438, 1979.

Ravenhill, Leonard, *Revival Praying,* Bethany House Publishing, Minneapolis, MN 55438, 1962.

*Ravenhill, Leonard, *Why Revival Tarries,* Bethany House Publishing, Minneapolis, MN 55438, 1959.

Revival Prayer Fellowship, *Newsheet #147,* W.B. Grant, 349 Latymer Ct., London, England W67LH

Riss, Richard, *The Latter Rain Movement of 1948 and the Mid-twentieth Century Evangelical Awakening,* National Library of Canada, Canadian Theses on Microfilm Service, 395 Wellington St., Ottawa, Ontario, Canada K1A ON4.

Robb, Edmon W., "Spiritual Sparks Ignite Some Mainstream Churches," *Christianity Today,* Carol Stream, IL 60188, August 8, 1981.

Roberts, Richard Owen, *Revival,* Tyndale House, Wheaton, IL 60188, 1983. He also has a very large library of books on revival.

Robison, James "Receive or Resist?," *Charisma,* December, 1983.

Revival Prayer Groups, I.H.C. Heritage House, Salem, OH 44460.

Schmul, H.E., *Handbook on Revival,* Schmul Publishing Co., Salem, OH 44460.

Shakarian, Demos, *The Happiest People On Earth,* Fleming H. Revell Co., Old Tappan, NJ 07675, 1975.

Smith, Timothy L., *Revivalism and Social Reform,* Abingdon Press, Nashville, TN 37202, 1980.

Spurgeon, Charles, "Genuine Revival," *Herald of His Coming,* Gospel Revivals, Inc., Los Angeles, CA 90051, May, 1983.

Stewart, James A., *Invasion of Wales by the Spirit,* Revival Literature, 159 Davenport Rd., Ashville, NC 28806.

Synan, Vinson, *Azusa Street Revival,* Logos, Plainfield, NJ 07060, 1980.

*Synan, Vinson, *In The Latter Day: The Outpouring of the Holy Spirit in the 20th Century,* Servant Books, P.O. Box 8617, Ann Arbor, MI 48107, 1984. The pentecostal and charismatic revivals.

Tari, Mel, *Like A Mighty Wind,* Creation House, Carol Stream, IL 60188, 1971. About the revival in Indonesia in the mid-1960's.

Truscott, Graham, *The Power of His Presence,* World Map Press, Burbank, CA 91502, 1969.

U.S. News & World Report, "A Revival of Religion on Campus," 2400 N. Street, N.W., Washington, D.C. 20037-1196, January 9, 1984.

U.S. News & World Report, "At Eastertide, A Resurgence of Religion," Washington, DC, April 30, 1984.

U.S. News & World Report, "Special Report: Religion's New Turn," Washington, DC, April 4, 1983.

Wallis, Arthur, *God's Chosen Fast,* Christian Literature Crusade, Fort Washington, PA 19034, 1968.

Wallis, Arthur, *In the Day of Thy Power,* CLC, Fort Washington, PA, 1956.

*Wallis, Arthur, *Rain From Heaven,* Hodder and Stoughton, London,

Warner, Wayne E., *Revival,* Harrison House, Tulsa, OK 74153.

Wilkerson, David, *Racing Toward Judgment*, Revell, Old Tappan, NJ 07675, 1971.

Wood, Dr. A. Skevington, "Characterstic of Holy Spirit Revival," *Convention Herald*, Salem, OH 44460, 1981.

Woolsey, Andrew, *Duncan Campbell, A Biography*, Hodder & Stoughton, London, England, 1974.

Youth With A Mission, "Nagaland Revival Continues," *Advance*, Issue 13, Holmsted Manor, Cuckfield, West Sussex, England RH17 5JF.

PART II — RESTORATION

A. Books that Substantiate the Restoration throughout Church History

Arnold, Aberhard, *The Early Anabaptists*, The Plough Publishing House, Rifton, NY 12471, 1984.

*Bartleman, Frank, *Another Wave of Revival*, Ed. By John G. Meyers, Whitaker House, Pittsburgh, and Colfax Streets, Springdale, PA 15144, 1982. How revivals cause restoration.

*Broadbent, E.H., *ThePilgrimChurch*, Pickering & Inglis Ltd., 29 Ludgate Hill, London, England, 1963. Restoration throughout Church history.

Brooks, Patricia O., *The Return of The Puritans*, WhitakerHouse, Springdale, PA 15144, 1976.

Burns, James, Revival, *Their Laws and Leaders*, Baker Book House, Grand Rapids, MI 49506, 1960. Some of the restoration leaders.

Beuhring, Dave, *Acts Alive*, Crown Ministries, Box 49, Euclid, MN 56722, 1986. A studay book on the Church in *The Acts*.

Christian History Magazine, Box 540, Worcester, PA 19490.

Discerning Times, Bread of Life Fellowship, P.O. Box 351, Shippensburg, PA, 17257-0351. A newspaper for the end-time Church.

*Durnbaugh, Donald F., *The Believers Church*, Herald Press, Scottdale, PA, 1968.

Flood, Robert, *America God Shed His Grace on Thee*, Moody Press, Chicago, IL 60645, 1975.

Frodsham, Stanley H., *With Signs Following*, Gospel Publishing House, Springfield, MO 65802, 1948. About the restoration of gifts of the Spirit to the Church in the late 1800's and early 1900's.

305

Fuller, David Otis, D.D., *A Treasury of Evangelical Writings,* Kregal Publications, Grand Rapids, MI 49501, 1961.

*Hamon, Dr. Bill, *The Eternal Church,* Christian International Publishers, P.O. Box 27398, Phoenix, AZ 85061, 1981.

Harnack, Adolf, *The Mission and Expansion of Christianity in the First Three Centuries,* 2 Vol., Putnam, NY 10016, 1981.

Harrell, David E., *All Things are Possible,* Indiana University Press, Bloomington, IN 47405, 1975. About the healing revivals of the 1940's and 50's.

*Iverson, Dick with Bill Scheidler, *Present Day Truths,* Bible Press, Portland, OR 97213, 1975. Detailed teaching of restoration.

Jackson, Jeremy, *No Other Foundation: the Church Through Twenty Centuries,* Crossway Books, Westchester, IL 60153, 1980. Church history.

*Latourette, Kenneth Scott, fwd. by Ralph D. Winter, *A History of Christianity, Vol. 1 and 2,* Harper & Row, New York, NY 10022, 1975. A comprehensive account of Church history.

Merricks, William S., *Edward Irving,* Scribe's Chamber Publications, P.O. Box 2123, East Peoria, IL 61611, 1983. A new release on a controversial forerunner to the Pentecostal movement.

McPherson, Aimee Semple, *The Story of My Life,* Words Books, Waco, TX 76796, 1973.

McPherson, Aimee Semple, comp. by Dr. Raymond L. Cox, *The Foursquare Gospel,* Heritage Committee, Foursquare Publications, Los Angeles, CA 90026, 1969. Contains Aimee's restoration message.

Mitchell, Robert Bryant, *Heritage and Horizons,* Open Bible Publishers, Des Moines, LA 50315, 1982. History of Open Bible Standard movement.

*Moyer, Elgin S., Th.D.M Ph.D., *Great Leaders of the Christian Church,* Moody Press, Chicago, IL 60645, 1951. Church history.

Schmitt, Charles, *Root out of Dry Ground - A History of the Church,* Charles Schmitt, 210 Third Ave., N.E., Grand Rapids, MI 55744, 1979.

*Shelley, Bruce L., *Church History in Plain Language,* Word Books Publisher, Waco, TX 76796, 1982. Easy to read.

Smith, Timothy L., *Revivalism & Social Welfare,* Abingdon Press, Nashville, TN 37202, 1957. Restoration of social reform in 1800's.

Snyder, Howard A., *The Radical Wesley,* Inter-Varsity Press, Downers Grove, IL 60515, 1980.

Synan, Vinson, *Aspects of Pentecostal - Charismatic Origins,* Logos International, Plainfield, NJ 07060, 1975.

Thompson, Bruce, *The Divine Plumbline,* Crown Ministries, P.O. Box 49, Euclid, MN 56722, 1983.

Williams, Rodman, *The Pentecostal Reality,* Logos International, Plainfield, NJ 07060, 1972.

World Book Encyclopedia, Childcraft International, Inc., Chicago, IL 1964, Vol. 1, p. 681, Vol. 2, p. 219, Vol. 5, p. 248, Vol. 6, p. 269, Vol. 8, p. 428-429, Vol. 12, p. 458-459, Vol. 13, p. 656-657, Vol. 14, p. 463, Vol. 15, p. 174, Vol. 16, p. 80, Vol. 20, p. 7.

B. Books That are Indicative of What God is Doing Today

Association of Christian Schools, P.O. Box 4097, Whittier, CA 90607.

Backus, William and Marie Chapian, *Telling Yourself The Truth,* Bethany Fellowship, Inc., Minneapolis, MN 55438, 1980. Helps renew the mind.

Baker, Don, *Beyond Forgiveness,* Multnomah Press, Portland, OR 97266, 1984. About redemptive church discipline.

Barna, George and McKoy, William Paul, *Vital Signs,* Crossway Books, Westchester, IL 60153, 1984. Emerging social trends and the future of American Christianity.

Bennett, Rita, *I'm Glad You Asked That,* Aglow Publications, Edmonds, WA, 1974; or direct from Rita Bennett, Box 576, Edmonds, WA 98020.

Biblical Blueprints Series, Dominion Press, 7112 Burns Street, Fort Worth, TX 76118. A series being published in 1986-87 giving biblical solutions for the problems facing our culture today.

*Billheimer, Paul E., *Destined for The Throne,* Christian Literature Crusade, Fort Washington, PA 19034, 1975. Intercession principles.

Bosworth, F.F., *Christ The Healer,* fwd. by R.V. Bosworth, Fleming H. Revell Company, Old Tappan, NJ 07675, 1973. About physical healing.

Bridges, Jerry, *The Pursuit of Holiness,* Navpress, Colorado Springs, CO 80934, 1978.

Carmody, John, *Ecology and Religion, Toward a New Christian Theology of Nature,* Paulist Press, Ramsey, NJ 07446, 1983.

Cho, Paul Yonggi, *More Than Numbers,* Word Books, Waco, TX 76796, 1984.

*Christenson, Larry, *The Christian Family,* Bethany Fellowship, Minneapolis, MN 55438, 1970.

Christian Life Magazine, ed. with co-op of C. Peter Wagner, *Signs and Wonders Today,* Christian Life Missions, Wheaton, IL 60187, 1982.

Cole, Edwin Louis, *Maximized Manhood,* Whitaker House, Springdale, PA 15144, 1982.

Colson, Charles W., "Whatever Became of Sin?," *Charisma,* February, 1984.

Days of Restoration, 1801 W. Euless Blvd., Euless, TX 76040. Magazine dedicated to restoration.

Derstine, Gerald, *Woman's Place In The Church,* Gospel Crusade Publications, Route 2, Box 279, Bradenton, FL 33505, 1977.

Dobson, James, *Dare to Discipline,* Tyndale House Publishers, Wheaton, IL 60187, 1970.

Dobson, James, *Hide and Seek,* Fleming H. Revell Company, Old Tappan, NJ 07675, 1970.

Edwards, Gene, *The Early Church,* Christian Books, Box 959, Augusta, ME 04330, 1974.

Eidsmore, John, *God and Caesar,* Goods News Publishers, Westchester, IL 60753, 1984. About Christian faith and political action.

Eidsmore, John, *The Christian Legal Advisor,* Mott Media, Milford, MI 48042, 1984.

Eldson, Ron, *Bent World, "A Christian Response the Environmental Crisis.,"* Inter-Varsity Press, Downers Grove, IL 60515, 1981.

*Fellowship Bible Church, *16 Tests of an Authentic New Testament Church,* Hegg Bros. Printing, Tacoma, WA 98407, 1980.

Foster, K. Neill, *Help! I Believe In Tongues,* Bethany Fellowship, Inc., Minneapolis, MN 55438, 1975.

Gesswein, Armin R., *With One Accord for One Place,* Christian Publications, Inc., Harrisburg, PA 17101, 1978. Importance of the local assembly.

Girard, Robert C., *Brethren, Hang Loose,* intro by Lawrence O. Richards, Zondervan Corp., Grand Rapids, MI 49506, 1972. New Testament church principles applied today.

Goslin, Thomas S., *The Church Without Walls*, Hope Publishing Co., Pasadena, CA 91106, 1984.

Graham, Billy, *Angels: God's Secret Agents*, Doubleday & Company, Inc., Garden City, NY 10017, 1975. Angels assisting Christians.

Grant, George, *In the Shadow of Plenty*, Dominion Press, Ft. Worth, TX, 1986. The Biblical blueprint for welfare.

Hagin, Kenneth, *The Woman Question*, Kenneth Hagin Evangelistic Assn., P.O. Box 50126, Tulsa, OK 74150, 1975.

Hallesby, O., *Temperament and the Christian Faith*, Augsburg Publishing House, Minneapolis, MN 55438, 1962.

Hammond, Frank & Ida Mae, *Pigs in the Parlor*, Impact Books, Inc., Kirkwood, MO 63122, 1973. On deliverance from demons-especially good on schizophrenia.

Hardisty, Margaret, *Forever My Love*, fwd. by Tim LaHaye, Harvest House Publishers, Irvine, CA 92707, 1975. What men should know about women.

Hartman, Jack, *Trust God for Your Finances*, Lamplight Publications, 912 Union St., Manchester, NH 03104.

Helfy, James C., *Textbooks on Trial*, S.P. Publications, Wheaton, IL 60187, 1976.

*Hegre, T.A., *The Cross and Sanctification*, fwd. by Norman P. Grubb, Bethany Fellowship, Inc., Minneapolis, MN 55438, 1960. The spirit-filled life.

Henley, Gary, *The Quiet Revolution*, Creation House, Inc., Carol Stream, IL, 60187, 1970. A return to house church principles.

Henry, Dr. Carl F.H., "The Road to Eternity," *Christianity Today*, 465 Gundersen Dr., Wheaton, IL 60188, July, 17, 1981.

Institute in Basic Youth Conflicts, *Basic Seminar Textbook*, Institute in Basic Youth Conflicts, Oakbrook, IL 60521.

Intercessors for America, Vol. II, No. 2, Elyria, OH, February 1, 1984.

Jackson, Dave & Neta, *Living Together in a World Falling Apart*, Creation House, Carol Stream, IL 60187, 1974.

Jepson, Dee, *Women: Beyond Equal Rights*, Word Books, Waco, TX 76796, 1984.

LaHaye, Tim, *How To Study the Bible For Yourself*, Harvest House Publishers, Irvine, CA 92714, 1976.

Laney, J. Carl, *A Guide to Church Discipline*, Bethany House

Publishers, Minneapolis, MN 55438, 1985. About Biblical discipline and restoration.

Langstaff, Alan, "A New Day Is Dawning for the Church," *Charisma*, 190 N. Westmonte Dr., Altamonte Springs, FL 32714 March, 1983.

Love, Robert, *How to Start Your Own School*, MacMillan Publishing Company, New York, NY 10022, 1973.

MacDonald, William, *True Discipleship*, Walterick Publishers, Kansas City, KS 66110, 1975. Being a genuine disciple of Jesus.

MacNutt, Father Francis, *Healing*, Bantam Books, Inc., Publ. with Ave Maria Press, New York, NY 10019, 1974. Physical and emotional healing.

Mahoney, Ralph, "Authority," *World Map Digest*, 900 N. Glenoaks, Burbank, CA 91502, Nov./Dec., 1983 and Jan/Feb 1984.

Marshall, Catherine, *The Helper*, Chosen Books, Lincoln, VA 22078, 1978. Holy Spirit in personal life.

Matthews, R. Arthur, *Born for Battle*, Send the Light, P.O. Box 48, Bromley, Kent, England, 1978.

McCrossan, T.J., BA, B.D., *Bodily Healing and the Atonement*, Hagin Ministries, Tulsa, OK 74150, 1982.

Montgomery, John Warwick, *Human Rights and Human Dignity*, Zondervan, Grand Rapids, ML 49506, 1986.

Moore, Waylon B., *Building Disciples Notebook*, Missions Unlimited, P.O. Box 8203, Tampa, FL 33604.

*Nee, Watchman, *The Normal Christian Church Life*, Christian Literature Crusade, Inc., Fort Washington, PA 19034, 1962. New Testament church principles.

Nee, Watchman, *Spiritual Authority*, Christian Fellowship Publishers, Hollis, NY 11423, 1972.

Orr, Dr. J. Edwin, "Playing the Good News Melody Off-Key," *Christianity Today*, Carol Stream, IL 60188,July, 1981.

Pape, Dorothy T., *In Search of God's Ideal Woman*, Inter-Varsity Press, Downers Grove, IL 60515, 1976. What the Bible teaches about women.

*Penn-Lewis, Jessie, *War On the Saints*, Christian Literature Crusade, Fort Washington, PA 19034, 1964.

**People of Destiny magazine*, 3515 Randolph Road, Wheaton, MD 20902.

Prophecy Today magazine, 175 Tower Bridge Road, London, England.

Roberts, Robert C., *Spirituality and Human Emotion,* Eerdmans Publishing House, Grand Rapids, MI 49503, 1983.

Rumble, Dale, *I Will Build My Church,* Fountain of Life, 79 E. Chester St., Kingston, NY 12401.

Rust, Eric C., *Nature: Garden or Desert,* An Essay in Environmental Theology, Word Books, Waco, TX 76796, 1971.

Salt Shakers, Inc., "Christian Jurisprudence." Vol. III, No.5-6, Portland, OR, May-June, 1983.

*Sanders, J. Oswald, *Spiritual Leadership,* (Revised Edition), The Moody Bible Institute, Chicago, IL 60645, 1980.

*Sandford, John & Paula, *The Transformation of the Inner Man,* Bridge Publishing, Inc., South Plainfield, NJ 07080, Comprehensive book on inner healing.

Sandford, John & Paula, *Healing the Wounded Spirit,* Bridge Publishing, 2500 Hamilton Blvd., South Plainfield, NJ 07080, 1985.

Sandford, John & Paula, *The Elijah Task,* Bridge Publishing, Plainfield, NJ 07080, 1977. About prophets.

Schaeffer, Edith, *Lifelines: Principles of the Ten Commandments for Today,* Ballantine Books, A Division of Random House, Inc., New York 10022, 1982.

*Schaeffer, Francis A., *The Complete Works of,* Crossway Books, Good News Publishing, Westchester, IL 60153, 1981.

Schaeffer, Franky, *A Time For Anger,* Crossway Books, A Division of Good News Publishing, Westchester, IL 60153, 1982. Restoration of the Church's prophetic role.

Searching Together, P.O. Box 548, St. Croix Falls, WI 54024. A magazine on issues of church renewal.

Sherrill, John L., *They Speak With Other Tongues,* Spire Books, Revell Company, Old Tappan, NJ 07675, 1964.

Sider, Ronald, *Evangelicals and Development Toward a Theology of Social Change,* Westminster Press, Philadelphia, PA 19107, 1982.

Smith, Daniel, *Bakht Singh of India,* International Students Press, Washingtong, DC. New Testament churches of India.

*Snyder, Howard A., *A Kingdom Manifesto,* Inter-Varsity Press, Downers Grove, IL 60515, 1985.

Snyder, Howard A., and Dan Runyon, *The Divided Flame: Wesleyans and the Charismatic Renewal,* Zondervan, Grand Rapids, MI 49506 1986.

Snyder, Howard A., and Dan Runyon, *Foresight,* Thomas Nelson, 1986.

*Snyder, Howard A., *The Problem of Wine Skins,* Inter-Varsity Press, Downers Grove, IL 60515, 1975. Proposed changes to today's Church.

Sojourners, P.O. Box 29272, Washington, DC 20017, Christian magazine to dedicated justice and peace.

Stabbert, Bruce, *The Team Concept,* Hegg Bros. Printing, Tacoma, WA 98407, 1982.

Stenberg, Odin, *A Church Without Walls,* Dimension Books, Bethany Fellowship, Inc., Minneapolis, MN 55438, 1976. About house churches.

Stott, John, *Involvement,* Revell, Old Tappan, NJ 07675, 1984.

Stube, Edwin B., *According to the Pattern,* available from CharisLife Box 12201, Portland, OR 97212.

Swindoll, Orville, *Times of Restoration,* Destiny Image, R.D. 2, Box 103, Shippenburg, PA 17257.

The Plough, a magazine published by the Hutterian Bruderhof, Rt. 213, Rifton, NY 12471. Covers a broad range of subjects dealing with discipleship and social responsibility.

*Thompson, Bruce, *The Divine Plumbline,* Crown Ministries, P.O. Box 49, Euclid, MN 56722, 1983.

Transformation, P.O. Box 1308-EQ, Fort Lee, NJ 07024. A magazine dedicated to evangelical social ethics.

U.S. News & World Report, 9465 Wilshire Blvd., Beverly Hills, CA 90212, February 13, 1984.

U.S. News & World Report, 9465 Wilshire Blvd., Beverly Hills, CA 90212, March 5, 1984.

Virgo, Terry, *Restoration in the Church,* Kingsway Publications, Eastbourne, E. Sussex, England, 1985.

*Wagner, C. Peter, *Your Spiritual Gifts,* Regal Books, Ventura, CA 93006, 1979.

Wallis, Arthur, *The Radical Christian,* Kingsway Publications, Eastbourne, England, 1981. About being totally sold out to God.

Walton, Rus, *One Nation Under God,* Third Century Publishers, Inc., Washington, DC 20013, 1975.

Whitehead, John W., *The Second American Revolution,* David C. Cook, Elgin, IL 60120, 1982. A call for the U.S. government to return to the founding fathers' committment to religious liberty and the original Judeo-Christian foundation.

Whitehead, John W., *The Stealing of America,* Crossway Books, Westchester, IL 60153, 1983. About the encroachment of the federal government into the areas of education, family life, and the church.

Williams, Don, *The Apostle Paul & Women In The Church,* Regal Books, Glendale, CA 91209, 1946.

Wilson, Carl, *With Christ in the School of Disciple Building,* Zondervan Publishing House, Grand Rapids, MI 49506, 1976.

*Wimber, John, *Power Evangelism,* Harper & Row Publishers, San Francisco, CA, 1985.

*Winter, Dr. Ralph, *The Two Structures of God's Redemptive Mission,* William Carey Library, Pasadena, CA 91104, 1976.

Yearbook of American and Canadian Churches, Abingdon Press, Nashville, TN 37202, 198

PART III — UNITY

Bakker, Jim, *Survival: Unite To Live,* New Leaf Press, P.O. Box 1045, Harrison, AR 72601.

Billheimer, Paul E., *Love Covers — A Viable Platform for Christian Unity,* Christian Literature Crusade, Fort Washington, PA 19034, 1981.

Cook, Jerry with Stanley C. Baldwin, *Love, Acceptance and Forgiveness,* Regal Books, Division of G/L Publications, Glendale, CA 91204, 1979.

Dodson, Edward, *In Search Of Unity,* Thomas Nelson, P.O. Box 141000, Nashville, TN 37214, 1985.

Hogg, William Richey, *Ecumenical Foundations,* Harper & Row, New York, NY, 10022, 1951.

*Houfe, Eric, *Vision for Unity,* Kingsway Publications, Ltd., Eastbourne, E. Sussex, Great Britain, 1980. Excellent on Christian unity.

Howard, David M., *The Dream That Would Not Die,* available from WEF International Office, P.O. Box WEF, Wheaton IL 60189. A history of the world evangelical movement.

Kurosaki, Kikochi, *One Body in Christ*, Banner Publications, Monroeville, PA 15146, 1968.

*McClung, Floyd, *Father, Make Us One*, Kingsway Publications, Ltd., Lottbridge Drove, Eastborne, E. Sussex BN23 6NT, England. About practical unity among Christians.

Mills, Dick, *The New Wave of the Holy Spirit*, Harrison House, Tulsa, OK, 74153, 1980.

Paulk, Earl, *That the World May Know*, Dimension Publishers, P.O. Box 7300, Atlanta, GA 30357,1987.

*Price, Keith A., *Co-operating in World Evangelization*, Whitefield House, London, England, 1983. About church and parachurch cooperation.

*White, Jerry A., *The Church and Parachurch — An Uneasy Marriage*, Multnomah Press, Portland, OR 97266, 1983.

PART IV — WORLD EVANGELIZATION

Adeney, Miriam, *God's Foreign Policy*, Wm. B. Eerdmans Publishing Co., Grand Rapids, MI 49503, 1983. Like so many other things in America, providing for the world's poor has become big business. Aid programs must respect other cultures. This book offers positive guidelines for identifying projects that work.

*Aldrich, Joseph C., *Life-Style Evangelism*, Multnomah Press, Portland, OR 97266, 1981.

*Allen, Roland, *Spontaneous Expansion of The Church*, Eerdmanns, Grand Rapids, MI 49503.

*Allen, Roland, *Missionary Methods*, Eerdmanns, Grand Rapids, MI 49503, 1962.

Area Handbooks, also called *Country Studies*, (a variety of countries are available) American University, Washington, DC or Pueblo Government Printing Office Bookstore, Majestic Building, 720 North Mail, Pueblo, CO 81003. This series provides detailed information on history, demographics, religion, society, government and economy.

Arn, Dr. Charles and Dr. Win Arn, *The Master's Plan for Making Disciples*, Pasadena, CA 91104. Church growth.

*Barrett, David C., *World Christian Encyclopedia*, Oxford University Press, Oxford, England, 1982. Most complete information on Christianity, nation-by-nation, ever published!

*Barrett, David C., *World-Class Cities and World Evangelization,* Newthorpe, P.O. Box 11657, Birmingham, AL 35202-1657, 1986.

Bartlotti, Len, *A Call for a Mission Renewal Movement,* International Journal of Frontier Missions, Pasadena, CA 91104, 1980.

Bauer, Arthur, *Making Mission Happen,* Friendship Press, 5820 Overbrook Avenue, Philadelphia, PA 19131, 1974.

Beaver, R. Pierce, *American Missions in Bicentennial Perspective,* William Carey Library, Pasadena, CA 91030, 1977.

Brother Andrew, *Battle for Africa,* Fleming H. Revell Co., Old Tappan, NJ 07675, 1977. Today's spiritual battle.

Bonnke, Reinhard, *Plundering Hell,* P.O. Box 3851, Laguna Hills, CA 92654.

Brother Andrew, *God's Smuggler,* The New American Library, Inc., New York, NY 10019, 1968. Getting the Bible behind closed doors.

*Bryant, David, *In The Gap,* Inter-Varsity Missions, Madison, WI 53703, 1979, 1981. The challenge of world evangelization.

*Bryant, David, *With Concerts of Prayer: Christians Joined For Spiritual Awakeninging World Evangelization,* Regal Books, Ventura, CA 93003, 1984.

Cho, Dr. Paul Y., *More Than Numbers,* Word Books, Waco, TX 76703, 1984.

Copeland, E. Luther, *World Missions and World Survival,* Broadman, 127 9th Ave. N., Nashville, TN 37234.

Christian Film and Video, P.O. Box 3000, Dept. Y, Denville, NJ 07834. A magazine giving the latest information on using the media for Christ.

*Coleman, Robert E., *The Master Plan Of Evangelism,* Fleming H. Revell Co., Old Tappan, NJ 07675, 1963. Jesus' strategy for world evangelization.

*Cunningham, Loren, *Is That Really You, God?,* Zondervan Corp., Grand Rapids, MI 49506, 1984.

*Dayton, Edward R., *That Everyone May Hear,* Missions Advanced Research and Communication Center (MARC), 919 W. Huntington Dr., Monrovia, CA 91016, 1983. Strategies for reaching people groups.

Decker, Ed, and Hunt, Dave, *The God Makers,* Harvest House Publishers, Eugene, OR 97402, 1984. Reaching Mormons.

315

Deckmann, David M. and Donnelly, Elizabeth Anne, *The Overseas List,* Augsburg Publishing House, 426 S. Fifth St., Minneapolis, MN 55415, 1979.

Departure, P.O. Box 15360, Richmond, VA 23227. Magazine dedicated to Christian travel.

*Duewel, Wesley L., *Touch the World Through Prayer,* Francis Asbury Press, Zondervan, Grand Rapids, MI 49506, 1986.

Directory of Religious Broadcasting, National Religious Broadcasters, CN 1926, Morristown, NJ 07960.

Elliot, Elizabeth, *The Shadow of the Almighty,* Zondervan, Grand Rapids, MI 49506, 1958.

EMIS, *A Bibliography of Articles on Islam,* P.O. Box 794, Wheaton, IL, 60189.

Engel, James F., and Norton, H. Wilbert, *What's Gone Wrong With The Harvest?,* Zondervan, Grand Rapids, MI, 49506, 1975. A communication strategy for the church and world evangelism.

Engstrom, Dr. Ted W., and Ed. R. Dayton, Editors, *The Christian Leadership Letter,* MARC Publications, 919 W. Huntington Dr., Monrovia, CA 91016.

Equipping the Saints, 5500 Sayle St., Greenville, TX 75401.

Evangelical Missions Quarterly, Vol. 20, No. 2, Evangelical Missions Information Service, Wheaton, IL 60189, April, 1984.

Fuller, Daniel P., *Give the Winds A Mighty Voice,* Word Books, Waco, TX 76703, 1972.

Gabel, Medard, *Hoping: Food For Everyone,* Anchor Books, 501 Franklin Ave., Garden City, NY 11530, 1979.

Glasser, Arthur F., *Crucial Dimensions in World Evangelization,* William Carey Library, Pasadena, CA 91104, 1976.

Gilliland, Dean S., *Pauline Theology & Mission Practice,* Baker Book House, Grand Rapids, MI 49506, 1983.

Godwin, David, E., *Church Planting Methods,* by Lifeshare Communications, P.O. Box 1067, DeSoto, TX 75115, 1984. P.O. Box 1067, DeSoto, TX 75115, 1984.

Graham, Billy, *A Biblical Standard For Evangelists,* World Wide Publications, Minneaspolis, MN 55403, 1984.

Green, Hollis L., *Why Wait Til Sunday,* Bethany Fellowship, Inc., 6820 Auto Club Road, Minneapolis, MN 55438, 1975.

316

Greenway, Roger S., *Apostles to the City,* Baker Book House, Grand Rapids, MI 49506, 1978. Guidelines for urban ministry.

Hall, Clarence W., *Miracle on the Sepik,* Gift Publications, Costa Mesa, CA, 1980. Missions biography about Bible translation work.

Harrison, Myron, *Developing Multinational Teams,* OMF Books, 404 S. Church St., Robesonia, PA 19551, 1985.

Hefley, James, *God's Tribesmen,* Holman Bible Publishers, Nashville, TN, 37234, 1974. Missions biography.

Hopler, Thom, *A World of Difference: Following Christ Beyond Your Cultural Walls,* Inter-Varsity Press, Downers Grove, IL 60515, 1978.

Houston Tom, *Africa: A Season for Hope,* MARC Publications, 919 W. Huntington Dr., Monrovia, CA 91016, 1986.

Howard, David M., *Student Power in World Mission,* Inter-Varsity Press, Downers Grove, IL 60515, 1979.

Hutchins, Clair and Gibson, John, *Winning the World,* World Mission Crusade, St. Petersburg, FL 33703-1739.

"International Bulletin of Missionary Research," P.O. Box 1308-E, Fort Lee, NJ 07024-9958. Excellent, scholarly missions information.

*Johnstone, P.J., *Operation World,* STL Publications, Bromley, Kent, England, 1986. Prayer data for every nation.

Johnstone, Patrick, *Transparencies on World Evangelization,* available from MARC, 919 W. Huntington Dr., Monrovia, CA 91016. Excellent.

Journey to the Nations, Caleb Project, 1605 E. Elizabeth St., Pasadena, CA 91104, 1984.

*Kane, J. Herbert, *A Global View of Christian Missions,* Baker Book House, Grand Rapids, MI 49506, 1971. History of missions, nation by nation.

*Kane, J. Herbert, *The Christian World Mission: Today and Tomorrow,* Baker Book House, Grand Rapids, MI 49506, 1981.

Kauffman, Paul E., *CHINA, The Emerging Challenge,* Baker Book House, Grand Rapids, MI 49506, 1982.

Keyes, Lawrence E., *The New Age Of Missions: A Study of Third World Missionary Societies,* William Carey Library, P.O. Box 40129, Pasadena, CA 91104.

King, Felicity and Maurice, *Primary Child-Care: A Manual for Health Workers,* Oxford University Press, TALC, Institute of Child Health, 30 Guilford, St., London, WV1N 1EH, England, 1978.

Knowles, Louis L., *A Guide to World Hunger Organizations,* Seeds/ Alternatives, 222 E. Lake Dr., Decatur, GA 30030.

Kraft, Charles H., *Christianity in Culture,* Orbis Books, Maryknoll, NY, 10545, 1979.

Kranse, Evangeline, *The Million-Dollar Living Room,* Tyndale House Publishers, Wheaton, IL 60187, 1984.

Krupp, Nate, *You Can Be A Soul Winner — Here's How!,* New Leaf Press, Inc., Harrison, AR 72601, 1978.

Kyle, John E., *Perspectives on the Unfinished Task,* Regal Books, Ventura, CA 93006, 1984.

*Lausanne Committee for World Evangelization, *The Lausanne Occasional Papers,* Lausanne Committee for World Evangelization, Wheaton, IL, 60189, 1980.

Lausanne Committee for World Evangelization, *The Thailand Report on Refugees,* Lausanne Committee for World Evangelization, Wheaton, IL 60189, 1980.

Lawrence, Carl, *The Church In China,* Bethany House Publishers, 6820 Auto Club Road, Minneapolis, MN 55438.

Luzbetak, Louis J., *The Church and Cultures,* William Carey Library, 1705 N. Sierra Bonita Ave., P.O. Box 40129, Pasadena, CA 91104, 1984.

Macagba, Dr. Rufino, *Health Care Guidelines For Use in Developing Countries,* MARC Publications, 919 W. Huntington Dr., Monrovia, CA 91016.

MAP International and World Concern make available helpful brochures, periodicals, books and bibliographies on the Christian approach to relief and development.

MARC, *Development Training for Practitioners,* MARC Publications, 919 W. Huntington Dr., Monrovia, CA 91016.

MARC, Directory, *North American Protestant Schools and Professors of Mission,* MARC Publications, Monrovia, CA 91016, 1982.

*MARC, *MARC Newsletter,* MARC Publications, Monrovia, CA 91016. Bi-monthly report on the work of MARC, news of mission research and strategic planning in missions.

MARC, *Missions Strategy of the Local Church,* MARC Publications, Monrovia, CA 91016.

MARC, *The Mission Handbook: North American Protestant Ministries Overseas,* MARC Publications, Monrovia, CA 91016.

*MARC, *World Christianity*, MARC Publications, Monrovia, CA 91016. Studies on the status of Christianity in each country. Now available: Middle East, Eastern Asia, South Asia, Central America and the Caribbean.

*MARC, *You Can So Get There From Here*, MARC Publications, Monrovia, CA 91016, 1979.

McBirnie, William Steuart, *The Search for The Twelve Apostles*, Tyndale House Publishers, Wheaton, IL 60189, 1973. Where they evangelized.

McCurry, Don M., *The Gospel and Islam*, MARC Publications, Monrovia, CA, 91016, 1979.

Mellis, Charles J., *Committed Communities*, William Carey Library, Pasadena, CA 91104, 1976. New approaches to missions.

Mitchell, Hubert, *Putting Your Faith on the Line*, Here's Life Publishers, San Bernardino, CA 92402, 1981.

Moore, Dr. Waylon B., *New Testament Follow-up*, Eerdmans Publishing Co., Grand Rapids, MI 49503, 1963.

Moore, Dr. Waylon B., *Multiplying Disciples: The New Testament Method for Church Growth*, Navpress, Colorado Springs, CO 80934, 1981.

*Murray, Andrew, *Key to the Missionary Problem*, Christian Literature Crusade, Fort Washington, PA 19034, 1979.

*Murray, Andrew, *State of the Church*, Christian Literature Crusade, Fort Washington, PA 19034. A cry for intercessors for world evangelization.

Myers, Dr. Bryant L., *Development Training for Practitioners*, MARC Publications, Monrovia, CA 91016. Contains a list of organizations involved in development training.

National Religious Broadcasters, *Directory of Religious Broadcasting*, Morristown, NJ 07960.

Nida, Eugene A., *Customs and Cultures*, William Carey Library, 1705 N. Sierra Bonita Ave., P.O. Box 40129, Pasadena, CA 91104, 1983.

Olsen, Bruce E., *Bruchko*, (Formerly: For This Cross I'll Kill You), Creation House, Carol Stream, IL 60188, 1973. An astonishing story of a 19 year old youth's capture by stone age Indians in South America and the fruit of his ministry which combined evangelism and development.

319

Palmer, Bernard, *Understanding the Islamic Explosion*, Horizon House Publishers, Beaverlodge, Alberta, Canada, 1980.

Parshall, Phil, *Bridges to Islam*, Baker Book House, P.O. Box 6287, Grand Rapids, MI 49506, 1983.

Pentecost, Edward C., *Reaching the Unreached*, World Mission Research Center, Dallas Theological Seminary, 3909 Swiss Ave., Dallas, TX, 75204.

People File Index, Global Mapping Project, 1605 Elizabeth St., Pasadena, CA 91104, 1986. A resource book giving information of Bible translation status of the people groups of the world.

Pippert, Rebecca Manley, *Out of the Salt Shaker Into the World*, Inter-Varsity Press, Downers Grove, IL 60515, 1979. Evangelism as a way life.

Population information available from Population Reference Bureau, Inc., 2213 M Street NW, Washington, DC 20037.

Portale, Joe, *The Go Manual*, Youth With A Mission, P.O. Box 1380, Lindale, TX, 75771, 1986. Service opportunities.

Pudiate, Rochunga, *My Billion Bible Dream*, Nelson Publishers, New York, NY, 1982.

Resources for Urban Ministry: A Biligraphy, MARC Publications, 919 W. Huntington Dr., Monrovia, CA 91016.

Richardson, Don, *Lords of the Earth*, Regal Books, A Division of G/L Publications, Ventura, CA 93006, 1977. Missions biography.

Richardson, Don, *Eternity in their Hearts*, Regal Books, A Division of G/L Publications, Ventura, CA 93006, 1978.

Rose, Larry K., *The Urban Challenge*, Reaching America's Cities With the Gospel, Broadman Press, Nashville, TN 37234, 1982.

Samuel, Vinay and Sugden, Chris, *Sharing Jesus in the Two Thirds World*, Eerdmans, Grand Rapids, MI 49503. From the 1982 Conference of Evangelical Missions Theologians.

Sider, Ronald J. (Ed.), *Cry Injustice: The Bible on Hunger and Poverty*, Paulist Press, Ramsey, NY 07446, 1980. Selected Biblical texts dealing with God's concern for the poor and hungry.

*Sider, Ronald J., *Rich Christian in an Age of Hunger*, Inter-Varsity Press, Downers Grove, IL 60515, 1977. A penetrating understanding of the American Christian's responsibility to the world's poor at this vital point in history.

Sine, Tom, *The Churchs in Response to Human Need,* MARC, Monrovia, CA 91016, 1983.

Stanton, Chris, *Mission Bridge,* Mission Bridge, 200 S. University Blvd., Denver, CO 80204. About a local church missionary training program.

Stott, John R. W., *Christian Mission in the Modern World,* Inter-Varsity Press, Downers Grove, IL 60515, 1975.

Summer Ministry Opportunities, Student Missionary Union, Biola University, 13800 Biola Ave., La Mirada, CA 90639.

Taylor, Mendell, *Exploring Evangelism,* Nazarene Publishing House, Kansas City, MO, 1964. History of evangelism.

Taylor, Robert T., *Wings for the Word,* Logos Int'l, Plainfield, NJ, 1978.

*The Missions Education Handbook, ACMC, Box ACMC, Wheaton, IL 60187.

The New Ethnologue, S.I.L., 7500 West Camp Wisdom Rd., Dallas, TX 75236. Information on the 5445 known languages of the world.

The Role of the Local Church in World Missions, Association of Church Missions Committees, P.O. Box ACMC, Wheaton, IL 60189.

The World Factbook, Central Intelligence Agency, Defense Intelligence Agency and the Department of State, United States Government Printing Office. This is a basic compact overview of all nations.

The World Today Series, Stryket-Post Publications, Inc., 888 Seventeenth St., NW, Washington, DC 20006. Available annually in August, $2.95 each.

Tillapaugh, Frank R., *Unleashing the Church,* Regal Books, Ventura, CA, 93006, 1982.

*Tucker, Ruth, *From Jerusalem to Irian Jaya,* Zondervan Publishing House, Grand Rapids, MI 49056, 1983. Missions biography for 2,000 years of history.

Vaughn, John N., *The World's 20 Largest Churches,* Baker Book House, Grand Rapids, M 49056, 1985.

Verwer, George, *For Distance Runners,* Tyndale House, Wheaton, IL 60187, 1984. A challenge to discipleship for completing the task of world evangelization by the founder of Operation Mobilization.

*Wagner, C. Peter, *On the Crest of the Wave,* Regal Books, Ventura, CA, 93006, 1983. The renewal of world evangelization today.

Wagner C. Peter, *Unreached Peoples, '79, '80, '81, '82, '83, '84,* David C. Cook Publishing Co., Elgin, IL 60120, 1978, 1980, 1981. Excellent data on unreached peoples.

*Wagner, C. Peter, *Spiritual Power and Church Growth,* Strang Communications Company, Altamonte Springs, FL 32714, 1986.

Wallstrom, Timothy C., *The Creation of A Student Movement to Evangelize the World,* William Carey Int'l University Press, 1539 E. Howard St., Pasadena, CA 91104, 1980.

Ward, Ted, *Living Overseas: A Book of Preparations,* The Free Press, 866 Third Ave., New York, NY 10022. Practical guide to overseas living, directed to missionaries.

Watson, David, *Called and Committed,* Harold Shaw Publishers, Wheaton,IL, 60188, 1982.

Werner, David, *Where There Is No Doctor,* Hesperian Foundation, P.O. Box 1692, Palo Alto, CA 94301, 1977.

When Disaster Strikes and Help Is Needed: A Guide to Climate Topography Food, Habits, Clothing, LICROSS/VOLAGS, Steering Committee for Disasters, P.O. Box 276, CH-1211, Geneva 19, Switzerland.

Wilson, Carl, *With Christ in the School of Disciple Building,* Zondervan Publishing House, Grand Rapids, MI 49506, 1978.

*Wilson, J. C., *Today's Tentmaker,* Tyndale House Publishers, 336 Gunderson Dr., Wheaton, IL 60187, 1979.

Wilson, Sam and Gordon Aeschliman, *The Hidden Half — Discovering the World of Unreached Peoples,* MARC Publications, 919 W. Huntington Dr., Monrovia, CA 91016.

*Winter, Ralph, *Perspectives on the World Christian Movement,* A Reader, William Carey Library, Pasadena, CA 91104, 1981. Articles from leading missions leaders.

Winter. Ralph, *Protestant Mission Societies: The American Experience,* William Carey Library, Pasadena, CA 91104, 1979. About various Proestant mission structures.

Winter, Ralph, *The 25 Unbelievable Years — 1945-1969,* William Carey Library, Pasadena, CA 91104, 1970. The changes in the world scene.

Winter, Roberta, *Once More Around Jericho,* William Carey Library, Pasadena, CA 91104, 1978. The story of the U.S. Center for World Mission.

Winter, Roberta, *The Kingdom Strikes Back, U.S.* Center for World Mission, 16053 Elizabeth St., Pasadena, CA 91104. The amazing story of the founding of the Center.

World-Wide Publications, *Let The Earth Hear His Voice,* World-Wide Publications, Minneapolis, MN 55403, 1975. Comprehensive reference volume on world evangelization.

Yohannan, K.P., *The Coming Revolution in World Missions,* Creation House, Altamonte Springs, FL 32714, 1986.

*Many additional, excellent books on world evangelization are available from William Carey Library Publications & Distributors, P.O. Box 41029, 1705 N. Sierra Bonita Avenue, Pasadena, CA 91104.

PART V — PERSECUTION

A. Coming Persecution

Adams, S.W., *The Federal Reserve System,* Gordon Press, New York, NY 10004, 1979. The purposes and functions of the FRS.

Allen, Gary, with Larry Abraham, *None Dare Call It Conspiracy,* Concord Press, Rossmoor, CA, 90740, 1971.Communists and international bankers' progress in taking over America.

Anderson, John O., *Cry of the Innocents,* Bridge Publishing, 2500 Hamilton Blvd., South Plainfield, NJ 07080, 1984. About abortion and God's judgment.

*Archer, Gleason L., Paul D. Feinburg, Douglas J. Moo, Richard R. Reiter, *The Rapture: Pre-, Mid-, or Post-Tribulation?,* Academie Books, A division of Zondervan, Grand Rapids, MI 49506.

Bible in the News, The Southwest Radio Church of the Air, P.O. Box 1144, Oklahoma City, OK 73101.

Bowen, William M., *Globalism: America's Demise,* Huntington House Inc., Shreveport, LA 71107, 1984.

Brother Andrew, *God's Smuggler,* Fleming H. Revell Co., Old Tappan, NJ 07675, 1974. God's marvelous protection of Brother Andrew's Bible smuggling behind the Iron Curtain.

Browne, Harry, *How You Can Profit from the Coming Devaluation,* Arlington House, New Rochelle, NY 10016, 1970.

Bue, Daniel, *The Coming Post-Industrial Society,* Basic Books New York, NY, 1973. A very complete presentation of the subject.

Cantelon, Willard, *The Day the Dollar Dies*, Logos International, Plainfield, NJ, 1973. Excellent picture of the coming cashless society.

CATO Institute, 224 Second St. SE, Washington, DC 20003. Write for the "Publications Catalog."

Christian Anti-Communism Crusade, P.O. Box 890, Long Beach, CA 90801-0890.

Cumby, Constance, *Hidden Dangers of the Rainbow*, Huntington House, Shreveport, LA 71107, 1983.

Delepine, Sheridan, *It Is Done*, Maranatha Press, Hood River, OR 97031, 1982.

Dudley, Johnny L., *The Harvest*, P.O. Box 19476, Jacksonville, FL 32245-9476, 1984.

Economic Advisor, Ministries, Inc., P.O. Box 4038, Montgomery, AL 36104. Phone number (205) 262-4891. A newsletter on finance, currency, and banking with highlights from Bible prophecy.

*End-Times News Digest, Omega Ministries, Box O, Eagle Point, OR 97524. Phone number (503) 826-9877. A news service for Christians giving a Spirit-filled analysis of news, world conditions, and prophecy.

F.R.E.E. (Fund to Restore an Educated Electorate), Box 8616, Waco, TX 76710. About the Council on Foreign Relations (CFR) and The Trilateral Commission.

*Ferris, James Jay, Inflation: The Ultimate Graven Image, New Leaf Press, Harrison, AR, 1982.

Fraley, Bob, *The Last Days in America*, Christian Life Services, 6438 E. Jenan Dr., Scottsdale, AZ 85254.

The FREEMAN, Ideas on Liberty, The Foundation for Economic Education, Inc., 30 South Broadway, Irvington-on-Hudson, NY. Articles on limited government and the free market. Free upon request.

Gilder, George, *Wealth and Poverty*, Basic Books, New York, NY 10022, 1981.

*Graham, Billy, *Approaching Hoofbeats — The Four Horsemen of the Apocalypse*, Word Books, Waco, TX 76796, 1983.

Gundry, Robert H., *The Church and The Tribulation*, Zondervan Publishing House, Grand Rapids, MI 49506, 1973. Very scholarly study of the church going through the tribulation.

Hagee, John C., *Like a Cleansing Fire*, Fleming H. Revell Co., Old Tappan, NJ 07675, 1974. Tells of climatic events the church of Jesus Christ may soon be experiencing.

*Hazlitt, Henry, *Economics in One Lesson*, Manor Books, Inc., New York, NY 10022, 1962.

Hill, Clifford, *The Day Comes*, Fount Paperbacks, William Collins Sons & Co., Glasgow, 1982. A prophetic view of the contemporary world.

Inflation Survival Letter, 410 First St. SE, Washington, DC 20003.

Kershner, Howard E., *Dividing the Wealth*, Druin-Adair Co., Old Greenwich, CT, 1971. Principles of free enterprise.

Krupp, Nate, *The Omega Generation*, New Leaf Press, Inc., Harrison, AR 72601, 1977. About coming persecution.

Ladd, George E., *The Blessed Hope*, William B. Eerdman's Publishing Co., Grand Rapids, MI 49503, 1984. Church going through the tribulation.

Lam, Nora, *China Cry*, Word, Incorporated, Waco, TX 76703, 1980. How God miraculously saved a Chinese Christian from a firing squad.

*Lightle, Steve, *Exodus II*, Hunter Books, Kingwood, TX 77339, 1983.

Lindsay, Hal, *The 1980's: Countdown to Armageddon*, Bantam Books, New York, NY 10019, 1980.

Lovett, C.S., *Latest Word on the Last Days*, Personal Christianity Chapel, Baldwin Park, CA, 1980.

Lyons, Eugene, *Worker's Paradise Lost*, Paperback Library, New York, NY 10009, 1967. Failure of the Communist system to bring answers to Russia.

MacPherson, Dave, *The Unbelievable Pre-Trib Origin*, Pedestal Press, Kansas City, MO, 1973.

McKeever, Jim, *Christians Will Go Through the Tribulation*, Omega Publications, Medford, OR 97501, 1978.

McKeever, Jim, *The Coming Climax of History*, Omega Publications, Medford, OR 97501, 1982.

Mogg, William Rees, *The Crisis of World Inflation,* Baxter, A World economic Service, Greenwich, CT, 1974.

Mooneyham, W. Stanley, *What Do You Say To a Hungry World?,* Word Books, Waco, TX 76796, 1973. An excellent presentation of the world's food shortage and what to do about it.

The New Order of Christ, Rte. 1, Box 9, Carlton, OR 97111. A Christian newsletter dedicated to preaching Jesus Christ and the Mark of the Beast.

News-Watch Alert, Maranatha Broadcaster, Inc., P.O. Box 25196, Northgate Station, Seattle, WA 98125. A news review and commentary from a Biblical viewpoint.

Nixon, President Richard M., *The Real War,* Warner Books, New York, NY 10103, 1980. An excellent treatise by the former U.S. President on the world-wide confrontation between freedom and Communism.

Noble, John, *I Was a Slave in Russia,* Cicero Bible Press, Broadview, IL, 1963. Ten years in Russian prison from 1945-1955.

Noble, John, *I Found God in Soviet Russia,* Zondervan Books, Grand Rapids, MI 49506, 1972. John Noble's conversion while in Russian prisons.

Novack, Michael, *The Spirit of Democratic Capitalism,* Simon and Schuster, New York, NY 10020, 1982.

Ontario Gazette, 9th Floor, Ferguson Block, Queen's Park, Toronto, Canada M7A 1N8. A newsletter about land buying in Canada.

Open Doors with Brother Andrew, P.O. Box 2020, Orange, CA 92669.

Pit, Jan, *Persecution: It Will Never Happen Here?,* Open Doors, P.O. Box 2020, Orange, CA 92669.

Pit, Jan, *Ready for the End Battle,* Open Doors, P.O. Box 2020, Orange, CA 92669.

Pugsley, John A., *The Alpha Strategy,* Stratford Press, Los Angeles, CA., 90064, 1980. The ultimate plan of financial self-defense.

*Relfe, Mary Stewart, *When Your Money Falls,* Ministries, Inc., Montgomery, AL 36105, 1981.

Rifkin, Jeremy, *Entropy,* The Viking Press, New York, NY 10012, 1980.

Rifkin, Jeremy, *The Emerging Order,* G.P. Putnam and Sons, New York, NY 10016, 1980.

Ritchie, David, *The Ring of Fire*, New American Library, (A Mentor Book), New York, NY and Scarborough, Ontario, 1981.

Roberts, W. Dayton, *RunningOut*, Regal Book, A Division of G/L Publ., Ventura, CA 93003, 1975. On the depleting natural resources of land, water, air, energy, metal, etc.

Robinson, Arthur, *Fighting Chance*, OISM, P.O. Box 1279, Cove Junction, OR 92523. About nuclear attack defense shelters.

Remnant Review, Box 467, Lynden, WA 98264. Newsletter on national finances.

The Ruff Times, Target Publishers, P.O. Box 2000, San Ramon, CA 94583. Phone number (800) 642-0204 from California; or (800) 227-0703 from other USA states. America's fastest growing advisory service, over 120,000 circulation.

The Reaper, P.O. Box 39026, Phoenix, AZ 85069.

Robertson, Pat, *The Secret Kingdom*, Bantam Books, New York, NY 10019, 1984.

Roxanne Brandt Newsletter, Roxanne Brandt Crusades, Inc., Naples, FL. Excellent on last days events.

*Rumble, Dale, *The Diakonate*, Torbay Publishing Ltd., 29 Milber Industrial Estate, Newton Abbot, Devon, England, TQ12 4SG. About the end-time Church.

*Schlink, M. Basilea, *The Eve of Persecution*, Creation House, Carol Stream, IL 60187, 1974. About preparing for coming persecution.

Schuller, Robert H. and Dunn, Paul David, *The Power of Being Debt Free*, Nelson Publishers, Nashville, TN, 1985.

Sharrit, John T., *Soon-coming, World Shaking Events!*, Christian Missionary Society, P.O. Box 4097, Phoenix, AZ 85030.

Sider, Ronald, *Rich Christians in an Age of Hunger*. Inter-Varisty Press; Downers Grove, IL 60515, 1977. The most persuasive presentation of the biblical case against hunger.

Simon, William E., *A Time of Truth*, McGraw-Hill Book Co., Readers Digest Press, New York, NY 10020 and Chicago, IL, 1978.

Sine, Tom, *The Mustard Seed Conspiracy*, Word Books, Waco, TX 76796, 1981.

Skousen, Cleon W., *The Naked Capitalist*, The Reviewer, 917 Berkeley St., Salt Lake City, UT, 1970. A look at the banking-Communist conspiracy and their progress toward world rule.

Stanton, Don E., *Mystery 666,* Maranatha Revival Crusade, Secunderabad, 1977.

Stormer, John A., *None Dare Call It Treason,* Liberty Bell Press, Florissant, MO 63033, 1964. Communist progress in infiltrating American society.

Stott, John R. W., ed., *The Year 2000,* Inter-Varsity Press, Downers Grove, IL 60515, 1983. Degeneration of human rights, global economics and hunger, dictatorships, etc., in the end-times.

S.W.I.F.T. Newsletter, (Society for Worldwide Interbank Financial Telecommunications S.C.), 81, Avenue Earnest Solvay, B-1310 La Hulpe, Brussels, Belgium. Tells of world-wide banking communications network.

Ten Boom, Corrie, *Marching Orders for the End Battle,* Christian Literature Crusade, Fort Washington, PA 19034, 1979.

Ten Boom, Corrie, *The Hiding Place,* Flemming H. Revell Co., Old Tappan, NJ 07675, 1971. Author's encounter with Naziism and Gods' protection.

The McAlvany Intelligence Advisor, P.O. Box 39810, Phoenix, AZ 85069.

The New American, 395 Concord Avenue, Belmont, MA 02178. Magazine giving trends in society leading to a one-world government.

Toffler, Alvin, *Future Shock,* Bantam Books, New York, NY 10019, 1971. The accelerated pace of life and its effects.

Tribulation Research, Box 12201, Portland, OR 97212. Facts and possibilities research of the "Acts 1:8 Church" in those God-sent end-times.

Ward, Larry,... *and There Will Be Famines,* Regal Books, A Division of G/L Publications, Ventura, CA 93003, 1973. Ever-increasing, world-wide food shortage.

Webber, Dr. David, *God's Timetable for the 1980's,* Huntington House, Inc., Lafayette, LA 70505.

Wilkerson, David, *Set the Trumpet to Thy Mouth,* World Challenge, Inc., P.O. Box 260, Lindale, TX 75771, 1985. A prophetic message calling America to repent.

Wilkerson, David, *The Vision,* Fleming H. Revell Co., Old Tappan, NJ 07675, 1974. A man's vision of end-time events.

Wolfe, Bertram D., *Three Who Made A Revolution,* Conservative Book

Club, 15 Oakland Ave., Harrison, NY 10528, 1984. On the Russian Revolution.

Woodrow, Ralph, *Great Prophecies of the Bible,* Woodrow Evangelistic Assn., Inc., P.O. Box 124, Riverside, CA 92502.

B. Preparedness

Abandoned school houses, write to the Department of Education in your state for inquiries.

Adams, Rex, *Michael Medicine Foods,* Progress Books, Ltd., Dept. MS-94A, 3200 Lawson Blvd., Oceanside, NY 11572.

Bargain Hunter's Review, 220 Delaware Ave., Buffalo, NY 14202. For American and Canadian land listings.

Campbell, Giraud Dr., *A Doctor's Proven New Home Cure For Arthritis,* Island Park Publishing, Dept. AR-2, 55A Saratoga Blvd., Island Park, NY 11558.

Carper, Jean, *The Brand Name Nutrition Center,* Bantam Books, Inc., New York, NY 10019, 1975. Brand name products and basic foods rated for vitamin, calorie and carbohydrate content.

Cumberland General Store, Route 3, Box 479, Crossville, TN 38555. One excellent source for equipment from stoves to pots.

Davis, Adelle, *Let's Cook It Right,* New American Library, New York, NY 10023, 1972.

Davis, Adelle, *Let's Eat Right and Keep Fit,* New American Library, New York, NY 10023, 1970.

*Emery, Carla, *Old Fashioned Receipe Book,* Bantam Books, Inc., New York, NY 10019, 1974. An encyclopedia of country living.

Ford Frank, *The Simpler Life Cookbook,* Harvest Press, Inc., P.O. Box 3535, Fort Worth, TX 76105, 1974.

Food Reserves, Inc., 710 SE 17th St. Causeway, Fort Lauderdale, FL 33316. Survival Storage foods — a complete selection of dehydrated and freeze dried foods.

Garden Way Research, Charlotte, VT 95445. Phone number (802) 425-2137. Catalog of gardening tools and farm tools.

Government Lands, 220 Delaware Ave., Buffalo, NY 14202. Government land in the United States and Canada that is available for $1 per acre. Greenbank, Anthony, *The Book of Survival,* New American Library, New York, NY 10023, 1970. How to survive in various emergencies, how to get along in the wild.

Hartman, Jack, *Trust God For Your Finances,* Word Associates, P.O. Box 3293, Manchester, NH 03105, 1983. Balanced presentation of God's laws of prosperity.

Health Foods Retailing, by Syndicate Magazines, Inc., 6 East 43rd St., New York, NY 10017. The official magazine of the National Nutritional Foods Association.

Hurd, Frank J., D.C. and Hurd, Rosalie, B.S., *Ten Talents,* Dr. Frank J. Hurd, Box 86A — Route 1, Chisholm, MN 55719, 1968. Natural Foods Cookbook.

Kadahs, Joseph M., *Enclcyopedia of Fruits, Vegetables, Nuts and Seeds For Healthful Living,* Parker Publ. Co., Inc., W. Nyack, NY 10944, 1973. Proper foods for correcting various physical problems.

Kern, Ken, *TheOwnerBuiltHome,* P.O. Box 550, Oakhurst, CA 93644. An invaluable guide for inexpensive construction.

Kodet, E. Russel and Dr. Angier, Bradford, *Being Your Own Wilderness Doctor,* Stackpole Books, Harrisburg, PA 17105, 1968. How to meet medical problems in the wilderness.

LaHaye, Tim, *The Race for the 21st Century,* Thomas Nelson, Nashville, TN, 1986.

Longacre, Doris, *More-With-Less Cookbook,* Herald Press, Scottsdale, PA 15683, 1976. 500 recipes for those concerned with wholesome eating in a world of limited resources.

McKeevor, James, *You Can Overcome,* Omega Ministries, Medford, OR 97501.

Mohoning County Canning Club, 3351 Orrin Ave., Youngstown, OH 44505. Canning equipment and price list.

*The Mother Earth News, The Mother News, Inc., 105 Stoney Mountain Rd., Hendersonville, NC 28739.

The following can be obtained from the above address:

Abraham, George and Kathy, *Organic Gardening Under Glass: Fruits, Vegetables, and Ornaments in the Greenhouse.*

Belanger, Jerome, D., *The Homesteader's Handbook to Raising Small Livestock,* For the beginner.

Blackburn, Graham, *The Illustrated Encyclopedia of Woodworking Handtools of Homemade Power.*

Ridley, Clifford, *How To Grow Your Own Groceries For $100 a Year.* Very good.

Rodale, Robert ed., *The Basic Book of Organic Gardening.* The Gardener'sCatalog. Very good.

Mother's General Store, Rou80 catalog, P.O. Box 546, Eagle Point, OR 97524.

Operation L.O.R.D., Creative Lifestyle Center, P.O. Box 504, Tacoma, WA 98401.

The Complete Book of Vitamins, Rodale Books, Emaus, PA 18049.

Back To Basics, Pleasantville, NY. Excellent "how-to" book. Preston, Robert L., *How to Prepare for the Coming Crash,* Hawkes Publishing, Inc., Salt Lake City, UT 84115, 1973. Physical preparation for coming economic collapse.

Recrominium, Inc., 2620 Post Road, Darien, CT 96820. Phone number (203) 669-2326. An architect-designed, completely self-contained vacation home that you can afford.

The Rodale Herb Book, Rodale Books, Emmaus, PA 18049.

Sauer, Wolfgang, *Prospering as God's Sharecropper,* Wolfgang Dieter Sauer, Tacoma, WA 1981.

Scher, Les., *Finding and Buying Your Place in the Country,* Collier, 866 Third Ave., New York, NY 1022, 1974. A comprehensive book on the subject.

Security Foods, 4911 W. 96th St., Overland Park, KS 66207.

Simpler Life, Arrowhead Mills, Inc., P.O. Box 2049, Hereford, TX 79045.

Skousen, Joel M., *The Survival Home Manual,* Survival Homes, 4270 Westcliff, Hood River, OR 97031. The most complete course on building and remodeling for self-sufficiency.

The Staff Of The Family Handyman Magazine, *America's Handyman Book,* Charles Scribner's Sons, New York, NY 10017, 1961. A basic, comprehensive guide to home maintenance and repair.

Summers, Bob, *Out Back with Jesus,* Harvest Press, Fort Worth, TX 76105, 1975. Getting ready for hard times.

Survival Supplies, P.O. Box 124, Provo, UT 84601.

The Complete Handbook for Earthquake Preparedness, Hands to Help, P.O. Box 3464, Orange CA 92665, 1986.

*Total Health Institute, 301 Crater Lake Ave., Medford, OR 97504.

Tobe, John H., *Proven Herbal Remedies,* Provoker Press, St. Catharines, Ontario, Canada, 1969. Herbal remedies for physical problems.

United Farm Agency, 612 W. 47th St., Kansas City, MO 64122. To find a low-cost farm.

U.S. Real Property Sales List, U.S. General Services Administration, Federal Property Resources Service, Washington, DC 20405.

Vibrant Living Unlimited, P.O. Box D, Eagle Point, OR 97524. Crown Valley Products.

Vita-Mix Corporation, 8615 Usher Rd., Cleveland, OH 44138.

Wheatgrass — God's Manna, National Medical-Physical Research Foundation, Inc., 25 Exeter St., Boston, MA 02116.

SCRIPTURE INDEX

This is a listing of where every Scripture is used in the body of the book.

Old Testament

Genesis
Ch 1-2	115
1:1	124
3:15	152
Ch 6-10	152
Ch 11	152
12:1-3	152
17:1	46
18:18	152
20:7	53
22:18	152
26:4	152
28:14	152
Ch 37-50	222
37:22	53
40:9-13	53
49:1	213
49:10	152

Exodus
4:7	53
15:20	100
19:4-6	46, 152
20:12	124

Leviticus
6:4-5	53,111

Numbers
6:2	100

27:11	100
35:25	53

Deuteronomy
11:14	34
17:18-20	203
22:2	53
28:10	152
30:2	53
30:7	219

Judges
4:4-10	100
4:14	100

1 Samuel
7:4-10	5
12:3	53

2 Samuel
9:7	53
16:3	53

1 Kings
12:21	54
20:34	54

2 Kings
5:1	100
8:6	54
22:8-20	100

336

340

341

GENERAL INDEX

This is a listing of where every major person, place, subject, and event are found in the body of the book.

346

347

355

359

ABOUT THE AUTHOR

Nate Krupp was born in 1935 in Fostoria, Ohio, in the United States of America. He was converted to Jesus Christ through the witness of two converted Jews in 1957, during his senior year at Purdue University, where he received a Bachelor of Science degree in Mechanical Engineering and was Student Body President. He was then an officer in the U.S. Navy Civil Engineer Corps during which time the Lord called him into full-time Christian ministry. This was followed by Christian training from The Navigators, at Marion College, and with Campus Crusade for Christ.

From 1961-1975, he founded Lay Evangelism, Inc., conducted Lay Evangelism Training Crusades with churches of many denominations throughout North America, and was involved in evangelism in Chicago. From 1976-1981, he was associated with Youth With A Mission (YWAM), teaching in their training schools and working with local churches and outreach teams in many parts of the world. From 1981-1983, he pastored a Foursquare Church in Salem, Oregon.

In 1983, he again became associated with YWAM, related to the Tacoma, Washington, center, where he was Director of the School of Church Ministries. He and is now ministering with his wife, Joanne, more widely throughout the Body of Christ, teaching the contents of this book and calling the Church to prayer.

He has worked closely with the National Association of Evangelicals, the Christian Holiness Association, the Full Gospel Business Men, and the Association of International Mission Services. He is the author of ten other books and booklets.

OTHER BOOKS AND BOOKLETS BY NATE KRUPP

A World to Win. The challenge of every believer—evangelism. Published by Bethany Fellowship, Minneapolis, MN, 55438, 1966. Out of print.

Bible Studies in Christian Discipleship. A 50-page question-and-answer-type Bible study on discipleship for the more mature Christian. New Leaf Press, P.O. Box 311, Green Forest, AR 72638, 1968.

Bible Studies for New Christians. A 48-page question-and-answer-type Bible study for New Christians. New Leaf Press, 1968.

Bible Studies for Soul Winners. A 44-page question-and-answer-type Bible study on the subject of evangelism. New Leaf Press, 1963.

Mastering the Word of God. A 40-page booklet on methods of Bible study, memory, and meditation. Available from Nate Krupp, 6813 N. 11th, Tacoma, WA 98406.

New Life Through Christ. A 16-page question-and-answer-type Bible study for the unsaved. Also as the first in a series for new Christians. New Leaf Press, 1968.

New Testament Survey Course. A 176-page study of the entire New Testament. Available from Nate Krupp, 6813 N. 11th, Tacoma, WA 98406.

The Omega Generation. About coming end-time persecution. New Leaf Press, 1977. Out of print.

The Way to God. A witnessing leaflet explaining the way of salvation. Available through Lay Evangelism, Inc., 1305 Dianne Drive, Bloomington, IL 61701.

You Can Be A Soul Winner. A 175-page book of practical evangelism know-how. Over 50,000 in print. New Leaf Press, 1962.

WORDS OF ENDORSEMENT

Every so often God uses a man to give His Body an important high level perspective on truth. This book is such a contribution on the subject of revival. Gaze from its vantage point at the march of history toward the consummation of all things in Christ's awakening and restoring power. It will inspire you to pray and to "occupy until He comes." Read it carefully and join with others who are seeking God's face for spiritual awakening.

—Ron Boehme
Renewal Ministries
Washington, DC

Here is an overview of evangelism beginning with the New Testament Church, with glimpses into great revival movements throughout history. Reading the account will challenge one to pray and work for an awakening in our day.

— Dr. Robert E. Coleman, Director
School of World Missions & Evangelism
Trinity Evanglical Divinity School

Nate Krupp has done the Christian world a valuable service in documenting renewal and revival through Church history. His book can save readers hundreds of hours of research in tracking down important information which, so far as I know, has never been put between the covers of a single volume before. His earnest burden to help the Church recover its New Testament fervor and format appears on almost every page. One need not adopt all the positions espoused in the book to appreciate its massive worth. I highly recommend it.

— Dr. Raymond L. Cox
Pastor & Historian
The International Church
of the Foursquare Gospel

I have known the author for many years. His personal life and ministry fit him for writing on this important topic. His passion for souls and desire to see the Church be the Church comes through these pages. Readers may not agree with everything in this book. I don't. But they will be gripped by the call of Christ for revival and world evangelism. The many Scriptural references, historical sketches, and current reference materials make this a useful tool to anyone who teaches others.

This volume is a contribution to Christians who want to be a part of God's ministry to a broken, hurting world. My prayer is that God will use it for His glory.

— Dr. Robert Crandall
Pastor & Educator
The Free Methodist Church

In The Church Triumphant at the End of the Age, the author has effectively raised the clarion call for "revival" for the Christian movement of our day. With clear historical perspective and intense evangelical zeal, he has adeptly moved across the lines marking the various theological zones of Christendom to embrace what all of us in Christ's body must earnestly desire, as he says, "The mighty, spiritual awakening which God longs to send to this earth."

The three essentials of humility, prayer, and holy living are threatened with profoundity as the elements which have previously opened heaven's presence upon the Church. The instructions for the present application of these truths to our need is powerfully presented.

I commend the author for his work and urge the wide circulation of this book.

—Dr. O.D. Emery
General Superintendent
The Wesleyan Church

Few books have dared to document so fully the incredible ways in which God has been working in His Church as we approach the year 2000. Should be required reading for any world Christian.

—Jay Gary
Executive Editor
WORLD CHRISTIAN magazine

The depth of research fairly oozes from the pages of this book. In concise, fast-moving style it gives the reader a sense of the sweep of Church history, telling the good news that God has had His people in every generation. The sovereign God is seen working, leading, arranging, revealing Himself along an ascending path toward the Church's full and permanent restoration. It made me feel good about where the Church is headed.

— Robert C. Girard
Church Renewal Specialist and Author

There is a fresh interest in prayer today. A kind of revival of prayer. Prayer which leads to revival. People want to learn about revival. What happens. What has happened in history as well as in Scripture. How can this help them? All this is what makes Nate Krupp's book, *The Church Triumphant at the End of the Age,* so important. It will enlighten and inspire your vision and prayer and faith for "revival in our time."

—Armin Gesswein
Minister's Prayer Fellowship

Big decisions need facts **and** the word of the Lord. I've made a big decision that has been greatly motivated by this book. Nate has convinced me with both facts **and** the word of the Lord that completion of the Great Commission will only come as the Church pays the price in desperate prayer for a mighty end times revival.
In the midst of this kind of prayer God will uncover His plans. What we **can't** do is plan first and pray later!

— Graham Kerr
Director C3 Design Team

A book that should be read and studied by every pastor, evangelist, Bible teacher, missionary...by heads of government world-wide...and by every serious Christian who sees the need for improving his own life and those around him, in preparation for the days ahead. Nate Krupp has been adequately prepared for researching and writing this book since the time when he turned his life over to the Lord as a student at Purdue University, and in the following years of faithfulness to his commitment, as he has participated in evangelization, pastoring, writing, and carrying the Word to every continent. The book is not only inspiring, but is also educational from the standpoint of God's plan for His Church from beginning up to the present and in the days ahead. MUST READING!

Paul ("Dad") Krupp
Nate's Father

Nate Krupp's vision of the climax of world history is in harmony both with the Scriptures, and with the prophetic hopes of past revival leaders. This book presents an image of a renewed church, restored in holiness, truth, and unity, responding faithfully under the pressures of persecution. This vision will foster both zeal and stability in the multitudes of Christians who take part in the final chapter of the Church's earthly history.

— Dr. Richard Lovelace
Professor of Church History
Gordon-Conwell Theological Seminary

In *The Church Triumphant at the End of the Age,* Nate Krupp has effectively compiled a powerful work that gives a thorough Biblical foundation and a clear historical perspective for Revival and Spiritual Awakening. Having served as Special Assistant in Prayer for Spiritual Awakening, Southern Baptist Convention, I gladly recommend this volume. I believe it will become a classic resource manual for the Body of Christ.

Glenn Sheppard, President
International Prayer Ministries
Atlanta, Georgia

I do not know any other one source where I could obtain so much information on the subject of Revival so quickly.

— *Ray E. Smith*
General Superintendent
Open Bible Standard Church

I am happy to commend Nate Krupp's latest book to the broader Church for two reasons.

First, the author's comprehensive vision reminds us that God is at work on a broad front today, and has been down through history.

Second, the book is written in a conciliator, optimistic tone. The author is note interested in beating up on people who may think differently on specific points, but rather in the question: What in the world is God doing in and through the Church today?

Two underlying theses of this book are: (1) We may expect a major, worldwide revival in coming years which will immediately precede Christ's second coming, and (2) God has been progressively restoring the Church to the New Testament model, particularly in the last few centuries. Whether the reader agrees fully with these or not, the author's evidence bears thoughtful consideration by all fairminded Christians. Go clearly is at work today in a variety of places and traditions, and we need to ask just what this means for Kingdom faithfulness in our Age. What is the Spirit saying to the churches?

The comprehensiveness, sensitivity, and essentially Biblical concept of the Church evident in these pages make this a useful study book for all careful, prayerful Christians.

— *Dr. Howard A. Snyder*
Church Renewal Specialist and Author

I agree with the major theses of *The Church Triumphant at the End of the Age*, namely that we have entered the period of the greatest spiritual harvest that history has ever known. And Nate Krupp has produced a major work which, if used as a text, can provide superb training for the harvesters when God calls. This book is informative, stimulating, and highly motivational. It is a timely work which has substantially advanced the fulfillment of the Great Commission.

— *Dr. C. Peter Wagner*
Fuller Theological Seminary
School of World Mission

What a privilege it has been for me to read Nate Krupp's manuscript. I catch the depth of his burden for the Church in its current state, and his heartfelt desire to see and help catalyze the Church toward the revival that must take place as prerequisite for ushering the "end of the age." It is a masterful collection of reference materials. The research that he has undertaken is a real service to the Body of Christ. I'm looking forward to keeping a copy close at hand. I'll be praying for the wide distribution and readership that it warrants.

He has clearly described the task confronting the Church. His listing of prerequisites for "fulfilling the task of the Great Commission" should be adopted by every Christian, local church, denomination, and agency; and this alone would certainly provide ample compensation for the years of committed effort the author has invested.

I trust this book will find a wide range of readership. It certainly warrants it. Church and Missions leaders, especially, need to take time to study and ponder the contents. In addition to providing an up-to-date status of world evangelization, it also provides vital keys for effecting a positive change in that status. Wherever its precepts and admonitions find a postive, obedient response, revival is certain to follow.

— *Bob Waymire*
Global Mapping Project